Vietnam War
Primary Sources

Vietnam War
Primary Sources

Kevin Hillstrom
and Laurie Collier
Hillstrom

Diane Sawinski, Editor

U·X·L®

AN IMPRINT OF THE GALE GROUP

DETROIT · SAN FRANCISCO · LONDON
BOSTON · WOODBRIDGE, CT

Vietnam War: Primary Sources

Ref
DS
557.7
H556
2001
v.4

Kevin Hillstrom and Laurie Collier Hillstrom

Staff

Diane Sawinski, *U•X•L Senior Editor*
Gerda-Ann Raffaelle, *U•X•L Editor*
Carol DeKane Nagel, *U•X•L Managing Editor*
Thomas L. Romig, *U•X•L Publisher*

Rita Wimberley, *Senior Buyer*
Dorothy Maki, *Manufacturing Manager*
Evi Seoud, *Assistant Manager, Composition Purchasing and Electronic Prepress*
Mary Beth Trimper, *Manager, Composition and Electronic Prepress*

Sarah Tomasek, *Permissions Specialist*
Michelle DiMercurio, *Senior Art Director*
Kenn Zorn, *Product Design Manager*
Dean Dauphinais, *Senior Editor, Imaging and Multimedia Content*
Pamela A. Reed, *Imaging Coordinator*
Robert Duncan, *Imaging Specialist*
Randy Bassett, *Imaging Supervisor*
Barbara J. Yarrow, *Manager, Imaging and Multimedia Content*

Linda Mahoney, LM Design, *Typesetting*

Front cover photographs: Walter Cronkite reproduced by permission of Archive Photos, Inc.; Kent State University shootings reproduced by permission of Corbis Corp. Back cover: Vietnamese woman with child reproduced by permission of AP/Wide World Photos.

Library of Congress Cataloging-in-Publication Data

Hillstrom, Kevin, 1963–

Vietnam War : primary sources / Kevin Hillstrom and Laurie Collier Hillstrom ; Diane Sawinski, editor.

p. cm.

Includes bibliographical references and index.

ISBN 0-7876-4887-6

1. Vietnamese Conflict, 1961–1975—Sources—Juvenile literature. [1. Vietnamese Conflict, 1961–1975—Sources.] I. Hillstrom, Laurie Collier, 1965– II. Sawinski, Diane M. III. Title.

DS557.4 .H55 2001

959.704'3—dc21

00-056377

Printed in the United States of America

10 9 8 7 6 5 4 3 2 1

Contents

Robert F. Kennedy, U.S. Senator and 1968 Democratic contender for the presidential nomination. Reproduced by permission of AP/Wide World Photos.

Tim O'Brien.
*Photograph by Jerry Bauer.
Reproduced by permission.*

Walter Cronkite reporting from Vietnam in 1968.
Reproduced by permission of Archive Photos.

Moving a wounded comrade.
Reproduced by permission of AP/Wide World Photos.

Reader's Guide

Vietnam War: Primary Sources presents thirteen full or excerpted documents from the Vietnam War era. These documents range from notable speeches that mark important points in the conflict to personal diaries and letters that reflect the hopes, dreams, fears, and experiences of ordinary soldiers and civilians. Some of the selections discuss highly personal issues, such as a young American's agonizing decision whether to report for military service or a Vietnamese girl's decision to join the Viet Cong. Others chronicle major events associated with the Vietnam War, like the Tet Offensive and the 1970 killings of four student protesters on the campus of Kent State University. Further, the works included in this volume present a wide range of perspectives on the conflict. For example, some entries provide insights into the feelings of Americans who served in Vietnam—including soldiers, nurses, and prisoners of war—while others provide a glimpse into the motivations of dedicated antiwar activists. Included are excerpts from civil rights leader Martin Luther King, Jr.'s 1967 antiwar speech at Riverside Church in New York City; President Richard M. Nixon's 1969 "Silent Majority" speech; Le Ly Hayslip's memoir about growing up in a war-torn Vietnamese village; and Admiral James Stockdale's memoir about his years in a Vietnamese prisoner-of-war camp.

The excerpts in *Primary Sources* are arranged in four chapters. Each of the chapters centers on a different theme. "Prelude to War" presents an overview of Vietnam's struggle for independence, the events that sparked the war, and the United States's early involvement in Vietnamese affairs. In this chapter, North Vietnamese leader Ho Chi Minh expresses his view of the war as a war of aggression waged by the U.S. government in a letter to the editor of the American magazine *Minority of One*. Excerpts in "The War at Home" are examples of how differently the war was regarded by individuals on the home front—from politicians to draft resisters. "The War in Vietnam" chapter looks at the range of personal experiences people in Vietnam had during the war. The impact of the war on both Vietnam and the United States is covered in "Legacies of the War."

Each excerpt included in *Vietnam War: Primary Sources* includes the following additional text:

- **Introductory material** places the document and its author in historical context.

- **"Things to remember while reading . . ."** offers readers important background information and directs them to central ideas in the text.

- **"What happened next . . ."** discusses the impact of the document and provides an account of subsequent historical events.

- **"Did you know . . ."** provides interesting facts about the document and its author.

- **"Sources"** presents citations used to compile the entry.

Entries in *Vietnam War: Primary Sources* include numerous sidebars, some focusing on the author of the featured document, others highlighting interesting, related information. Nearly seventy photos illustrate the text, and each excerpt has a glossary that runs alongside the reprinted document defining unfamiliar terms and ideas contained in the material. The volume begins with a timeline, "Words to Know" section, and a "Research and Activity Ideas" section. It concludes with a "Where to Learn More" section and a subject index so the reader can easily find the people, places, and events disussed throughout *Vietnam War: Primary Sources*.

Vietnam War Reference Library

Vietnam War: Primary Sources is only one component of the three-part U•X•L Vietnam War Reference Library. The other two titles in this set are:

- *Vietnam War: Almanac* presents a comprehensive overview of the Vietnam War. The volume's sixteen chapters cover all aspects of the conflict, from the reasons behind American involvement, to the antiwar protests that rocked the nation, to the fall of Saigon to Communist forces in 1975. The chapters are arranged chronologically and explore such topics as Vietnam's struggles under French colonial rule, the introduction of U.S. combat troops in 1965, the Tet Offensive, and the lasting impact of the war on both the United States and Vietnam. Interspersed are four chapters that cover the growth of the American antiwar movement, the experiences of U.S. soldiers in Vietnam, Vietnam veterans in American society, and the effect of the war on Vietnam's land and people. The Almanac also contains "Words to Know" and "People to Know" sections, a timeline, research and activity ideas, and a subject index.

- *Vietnam War: Biographies* is a two-volume set featuring profiles of sixty important figures from the Vietnam War era. The essays cover such key people as politicians Ho Chi Minh, Lyndon B. Johnson, Robert S. McNamara, Ngo Dinh Diem, and Richard M. Nixon; military leaders William Westmoreland and Vo Nguyen Giap; antiwar activists Joan Baez, David Dellinger, and Abbie Hoffman; journalists Frances FitzGerald, David Halberstam, and Neil Sheehan; and prominent veterans Ron Kovic, Tim O'Brien, John McCain, and Oliver Stone. The volumes are filled with photographs, sidebars, individual "Where to Learn More" sections, and an index.

- A cumulative index of all three titles in the U•X•L Vietnam War Reference Library is also available.

Acknowledgments

The authors extend thanks to U•X•L Senior Editor Diane Sawinski and U•X•L Publisher Tom Romig at the Gale Group for their assistance throughout the production of this series.

Comments and Suggestions

We welcome your comments on *Vietnam War: Primary Sources* and suggestions for other topics in history to consider. Please write: Editors, *Vietnam War: Primary Sources,* U•X•L, 27500 Drake Rd., Farmington Hills, Michigan 48331–3535; call toll-free 800–877–4253; fax to 248–414–5043; or send e-mail via http://www.galegroup.com.

Vietnam War Timeline

1859 The French capture Saigon.

1862 Under the Treaty of Saigon, Vietnam gives control of three eastern provinces to France.

1863 France makes Cambodia a French colony.

1883 Under the Treaty of Hue, France expands its control over all of Vietnam.

1887 France turns its holdings in Southeast Asia into one colony, called Indochina.

1893 France makes Laos a French colony.

1930 Vietnamese nationalist Ho Chi Minh creates the Indochinese Communist Party to oppose French colonial rule.

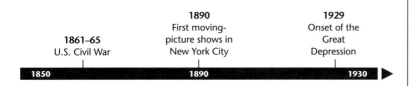

1861–65 U.S. Civil War

1890 First moving-picture shows in New York City

1929 Onset of the Great Depression

1850 — 1890 — 1930 ▶

Bao Dai.
Reproduced by permission of Archive Photos.

1940 Japan occupies Indochina during World War II.

1941 The Communist-led Vietnamese nationalist organization known as the Viet Minh is established.

March 1945 Emperor Bao Dai proclaims Vietnam an independent nation under Japan's protection.

April 1945 U.S. President Franklin Roosevelt dies; Harry S. Truman takes office.

August 1945 Japan surrenders to end World War II.

August 1945 Bao Dai is removed from power in the August Revolution.

September 1945 Ho Chi Minh establishes the Democratic Republic of Vietnam and declares himself president. France and most other Western powers do not recognize the new nation.

September 1945 U.S. Army Major A. Peter Dewey becomes the first American soldier to die in Vietnam.

March 1946 France declares Vietnam an independent state within the French Union.

November 1946 The First Indochina War begins with a Viet Minh attack on French forces in Hanoi.

1949 France creates the independent State of Vietnam under Bao Dai.

January 1950 Communist countries China, Yugoslavia, and the Soviet Union formally recognize the Democratic Republic of Vietnam under Ho Chi Minh.

February 1950 Democratic countries Great Britain and the United States formally recognize the State of Vietnam under Bao Dai.

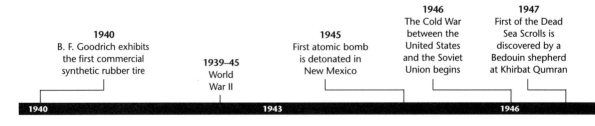

1940
B. F. Goodrich exhibits the first commercial synthetic rubber tire

1939–45
World War II

1945
First atomic bomb is detonated in New Mexico

1946
The Cold War between the United States and the Soviet Union begins

1947
First of the Dead Sea Scrolls is discovered by a Bedouin shepherd at Khirbat Qumran

1940   1943   1946

May 1950 The United States begins providing military and economic aid to French forces in Vietnam.

1952 Dwight D. Eisenhower becomes president of the United States.

March 1954 The Viet Minh set up a siege of the French outpost at Dien Bien Phu.

May 1954 Viet Minh forces defeat the French in the Battle of Dien Bien Phu.

June 1954 Bao Dai selects Ngo Dinh Diem as prime minister of the State of Vietnam.

July 1954 The Geneva Accords divide Vietnam into two sections: North Vietnam, led by Communists under Ho Chi Minh; and South Vietnam, led by a U.S.-supported government under Ngo Dinh Diem.

July 1954 Laos and Cambodia are granted full independence from France.

October 1954 French troops are withdrawn from Vietnam.

July 1955 Ngo Dinh Diem refuses to proceed with national elections required by the Geneva Accords.

September 1955 Cambodia gains independence from France; Norodom Sihanouk becomes prime minister.

October 1955 Diem takes control of the South Vietnamese government from Bao Dai and establishes the Republic of Vietnam.

November 1955 The U.S. Military Advisory Group—Vietnam (MAGV) is formed.

1957 Communist rebels begin fighting for control of South Vietnam.

French headquarters at Dien Bien Phu captured by Viet Minh.
Reproduced by permission of AP/World Wide Photos.

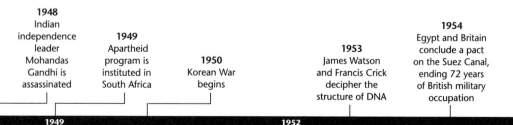

1948
Indian independence leader Mohandas Gandhi is assassinated

1949
Apartheid program is instituted in South Africa

1950
Korean War begins

1953
James Watson and Francis Crick decipher the structure of DNA

1954
Egypt and Britain conclude a pact on the Suez Canal, ending 72 years of British military occupation

1949   1952   1955

Ho Chi Minh.
*Reproduced by permission of
the International Portrait
Gallery.*

1959 In neighboring Laos construction begins on the Ho Chi Minh Trail, a major supply and communications route for Communist forces.

Novermber 1960 Rebels try to overthrow the Diem government.

Novermber 1960 John F. Kennedy becomes president of the United States.

December 1960 The National Liberation Front is established in North Vietnam to overthrow Diem and reunite the two parts of Vietnam.

1961 Vietnamese peasant **Le Ly Hayslip,** like other villagers, feels caught in the middle of the dispute between the Viet Cong guerila fighters and the ARVN forces.

1961 Kennedy offers military assistance to Diem and sends the first U.S. advisors to South Vietnam.

1962 U.S. Military Assistance Command—Vietnam (MACV) is established.

1962 The South Vietnam government and the United States' Central Intelligence Agency (CIA) launch the Strategic Hamlets resettlement program to reduce support for Viet Cong guerrillas in rural farming communities.

January 1963 The Battle of Ap Bac brings American public attention to Vietnam.

April 1963 Buddhists begin demonstrating against the Diem government.

June 1963 The suicide of a Buddhist monk draws international attention to the situation in Vietnam.

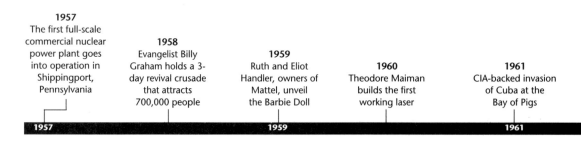

1957
The first full-scale commercial nuclear power plant goes into operation in Shippingport, Pennsylvania

1958
Evangelist Billy Graham holds a 3-day revival crusade that attracts 700,000 people

1959
Ruth and Eliot Handler, owners of Mattel, unveil the Barbie Doll

1960
Theodore Maiman builds the first working laser

1961
CIA-backed invasion of Cuba at the Bay of Pigs

1957   1959   1961

November 1963 Ngo Dinh Diem and other members of his government are assassinated; the Military Revolutionary Council takes control of South Vietnam.

November 1963 Kennedy is assassinated; Lyndon B. Johnson takes office.

May 1964 Ho Chi Minh makes an appeal to the American people in a letter to the editor of *Minority of One* magazine.

August 1964 North Vietnamese patrol boats reportedly attack American warships in the Gulf of Tonkin.

August 1964 The U.S. Congress passes the Tonkin Gulf Resolution, which allows Johnson to use any means necessary to prevent North Vietnamese aggression.

November 1964 Johnson is reelected president of the United States.

February 1965 Viet Cong guerillas ambush a U.S. base at Pleiku; the U.S. military retaliates with air attacks.

March 1965 The American bombing campaign known as Operation Rolling Thunder begins over North Vietnam.

March 1965 The first U.S. combat troops are sent to Vietnam.

March 1965 Philip Caputo arrives in Vietnam with one of the first groups of U.S. Marines.

March 1965 Faculty of the University of Michigan organize a teach-in to protest the war.

August 1965 Henry Cabot Lodge is appointed as American ambassador to South Vietnam.

September 1965 American pilot **James Stockdale** is shot down over North Vietnam and taken prisoner.

November 1965 Antiwar demonstrations become widespread in the United States.

An American GI.
Reproduced by permission of Archive Photos.

1963
Freedom March
held in
Washington, D.C.

1964
G.I. Joe toy figure
is introduced by
toymaker Hasbro

1965
Recording of
"Satisfaction" makes the
Rolling Stones rock stars

1963   1964   1965

Martin Luther King, Jr.
Reproduced by permission of AP/Wide World Photos.

November 1966 The U.S. military launches Project 100,000, a controversial program designed to recruit the poor and minorities into the service.

1967 Heavyweight boxing champion Muhammad Ali refuses to honor his draft notice, is convicted of draft resistance, and loses his boxing license.

April 1967 Civil rights leader **Martin Luther King, Jr.**, speaks out against the war in a speech at Riverside Church in New York City

September 1967 Nguyen Van Thieu becomes president of South Vietnam.

October 1967 The March on the Pentagon draws 50,000 anti-war protesters to Washington, D.C.

January 1968 The Siege of Khe Sanh (in South Vietnam) begins.

January 1968 North Vietnamese forces launch the Tet Offensive.

January 1968 The Battle for Hue (in South Vietnam) begins.

February 1968 Clark Clifford replaces Robert McNamara as U.S. Secretary of Defense.

February 1968 **Senator Robert F. Kennedy** speaks out against U.S. government support for South Vietnamese leader Ngo Dinh Diem.

February 1968 Influential newsman **Walter Cronkite** broadcasts an editorial against the war on the *CBS Evening News*.

March 1968 U.S. troops kill hundreds of Vietnamese civilians in the My Lai Massacre.

March 1968 President Johnson announces he will not seek reelection.

April 1968 Civil rights leader, Martin Luther King, Jr., is assassinated.

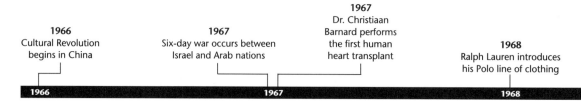

1966
Cultural Revolution begins in China

1967
Six-day war occurs between Israel and Arab nations

1967
Dr. Christiaan Barnard performs the first human heart transplant

1968
Ralph Lauren introduces his Polo line of clothing

1966   1967   1968

May 1968 The United States and North Vietnam open peace negotiations in Paris, France.

June 1968 U.S. Senator and Democratic presidential candidate Robert F. Kennedy is assassinated.

August 1968 Antiwar protesters disrupt the Democratic National Convention in Chicago.

October 1968 President Johnson announces an end to the bombing of North Vietnam.

November 1968 Richard M. Nixon is elected president of the United States.

1969 **Tim O'Brien** is sent to Vietnam as an American combat soldier.

February 1969 Secret bombing of Cambodia begins.

April 1969 U.S. troop levels in Vietnam peak at 543,400.

June 1969 Nixon puts his Vietnamization policy into effect, reducing U.S. troop levels by 25,000.

September 1969 North Vietnamese military leader and president Ho Chi Minh dies.

September 1969 The treatment of American prisoners of war (POWs) in North Vietnam begins to improve following Ho's death.

April 1970 Lon Nol seizes power from Norodom Sihanouk in Cambodia.

April 1970 Nixon authorizes American troops to invade Cambodia.

May 1970 The National Guard kills four student protesters during an antiwar demonstration at Kent State University in Ohio. **Bill Rubenstein** recalls the event in his essay, "Tragedy at Kent."

A young man burning his draft card.
Reproduced by permission of AP/Wide World Photos.

Tear gas being used by National Guardsmen on Kent State University students.
Reproduced by permission of AP/Wide World Photos.

1969
U.S. astronaut Neil Armstrong walks on the moon

August 1969
Woodstock Music Fair attracts three hundred thousand people

1970
Marxist politician Salvador Allende is elected president of Chile

1971
Greenpeace founded in Vancouver, Canada

1969	1970	1971

Kent State Four—Nixon's "Silent Minority"
Kent State University. Public Domain.

May 1970 About 200 pro-war construction workers, known as "Hard Hats," attack antiwar protesters in New York City.

June 1970 U.S. troops withdraw from Cambodia.

October 1970 Antiwar groups hold the first Moratorium Day protests.

June 1970 The U.S. Supreme Court overturns Muhammad Ali's conviction for resisting the draft.

November 1970 President **Richard M. Nixon** makes his "Silent Majority" speech.

November 1970 The My Lai Massacre is revealed to the American people. Lt. William Calley is put on trial for his role in the massacre.

November 1970 Lt. William Calley is put on trial for his role in the My Lai Massacre.

December 1970 The U.S. Congress repeals the Tonkin Gulf Resolution.

1971 The *New York Times* begins publishing the Pentagon Papers.

1971 Nixon eliminates student deferments for the military draft.

March 1972 North Vietnamese troops begin the Easter Offensive.

June 1972 Republican agents associated with Nixon break into the Democratic presidential campaign headquarters at the Watergate Hotel in Washington, D.C.

August 1972 The last U.S. combat troops withdraw from Vietnam.

November 1972 Nixon is reelected president of the United States.

1972
President Nixon makes historic visit to China

1973
Artist Pablo Picasso dies

1973
Members of the American Indian Movement (AIM) occupy Wounded Knee, South Dakota, to protest corrupt tribal government

1974
Anthropologists discover "Lucy," a hominid skeleton more than three million years old

1972   1973   1974

December 1972 U.S. warplanes begin the Christmas bombing campaign.

January 1973 The United States and North Vietnam sign the Paris Peace Accords.

January 1973 The U.S. government formally ends the military draft.

February 1973 North Vietnam releases American prisoners of war (POWs).

June 1973 The U.S. Congress passes the Case-Church Amendment, prohibiting further American military involvement in Southeast Asia.

November 1973 The U.S. Congress passes the War Powers Act over Nixon's veto, reducing the president's authority to commit U.S. military forces.

August 1974 Threatened with impeachment over the Watergate scandal, Nixon resigns from office; Gerald R. Ford becomes president of the United States.

September 1974 Ford pardons Nixon.

1975 In a civil trial, the Ohio National Guard is found not legally responsible for shooting four students to death on the campus of Kent State University.

1975 The U.S. House of Representatives forms a special committee to investigate claims that American prisoners of war are still being held in North Vietnam.

March 1975 North Vietnamese forces capture Hue, Da Nang, and other South Vietnamese cities.

March 1975 President Nguyen Van Thieu orders South Vietnamese forces to withdraw from the central provinces, causing the "Convoy of Tears."

South Vietnamese fleeing Saigon.
Reproduced by permission of Corbis-Bettman.

Military police confront peace protestors.
Reproduced by permission of Corbis Corporation.

1975
Cartoonist Gary Trudeau wins the Pulitzer Prize for his satirical comic strip, *Doonesbury*

1975
Bill Gates organizes Microsoft Corp.

1976
Viking I and *Viking II* space probes land on Mars

1977
Steven Jobs and Steve Wozniak found the Apple Computer Co.

1975   1976   1977

Maya Lin, designer of the Vietnam Veterans Memorial. *Reproduced by permission of AP/Wide World Photos.*

April 1975 The U.S. Embassy in Saigon is evacuated by military helicopters.

April 1975 North Vietnamese forces capture the South Vietnamese capital of Saigon to win the Vietnam War.

April 1975 Communist Khmer Rouge rebels capture the capital of Phnom Penh and take control of Cambodia.

August 1975 The Communist-led Pathet Lao take control of Laos.

July 1976 Vietnam is reunited as one country under Communist rule, called the Socialist Republic of Vietnam.

August 1976 Vietnamese businessman **Phuong Hoang** and his family flee their homeland after the Communist takeover.

November 1976 Jimmy Carter is elected president of the United States.

1977 Carter pardons most Vietnam War draft evaders.

1977 **Philip Caputo** publishes *A Rumor of War* about his experiences as a combat soldier in Vietnam.

1978 Thousands of refugees known as "boat people" flee from Vietnam, creating an international crisis.

1978 Vietnam invades Cambodia and takes control of the government away from the violent Khmer Rouge.

1979 China reacts to the Vietnamese invasion of Cambodia by invading northern Vietnam.

1979 A group of female veterans form the Vietnam Veterans Association Women's Project to bring attention to the issues they face.

| **1978** First "test tube" baby is born | **1979** Margaret Thatcher becomes prime minister of Great Britain | **1980** *Voyager I* space probe photographs Saturn | **1981** Acquired Immune Deficiency Syndrome (AIDS) is diagnosed for the first time | **1982** Magnetic Resonance Imaging (MRI) machines are introduced |

1978   1980   1982

1979   Several Southeast Asian nations announce that they will no longer accept Vietnamese refugees.

1980   The Ohio National Guard reaches a settlement with the families of four students shot to death on the campus of Kent State University in 1970.

1980   Jimmy Carter signs the Refugee Assistance Act, which increases the number of Indochinese refugees allowed into the United States and provides for their care.

1980   Ronald Reagan is elected president of the United States.

1982   The Vietnam Veterans Memorial is dedicated in Washington, D.C.

1984   American Vietnam veterans reach an out-of-court settlement with chemical companies over health problems related to their wartime exposure to the poisonous herbicide Agent Orange.

July 1985   **Linda Phillips Palo** leaves a letter to her three best friends who died in the Vietnam War at the Vietnam Veterans Memorial.

1986   Nguyen Van Linh becomes head of the Communist Party in Vietnam and introduces the *Doi Moi* economic reforms.

1987   Civilian relief worker **Julie Forsythe** recalls her experiences in Vietnam in an interview with Kathryn Marshall.

1988   George Bush becomes president of the United States.

1989   Vietnam withdraws its troops from Cambodia.

A U.S. Marine veteran at the replica of the Vietnam Veterans Memorial Wall in Brooklyn, New York.
Reproduced by permission of AP/Wide World Photos.

1984
Toxic gas leak kills 2,500 in Bhopal, India

1985
Coca Cola Co. changes its original formula, but public opinion forces it to change it back

1986
Space shuttle *Challenger* explodes seconds after takeoff killing all seven crew members including teacher, Christa McAuliffe

1988
Colin Powell becomes the first African American four-star general

1984   1986   1988

1990 **Tim O'Brien** publishes *The Things They Carried,* a collection of stories about his experiences as a combat soldier in Vietnam.

1992 Bill Clinton is elected president of the United States.

1993 The United Nations sponsors free elections in Cambodia.

1993 A bronze statue is dedicated in Washington, D.C., as a memorial to the American women who served in Vietnam.

1994 Clinton ends the economic embargo against trade with Vietnam.

1995 The United States restores full diplomatic relations with Vietnam.

July 2000 The United States and Vietnam sign a sweeping trade agreement.

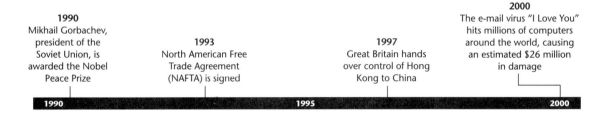

1990
Mikhail Gorbachev, president of the Soviet Union, is awarded the Nobel Peace Prize

1993
North American Free Trade Agreement (NAFTA) is signed

1997
Great Britain hands over control of Hong Kong to China

2000
The e-mail virus "I Love You" hits millions of computers around the world, causing an estimated $26 million in damage

1990   1995   2000

Words to Know

A

ARVN: The South Vietnamese army, officially known as the Army of the Republic of South Vietnam. The ARVN fought on the same side as U.S. troops during the Vietnam War.

B

Buddhism: A religion based on the teaching of Gautama Buddha, in which followers seek moral purity and spiritual enlightenment.

C

Cambodia: Southeast Asian nation located on the western border of South Vietnam. During the Vietnam War, Cambodia experienced its own civil war between its pro-U.S. government forces and Communist rebels known as the Khmer Rouge.

Cold War: A period of intense rivalry between the United States and the Soviet Union as both nations competed to spread their political philosophies and influence around the world after the end of World War II. The climate of distrust and hostility between the two nations and their allies dominated international politics until the 1980s.

Colonialism: A practice in which one country assumes political control over another country. Most colonial powers established colonies in foreign lands in order to take possession of valuable natural resources and increase their own power. They often showed little concern for the rights and well-being of the native people.

Communism: A political system in which the government controls all resources and means of producing wealth. By eliminating private property, this system is designed to create an equal society with no social classes. However, Communist governments in practice often limit personal freedom and individual rights.

Coup d'état: A sudden, decisive attempt to overthrow an existing government.

D

Dien Bien Phu: A French fort in northwestern Vietnam that was the site of a major battle in the Indochina War in 1954.

Domino Theory: A political theory that held that the fall of one country's government to communism usually triggered similar collapses in neighboring countries, as if the nations were dominoes falling in sequence.

Draft: The process of selecting from a qualified pool of individuals people to serve in the military.

E

Escalation: A policy of increasing the size, scope, and intensity of military activity.

G

Great Society: A set of social programs proposed by President Lyndon Johnson designed to end segregation and reduce poverty in the United States.

H

Hanoi: The capital city of Communist North Vietnam. Also an unofficial shorthand way of referring to the North Vietnamese government.

I

Indochina: The name sometimes given to the peninsula between India and China in Southeast Asia. The term narrowly refers to Cambodia, Laos, and Vietnam, which were united under the name French Indochina during the colonial period, 1893–1954.

Indochina War: Later known as the First Indochina War (the Vietnam War became the Second Indochina War), this conflict took place between France and Communist-led Viet Minh forces in Vietnam, 1946–54.

K

Khmer Rouge: Communist-led rebel forces that fought for control of Cambodia during the Vietnam War years. The Khmer Rouge overthrew the U.S.-backed government of Lon Nol in 1975.

L

Laos: A Southeast Asian nation located on the western border of North Vietnam. During the Vietnam War, Laos experienced its own civil war between U.S.-backed forces and Communist rebels known as the Pathet Lao.

M

MIAs: Soldiers classified as "missing in action," meaning that their status is unknown to military leaders or that their bodies have not been recovered.

Military Revolutionary Council: A group of South Vietnamese military officers that overthrew President Ngo Dinh Diem and took control of South Vietnam's government in 1963.

N

Nationalism: A feeling of intense loyalty and devotion to a country or homeland. Some people argued that nationalism, rather than communism, was the main factor that caused the Viet Minh to fight the French for control of Vietnam.

North Vietnam: The Geneva Accords of 1954, which ended the First Indochina War, divided the nation of Vietnam into two sections. The northern section, which was led by a Communist government under Ho Chi Minh, was officially known as the Democratic Republic of Vietnam but was usually called North Vietnam.

NVA: The North Vietnamese Army, which assisted the Viet Cong guerilla fighters in trying to conquer South Vietnam. These forces opposed the United States in the Vietnam War.

O

Offensive: A sudden, aggressive attack by one side during a war.

P

Pentagon Papers: A set of secret U.S. Department of Defense documents that explained American military policy toward Vietnam from 1945 to 1968. They created a controversy when they were leaked to the national media in 1971.

Post-Traumatic Stress Syndrome (PTSS): A set of psychological problems that are caused by exposure to a dangerous or disturbing situation, such as combat. People who suffer from PTSS may experience symptoms of depression, flashbacks, nightmares, and angry outbursts.

S

Saigon: The capital city of U.S.-supported South Vietnam. Also an unofficial shorthand way of referring to the South Vietnamese government.

Silent Majority: A term used by President Richard Nixon to describe the large number of American people he believed quietly supported his Vietnam War policies. In contrast, Nixon referred to the antiwar movement in the United States as a vocal minority.

Socialist Republic of Vietnam (SRV): The country created in 1976, after North Vietnam won the Vietnam War and reunited with South Vietnam.

South Vietnam: Created under the Geneva Accords of 1954, the southern section of Vietnam was known as the Republic of South Vietnam. It was led by a U.S.-supported government.

Strategic hamlets: South Vietnamese villages surrounded by barbed wire and other defenses as part of an American strategy of keeping Viet Cong guerillas from circulating among the people.

T

Tonkin Gulf Resolution: Passed by Congress after U.S. Navy ships supposedly came under attack in the Gulf of Tonkin, this resolution gave President Lyndon Johnson the authority to wage war against North Vietnam.

V

Veteran: A former member of the armed forces.

Veterans Administration: A U.S. government agency responsible for providing medical care, insurance, pensions, and other benefits to American veterans of Vietnam and other wars.

Viet Cong: Vietnamese Communist guerilla fighters who worked with the North Vietnamese Army to conquer South Vietnam.

Viet Minh: Communist-led nationalist group that worked to gain Vietnam's independence from French colonial rule.

Vietnamization: A policy proposed by President Richard Nixon that involved returning responsibility for the war to the South Vietnamese. It was intended to allow the United States to reduce its military involvement without allowing the country to fall to communism.

W

Watergate: A political scandal that forced U.S. President Richard Nixon to resign from office in 1974. In June 1972, Republican agents associated with Nixon's reelection campaign broke into the Democratic campaign headquarters in the Watergate Hotel in Washington, D.C., to gather secret information. Nixon and several members of his administration attempted to cover up the burglary.

Research and Activity Ideas

In his letter to the American people, North Vietnamese leader Ho Chi Minh claims that his Communist government would bring freedom and independence to the Vietnamese people. Write a paper comparing Ho's vision of Vietnam under Communist rule with Phuong Hoang's experiences in South Vietnam after the Communist takeover. Did the North Vietnamese deliver on Ho's promises once they won the war? If you were in Phuong Hoang's position, would you have decided to leave Vietnam as a refugee?

Imagine that you are an American citizen who has just watched President Richard Nixon's "Silent Majority" speech on television in 1969. Write a letter to Nixon expressing your views about the Vietnam War and his administration's policies. If you wish, write your letter from the perspective of an antiwar protester, an American soldier stationed in Vietnam, a young person whose brother has been killed in Vietnam, a veteran of World War II, a government official, or the president of a company that manufactures military equipment.

The design of the Vietnam Veterans Memorial was very controversial when it was first proposed. Since then, however, the Wall has been widely recognized as a powerful tribute to the Americans who lost their lives in Vietnam. In fact, one retired three-star general called it "exactly the right memorial for that war." Why would the general say this? Do you agree or disagree? What is it about the Vietnam War that makes a polished black granite wall seem more appropriate than a traditional, patriotic statue? Write a one-page essay considering these questions.

During the Vietnam War, the peasants in rural South Vietnamese villages were often caught in the middle as the Viet Cong guerilla fighters and South Vietnamese government forces competed for their loyalty. Pretend that you are one of these villagers during the early years of the war. Keep a diary of your imaginary experiences as you try to maintain a normal life while facing threats of violence from both sides. Do you favor one side or the other? Why?

Many people criticized Martin Luther King's decision to link the American civil rights movement with the growing antiwar movement in 1967. Make a list of the reasons King believed that the two movements should be connected. Make another list of the reasons that fellow black leaders, U.S. government officials, and members of antiwar groups disagreed with his view. Which one seems to be the stronger position?

Select three students to perform a skit in front of the class. One student will play the role of a college student who has just returned home from Kent State University in May 1970. The other two students will play the roles of his or her parents. The college student should discuss his or her views of the antiwar demonstrations in which four fellow students were killed by Ohio National Guard troops. At least one of the parents should take the position that the demonstrators were to blame for the violence on the campus.

Like many other U.S. soldiers, former Marine Philip Caputo was involved in several acts of violence against Vietnamese civilians during the Vietnam War. Pretend that

Caputo has been charged with war crimes for actions he committed during his military service. Divide the class into groups and stage a mock trial. Be sure to introduce evidence about his experiences as a combat soldier in Vietnam, and his feelings about what he did. Does the jury find him innocent or guilty?

Give an oral presentation to the class in which you recite a speech or poem from the Vietnam War era. Another option might be to play a tape of a popular song connected to the war—such as "The Ballad of the Green Berets" by Barry Sadler, "Born in the U.S.A" by Bruce Springsteen, "Fortunate Son" by Creedence Clearwater Revival, "The Unknown Soldier" by the Doors, "The Big Parade" by 10,000 Maniacs, or "Ohio" by Crosby, Stills, Nash, and Young—and discuss the lyrics with the class.

Imagine that you are an American pilot who was held as a prisoner of war in North Vietnam for five years. How do you think you would feel about the way the war ended? Would you be glad that no more American soldiers were going to be captured or killed? Or would you be angry that you sacrificed years of your life only to have the American war effort end in defeat? How would you feel about the U.S. government reestablishing normal diplomatic relations with Vietnam? If you wish, research the views of actual POWs like James Stockdale and John McCain on these questions. Write an essay explaining your answers.

In the excerpt from his book *The Things They Carried*, Tim O'Brien describes his agonizing decision to report for military service rather than flee to Canada. He opposes the war, yet he decides to honor his draft notice and serve in Vietnam because he is afraid of what his parents and other people will think of him if he evades the draft. Think of a situation in which you felt pressured to do something you did not want to do by other people's expectations. Write an essay explaining the situation you faced, the decision you made, what the consequences were, and how you feel about it now.

Pick one year of the Vietnam War and create a collage of pictures and other images representing the events of that year. For example, a collage for 1968 might include images from the Tet Offensive, the My Lai Massacre, the assassinations of Martin Luther King Jr. and Robert F. Kennedy, the Democratic National Convention in Chicago, and Richard Nixon's election to the presidency.

Vietnam War
Primary Sources

Prelude to War

Long before American soldiers arrived in Vietnam in the 1960s, the Vietnamese people had endured centuries of violent struggle for control of their country. The most recent of these struggles took place from 1946 to 1954, when Vietnamese Communists—known as Viet Minh—fought to free the country from more than one hundred years of French colonial rule.

In 1954 war-weary France gave up its claims on Vietnam. Ho Chi Minh and his lieutenants rejoiced at their victory and prepared to establish Communist rule over the entire nation. But the United States and other democratic nations objected to this plan because they did not want Vietnam controlled by Communists. The view at the time was that if one country fell to Communist control, others would follow. As a result, Ho Chi Minh and the Vietnamese Communists were forced to accept a compromise—the Geneva Accords—in which they received only the northern half of the country. The southern portion of the country went to non-Communists. This arrangement was only supposed to be temporary. The treaty called for national elections to be held in 1956 to create a single Vietnamese government. However, South Vietnam and its American supporters refused to hold the elections because of fears that Ho Chi Minh would win.

Before long, North and South Vietnam were engaged in a fierce fight for control of the divided nation. As this battle progressed, the U.S. government provided financial aid and military advisors to South Vietnam. America's involvement angered Ho Chi Minh and the North Vietnamese Communists. They maintained that the United States was interfering with the internal affairs of their country, just as China and France had done in earlier times. Ho Chi Minh explained these sentiments in a letter that was published in the May 1964 issue of an American magazine called *Minority of One*.

Ho Chi Minh

Excerpt from a letter to the editor of the American magazine Minority of One
Published in the May 1964 issue

Vietnam has a long history of being controlled by other countries. For example, it was ruled by neighboring China during ancient times, it was a colony of France during the late nineteenth and early twentieth centuries, and it was occupied by Japan during World War II. All through their nation's history, the Vietnamese people have struggled to gain their independence from foreign powers. Some historians consider the Vietnam War to be another example of the Vietnamese fighting to achieve independence and self-rule. In that war, the historians argue, the foreign country that was using its power to control Vietnam was the United States.

North Vietnamese Communist leader Ho Chi Minh often characterized the war as a revolution to overthrow the U.S.-sponsored government in South Vietnam and thus free the country from foreign control. "For the defense of the independence of the fatherland and for the fulfillment of our obligation to the peoples struggling against U.S. imperialism [the practice of extending power or influence over other countries], our people and army, united as one man, will resolutely fight until complete victory, whatever the sacrifices and hardships

"The Vietnamese people thank the workers', youth, students', and women's organizations, as well as progressive intellectuals, congressmen, and clergymen in the United States who have courageously raised their voices, staged demonstrations, exposed the criminal policy of aggression pursued by the U.S. government."

may be," he stated. "In the past we defeated the Japanese fascists [brutal dictators] and the French colonialists . . . . Our people's struggle against U.S. aggression for national salvation is sure to win a total victory."

Some people believe that this view of the war as a fight for independence explains why North Vietnam fought with such patience and determination. The United States and the South Vietnamese government it supported had superior weapons and equipment during the Vietnam War. But the North Vietnamese were strongly motivated by their desire to reunite the country and bring independence to their people. They were able to gain the support of many peasants in the South by encouraging them to view the Americans as foreign invaders, like the Chinese or the French.

North Vietnamese leaders knew that U.S. military involvement in Vietnam could not last forever, because the American people would eventually pressure the government to bring the troops home. As a result, North Vietnam was determined to continue fighting as long as necessary to achieve its goals of independence and self-rule. "Your mission is to fight for five years or even ten or twenty years," Ho told his people. Their patience finally paid off in 1975, when North Vietnamese Communist forces captured the South Vietnamese capital of Saigon to win the Vietnam War.

A first bid for independence

Vietnam almost succeeded in becoming an independent nation thirty years earlier, in 1945. During World War II, Japanese forces moved into Vietnam, which was then a colony of France. In fact, France had controlled all of Indochina (the region of Southeast Asia that included Vietnam, Cambodia, and Laos) for nearly a century. But during World War II Germany seized control of France. As a result, the French were unable to protect their colonies in Southeast Asia. France's problems enabled Japan to occupy Vietnam and set up military bases there in 1940.

In 1945, however, the Allied forces (which mainly consisted of the United States, Great Britain, and the Soviet Union) defeated both Germany and Japan to win World War II. As soon as Japan was defeated, Vietnamese Communists

A French soldier and a Communist Viet Minh soldier at Trung-gia, where the French and Viet Minh held a meeting in 1954 to arrange a truce.
Reproduced by permission of Corbis-Bettmann.

under Ho Chi Minh—known as the Viet Minh—launched a revolution to regain control of Vietnam. "The hour is decisive for the destiny of the nation," Ho Chi Minh told his people. "Let us all arise and bend all efforts to liberate ourselves."

This so-called August Revolution was successful, as the Viet Minh took control of large areas of the country. In September 1945 Ho formally declared Vietnam's independence from

The Vietnamese Declaration of Independence

In 1945, after the Allied forces defeated Japan to end World War II, Ho Chi Minh took advantage of the opportunity to declare Vietnam's independence from foreign control. He knew that Japan would be forced to end its occupation of Vietnam. He hoped that the Allies would then support Vietnam's bid for independence rather than allowing France to regain control over its former colony. As a way of appealing to the United States and other democratic nations, Ho quoted from the American Declaration of Independence in his statement. The following is an excerpt from the Vietnamese Declaration of Independence, issued by Ho Chi Minh on September 2, 1945:

> All men are created equal; they are endowed by their Creator with certain unalienable Rights; among these are Life, Liberty, and the pursuit of Happiness.
>
> This immortal statement was made in the Declaration of Independence of the United States of America in 1776. In a broader sense, this means: All the peoples on earth are equal from birth, all the peoples have a right to live, to be happy and free.

> The Declaration of the French Revolution made in 1791 on the Rights of Man and the Citizen also states: "All men are born free and with equal rights, and must always remain free and have equal rights."
>
> Those are undeniable truths.
>
> Nevertheless, for more than eighty years, the French imperialists, abusing the standard of Liberty, Equality, and Fraternity [brotherhood], have violated our Fatherland and oppressed our fellow citizens. They have acted contrary to the ideals of humanity and justice.
>
> In the field of politics, they have deprived our people of every democratic liberty. . . .
>
> In the field of economics, they have fleeced [cheated] us to the backbone, impoverished [reduced to poverty] our people and devastated our land.
>
> They have robbed us of our rice fields, our mines, our forests, and our raw materials. . . .
>
> In the autumn of 1940, when the Japanese fascists [brutal dictators] violated Indochina's territory to establish new bases in their fight against the Allies, the French imperialists [people who seek to extend

both the French and the Japanese. He announced that the nation would be known as the Democratic Republic of Vietnam, with a capital in the northern city of Hanoi. In his speech Ho used quotes from the American Declaration of Independence. Some people felt that this proved that Ho's main motivation was securing the freedom of his people, rather than creating a Communist state. But others claimed that Ho was only trying to gain *their power or influence over others] went down on their bended knees and handed over our country to them. . . .*

After the Japanese had surrendered to the Allies, our whole people rose to regain our national sovereignty [independence and self-rule] and to found the Democratic Republic of Vietnam.

The truth is that we have wrested [taken] our independence from the Japanese and not from the French.

The French have fled, the Japanese have capitulated [surrendered], Emperor Bao Dai has abdicated [given up claim to the throne]. Our people have broken the chains which for nearly a century have fettered [restrained] them and have won independence for the Fatherland. Our people at the same time have overthrown the monarchic regime [a government ruled by a king or queen] that has reigned supreme for dozens of centuries. In its place has been established the present Democratic Republic.

For these reasons, we, members of the Provisional Government, representing the whole Vietnamese people, declare that from now on we break off all relations of a colonial character with France . . . and we abolish all the special

rights the French have unlawfully acquired in our Fatherland.

The whole Vietnamese people, animated [energized] by a common purpose, are determined to fight to the bitter end against any attempt by the French colonialists to reconquer their country.

We are convinced that the Allied nations, which at Teheran and San Francisco [sites of peace negotiations following World War II] have acknowledged the principles of self-determination and equality of nations, will not refuse to acknowledge the independence of Vietnam.

A people who have courageously opposed French domination for more than eighty years, a people who have fought side by side with the Allies against the fascists during these last years, such a people must be free and independent.

For these reasons, we, members of the Provisional Government of the Democratic Republic of Vietnam, solemnly declare to the world that Vietnam has the right to be a free and independent country—and in fact it is so already. The entire Vietnamese people are determined to mobilize all their physical and mental strength, to sacrifice their lives and property in order to safeguard their independence and liberty.

the support of the United States by quoting from the famous American document. "Was it admiration for the ideals of the United States? Only a pragmatic [practical] gesture to enhance his bid for American support? The legend of Ho Chi Minh permits either answer," Henry Kamm wrote in *Dragon Ascending.*

In any case, it soon became clear that France—which had suffered a great deal of damage to its land, economy, and

Crowds in Saigon await the proclamation of the Republic of Vietnam in 1955.

Reproduced by permission of Corbis Corporation.

reputation as a world leader during World War II—was not willing to give up its former colony. After a year of negotiations between Ho and the French government, war erupted in Vietnam in late 1946. During this conflict, which became known as the First Indochina War, two different Vietnamese governments emerged to compete for the support of the people. One was Ho's Communist government, based in Hanoi. The other was a French-supported government led by Bao Dai, based in the southern city of Saigon. The United States recognized Bao Dai and his government as the legitimate leaders of Vietnam.

The Geneva Accords

But Ho and his Viet Minh forces continued fighting to gain Vietnam's independence from French rule. The war continued until 1954, when the Viet Minh finally defeated the French at the decisive Battle of Dien Bien Phu. Afterward, representatives from Vietnam, France, the United States, and other nations met in Geneva, Switzerland, to negotiate a peace agreement to end the Indochina War. The Geneva Accords divided Vietnam into two sections along the 17th parallel. Ho's Communist government controlled the area north of the line—known as the Democratic Republic of Vietnam or North Vietnam. A U.S.-supported government under Ngo Dinh Diem controlled the area south of the line—known as the Republic of Vietnam or South Vietnam. The Geneva Accords also provided for nationwide free elections to be held two years later, in July 1956, with the goal of reunifying Vietnam under a single government.

In the meantime, however, the United States and the Soviet Union had become involved in an intense rivalry known as the Cold War. Both nations competed to spread their political philosophies and influence around the world after the end of World War II. For this reason, the U.S. government began to worry about the spread of communism in Southeast Asia. It believed that if a Communist government came to power in Vietnam, then Communist forces would soon take control of other nearby nations as well. They felt that this situation would threaten the national security of the United States by increasing the strength of the Soviet Union.

U.S. government leaders knew that Ho held strong Communist beliefs. They also realized that he had connections in the Soviet Union and enjoyed great popularity across Asia. As a result, American officials feared Ho and became determined to prevent him from establishing a Communist government over all of Vietnam. Instead, the United States government provided financial aid and military advisors to Diem's government in the South. When it became clear that Diem would lose a national election to Ho, the United States and its South Vietnamese allies refused to hold the elections that were required under the Geneva Accords.

Ho and the North Vietnamese Communists became very angry when the deadline for free elections passed and no action was taken. They felt that by refusing to honor the Geneva Accords, the United States was interfering with the internal affairs of their country. Some people in South Vietnam felt the same way, especially after Diem's government began restricting their personal freedom and using violence to

North Vietnamese soldiers patrolling Hanoi.
Reproduced by permission of Corbis Corporation.

silence its enemies. In addition, some people who had supported the Viet Minh during the war against France had remained in the South afterward. These Communist supporters mingled with the South Vietnamese people and encouraged them to rise up against Diem and force him to hold elections. Diem renamed these Communists the Viet Cong.

In 1960 the National Liberation Front (NLF) was formed in order to organize the various groups that opposed

Diem's government. By that time the Viet Cong had entered an armed struggle against Diem and his American military advisors. As opposition to Diem grew, the Communist guerilla fighters were able to gain control of large areas of the South Vietnamese countryside. The U.S. government responded by sending in Army Special Forces units, known as the Green Berets, to confront the guerillas and help Diem maintain control. The Americans also took steps to reduce the support for the Viet Cong in the countryside. For example, they moved peasants into fortified compounds known as Strategic Hamlets. But this program uprooted the peasants from their traditional lands and forced them to depend on the Americans. In fact, some people claim that this plan actually increased support for the Communist rebels.

The United States continued increasing its financial and military support for South Vietnam over the next several years. "By the middle of 1964, the United States had formed in South Vietnam the largest military and civilian [non-military] advisory team ever assembled abroad in 'peacetime,'" Sanford Wexler wrote in *The Vietnam War: An Eyewitness History*. The U.S. government was more determined than ever to prevent the Communists from gaining control of Vietnam. But Ho refused to negotiate any settlement that did not include a complete withdrawal of American forces and Communist participation in the South Vietnamese government. The North Vietnamese were equally determined to continue fighting until they achieved their goal of an independent, unified Vietnam under Communist rule.

Things to remember while reading the excerpt from Ho Chi Minh's letter:

- In his letter Ho Chi Minh characterizes the situation in Vietnam as a "war of aggression" by the United States against the Vietnamese people. Throughout the Vietnam War, North Vietnamese leaders often claimed that they were involved in a nationalist movement to liberate their country from foreign invaders. Ho says that by refusing to honor the Geneva Accords, the U.S. government is interfering with the natural process of reunifying his country under one government. He claims that the American actions endanger not only Vietnamese independence, but also the United States' reputation in the world.

- Ho makes a distinction between the American people and the U.S. government. He is aware that many Americans oppose U.S. involvement in Vietnam. He asks these people to demand that the U.S. government withdraw its forces and allow his country to move toward independence and self-rule. Throughout the Vietnam War many U.S. political leaders criticized the American antiwar movement. They claimed that it limited their ability to fight the war and added to the strength and determination of North Vietnam. Ho's statement makes it clear that he did feel some hope that a strong antiwar movement in the United States could eventually help him achieve his goals.

- Ho refers to the South Vietnamese government and army as agents of the United States. He claims that U.S. and South Vietnamese leaders are working together to dominate the Vietnamese people against their will. In fact, he says that the United States is simply planning to turn Vietnam into a new colony to replace the one abandoned by the French ten years earlier. At the same time, Ho refers to the Viet Cong guerilla fighters and South Vietnamese people who support the Communists as "heroic" and "patriotic." He even makes it seem as if the people of South Vietnam are fighting to end U.S. aggression on their own. In reality, however, the Viet Cong enjoyed broad support from North Vietnam throughout the war. In addition, many people in South Vietnam did not support the Communists, and some strongly favored the U.S. presence in their country.

- In May 1964, when Ho wrote this letter, the U.S. presence in Vietnam consisted of about 25,000 military advisors and some helicopters and other equipment. The United States did not send combat troops into Vietnam to wage an all-out ground war until later in 1964.

- In his letter Ho claims that between 1954 and 1964 the American and South Vietnamese forces killed 160,000 people and either tortured or arrested over one million others. These figures are hotly disputed by the other side. The South Vietnamese government and its American military advisors would argue that nowhere near this many people had been victims of the war. In addition, they would blame the Viet Cong guerillas for much of the violence that did occur in South Vietnam during these years.

Excerpt from Ho Chi Minh's letter to the editor of Minority of One:

Dear Mr. Editor,

*I sincerely thank your paper for affording me an opportunity to talk with the American people on the present situation in South Vietnam. From Vietnam, some ten thousand miles away from the United States, I wish to **convey** to our American friends greetings of friendship together with this **earnest** appeal.*

*I hope that you will more clearly realize the bitter truth about South Vietnam which **constitutes** one half of our fatherland. An extremely **atrocious** war is raging there, a war which turns out to be the biggest, the most **protracted**, and the bloodiest one now going on in the world. This so-called "**special war**" is actually a war of aggression waged by the U.S. Government and its agents, a war which is daily causing grief and suffering to our fourteen million **compatriots** in South Vietnam, and in which thousands of American youths have been killed or wounded. This "special war" is reducing to ashes our villages, destroying our fields, and devastating one half of our country; it has cost the American people thousands of millions of dollars. Furthermore, this war which is **replete** with horrible crimes, has not only **infringed** upon the freedom and independence of our compatriots in South Vietnam, but also **besmeared** the good reputation and good traditions of the American people.*

The Vietnamese people are well aware that the American people want to live in peace and friendship with all other nations. I have been to the United States, and I understand that the Americans are a talented people strongly attached to justice.

*The Vietnamese people never confuse the justice-loving American people and the U.S. Government which has committed numerous crimes against them in the past ten years. Those very **saboteurs** of our nation's independence and freedom are also the people who*

Convey: Express.

Earnest: Sincere.

Constitutes: Forms or makes up.

Atrocious: Extremely cruel or brutal.

Protracted: Extended or drawn out.

Special war: A term used to describe American military involvement in Vietnam during the early 1960s, when U.S. Army Special Forces were sent to train the local people to resist guerilla warfare.

Compatriots: Countrymen; fellow people of Vietnam.

Replete: Full.

Infringed: Interfered with or limited.

Besmeared: Smeared or soiled.

Saboteurs: People who commit sabotage, or engage in deliberate destruction in order to harm others.

Unalienable: Not able to be given up or transferred.

Viz: An abbreviation of the Latin term *videlicet,* meaning namely or specifically.

Colonialist: A country that assumes political control over another country.

Dienbienphu: A French military post in northwestern Vietnam that was the site of a decisive Vietnamese victory during the First Indochina War in 1954.

Geneva Accords: The 1954 peace treaty that ended the First Indochina War and divided the nation of Vietnam into two sections at the 17th parallel.

Sovereignty: Independence and self-government.

Lao: The people of Laos, a country located on Vietnam's western border.

Cambodian: The people of Cambodia, a country located on Vietnam's western border.

Demarcation: Separation.

Democratic Republic of Vietnam: North Vietnam, of which Ho Chi Minh was the leader.

National construction: Nation building.

Saigon: The capital city of South Vietnam.

Partition: Division or separation.

have betrayed the Declaration of Independence of the United States which highlights the truth that "all men are created equal," and the **unalienable** Rights of man, **viz.** "Life, Liberty, and the pursuit of Happiness."

It is common knowledge that in 1954, the Vietnamese people and army defeated the forces of the French **colonialist** aggressors in the **Dienbienphu** battle. Subsequently, the 1954 Geneva Conference on Indochina was held with the participation of nine countries including the United States. The **Geneva Accords** were concluded and the participating countries, the United States included, solemnly undertook to respect the unalienable national rights, namely independence, **sovereignty**, unity, and territorial integrity [completeness] of the Vietnamese as well as the **Lao** and **Cambodian** peoples. The Agreements also stipulate that the 17th Parallel is to be only a provisional [temporary] military **demarcation** line between the Northern and Southern zones of Vietnam and that in 1956 the administrations of the two zones should hold general elections to bring about the peaceful reunification of the country.

Loyal to the interests of peace and to the supreme national interests of the fatherland, the Government of the **Democratic Republic of Vietnam** ever since the signing of the Geneva Agreements has been unswervingly standing for respect and correct implementation of the said Agreements, and it firmly demands that the other parties should do the same.

After the Geneva Conference, the Vietnamese people should have been in a position to live in peace and to devote themselves to **national construction**. But the U.S. Government has trampled underfoot the Geneva Agreements . . . . Early in 1962, it openly established in **Saigon** a U.S. military command to take into its hands the reins directing the war in South Vietnam. It has more and more brazenly intervened in that part of our country where it has fostered [encouraged] a gang of henchmen [followers] to carry out its policy and massacre our compatriots. They have sabotaged the Geneva Agreements, prolonged the **partition** of our country, and thus caused heart-rending sufferings to an entire people.

Over the past ten years, our people in North Vietnam, having become masters of their own life, have been in a position to live in peace, to develop economy and culture and to build up a new life of welfare and happiness. Meanwhile, our compatriots in South Vietnam, who had, together with the whole nation, gone through nine years of hard and heroic resistance war against the French colonialist invaders, have had to undergo ten more years of an atrocious war unleashed by the U.S. **imperialists** and their agents. It is due to the latter that over 160,000 compatriots of ours in South Vietnam have been killed, 680,000 tortured to **infirmity** and 370,000 others jailed. The victims include many old folk, women, and children.

At present, this horrible war of aggression has become fiercer under the impulse [driving force] and command of 25,000 U.S. officers and servicemen with the use of U.S. aircraft, tanks, arms, ammunition, and chemical poisons, and of the over 600,000 strong **mercenary** army of the South Vietnam administration, agent of the United States.

For ten years now, U.S. Governments and their agents have tried to crush the resistance of a heroic people by the use of brutal force. They want to turn our fourteen million compatriots in South Vietnam into slaves, and the southern part of our country into a new-type colony and a military base with a view to menacing the independence of the **Indochinese** and other Southeast Asian countries and attacking North Vietnam . . . .

But facts have shown that the path of aggression followed by the U.S. imperialists in South Vietnam is only a dark "tunnel" as admitted by the late President John Kennedy.

The heroic people of South Vietnam are resolved not to balk at the guns of the aggressors and **traitors**. Our compatriots would rather sacrifice everything than live in slavery. So far, under the leadership of the **National Front for Liberation**, the **patriotic forces** in South Vietnam have daily grown in strength and enjoy an increasing prestige at home and abroad. More than half of the population and over two-thirds of the territory of South Vietnam have been **liberated**. Over the past three years alone, the South Vietnam **Liberation Armed Forces** and people have wiped out or disintegrated hundreds of thousands of enemy troops, thousands of U.S. officers and servicemen have been killed or wounded. The Liberation Armed Forces have shot down hundreds of aircraft and captured tens of thousands of U.S.-made weapons of various kinds. All the strategies and tactics applied by the United States in South Vietnam have completely failed. Of the 8,000 **strategic hamlets** already set up (which are in fact fascist-like concentration camps) over 80 percent have been destroyed. All these victories of the patriotic forces in South Vietnam amply show that the people of South Vietnam by themselves are fully in a position to thwart [defeat] all aggressive

Imperialists: People who seek to extend their power or influence over others.

Infirmity: Frailty or feebleness.

Mercenary: Soldiers hired to serve a foreign country.

Indochinese: People of the Indochina Peninsula, which includes Vietnam, Cambodia, and Laos.

Traitors: People who are disloyal to their country; in this case, South Vietnamese who support the Americans.

National Front for Liberation: A nationalist organization designed to rally the South Vietnamese people to overthrow the government and reunify the country under Communist rule.

Patriotic forces: People in South Vietnam who supported the Communist cause, including the Viet Cong.

Liberated: Freed from the control of the South Vietnamese government and its American allies.

Liberation Armed Forces: Vietnamese Communist guerilla fighters, also known as Viet Cong, who worked with the North Vietnamese Army to conquer South Vietnam.

Strategic hamlets: South Vietnamese villages surrounded by barbed wire and other defenses as part of an American strategy of keeping Viet Cong guerillas from circulating among the people.

Ho Chi Minh: Nationalist or Communist?

Experts on the Vietnam War have often debated the question of whether Ho Chi Minh was motivated primarily by nationalism (an intense feeling of loyalty to a country) or communism. There is little doubt that Ho believed strongly in the Communist political system, in which the government controls all resources and means of producing wealth. By eliminating private property, this system is designed to create an equal society with no social classes. But Ho also felt a deep passion for Vietnam and truly wanted to bring independence to his people. He often downplayed his Communist beliefs in order to appeal to the patriotic feelings of the Vietnamese people. He also emphasized his nationalism as he tried to gain the support of democratic nations like the United States.

In his book *Dragon Ascending* Henry Kamm noted that historians may never know the truth behind Ho's motivations: "What is certain is his single-minded passion for the independence of his people, by peaceful means if possible, by war if necessary. Rightly or wrongly . . . he convinced himself . . . that Vietnam's road to independence could only be Communist." But other experts claim that Ho's main goal was to institute a Communist government in Vietnam, and that his nationalist feelings were of secondary importance. "Ho was a Vietnamese Communist, not a Communist Vietnamese," Albert Marrin wrote in *America and Vietnam: The Elephant and the Tiger.* "There is an important difference here. Being a Communist Vietnamese would have meant patriotism came first. Ho certainly loved his country, but patriotism was no longer his chief concern. It had become a means to an end, a way of uniting people. . . . His chief loyalty, however, was to communism."

By many accounts, both nationalism and communism played important roles in determining Ho's actions before and during the Vietnam War. Perhaps a more important factor in causing the war was the U.S. government's view of Ho's motivations. If American leaders had not believed that Ho was first and foremost a Communist, they may not have tried to prevent him from gaining control over Vietnam. Nationwide elections might have taken place in 1956, as outlined in the Geneva Accords, and the United States might never have become involved in Vietnam. "If Ho was sincere [in telling U.S. officials that he was motivated by nationalism], then Washington's later actions were both foolish and unnecessary," Marrin stated. "Indeed, next to the Civil War, they produced the worst tragedy in our nation's history."

maneuvers and plans of the U.S. imperialists, and that the war of aggression now being waged by the U.S. Government and its agents is a hopeless war doomed to defeat. Such signboards as "anticommunism," "for democracy and freedom," and **slanderous allegations** about "intervention" or "aggression" by the North in South Vietnam which they resort to as a cover to their crimes, can deceive no one. And in spite of several **"changes of horses,"** the U.S. imperialists cannot help being increasingly bogged down in South Vietnam, nor can they conceal their repeated setbacks from the American people who have come to be more and more aware of the truth.

That is the reason why the movement of struggle of the American people for the ending of the dirty war of aggression in South Vietnam is gaining momentum. And among the U.S. ruling circle themselves, more and more voices are being raised against the policy of blindly pursuing this hopeless war. From the bottom of their hearts, the Vietnamese people thank the workers', youth, students', and women's organizations, as well as **progressive** intellectuals, congressmen, and clergymen in the United States who have courageously raised their voices, staged demonstrations, exposed the criminal policy of aggression pursued by the U.S. government, and expressed their support for the just struggle of the patriotic forces in South Vietnam.

I wish to add the following for our American friends: Not only do we suffer because of the hardships and sacrifices imposed on our compatriots in South Vietnam, we also feel pity and sympathy for the American mothers and wives who have lost their sons or husbands in the unjust war carried out in South Vietnam by the U.S. **militarists.**

One cannot allow the U.S. Government and its agents to go on indefinitely perpetrating [carrying out] their dark designs. It is high time to stay [stop] their bloody hands. Of course, first of all our compatriots in South Vietnam must fight to the end for their own liberation.

Ho Chi Minh.
Reproduced by permission of the International Portrait Gallery.

Slanderous allegations: False charges that could damage someone's reputation.

Changes of horses: A reference to the U.S. government's support for several different governments in South Vietnam.

Progressive: Forward-thinking; people who believe in political and social change.

Militarists: People who favor the use of aggressive military action.

*But you, American people, are also victims of the U.S. imperialists, so together with the Vietnamese people, you should **resolutely** struggle against the **bellicose** and aggressive militarists in your own country. Demand an immediate end to the dirty war in South Vietnam! Demand the immediate withdrawal of all U.S. troops of aggression and all U.S. arms from South Vietnam!*

*Demand that the U.S. Government let the Vietnamese people decide themselves their own internal affairs. The provisions of the 1954 Geneva Agreements on Vietnam recognizing the unalienable national rights of the Vietnamese people must be strictly respected. That is the only solution to the South Vietnam question which does not involve **face-losing** for the United States.*

*I hope that this urgent appeal will reach the American people. Once again I wish to thank all American progressive intellectuals and people who, for the sake of justice and freedom, peace and the friendship between our two peoples, have **valiantly** opposed the U.S. Government's policy of aggression in South Vietnam.*

I send you my best greetings.

Resolutely: With great determination.

Bellicose: Argumentative; inclined to start fights.

Face-losing: Embarrassment.

Valiantly: With great courage.

What happened next . . .

The situation in Vietnam continued to escalate into war after Ho wrote his letter in 1964. In August of that year North Vietnamese patrol boats allegedly fired upon American ships in the Tonkin Gulf off the coast of Vietnam. Today, most historians believe that this attack never occurred. Nevertheless, President Lyndon Johnson (1908–1973) used reports of this incident to convince the U.S. Congress to pass the Tonkin Gulf Resolution, which gave him broad authority to wage war in Vietnam. Under this authority Johnson launched a large-scale bombing campaign against North Vietnam and sent U.S. combat troops into Vietnam in early 1965. In the meantime, Ho decided to send regular North Vietnamese Army (NVA) forces into South Vietnam in order to help the Viet Cong fight the Americans.

Over time, the Vietnam War became a source of heated debate within the United States. As the number of killed and wounded American soldiers rose, the American people grew weary of the war and pressured the government to end its involvement. In 1973 President Richard Nixon (1913–1994) withdrew the last American troops from Vietnam. Two years later, North Vietnamese forces captured Saigon to win the war. North Vietnamese leaders then took steps to reunite the country as an independent nation under Communist rule—the mission that Ho Chi Minh had set out to accomplish thirty years earlier.

Did you know . . .

- Ho Chi Minh's name at birth was Nguyen That Thanh, which means "Nguyen Who Will Be Victorious" in Vietnamese. He went by a variety of other names during his career as a revolutionary, but he became best known under the name Ho Chi Minh, which means "He Who Enlightens."

- Ho Chi Minh spent much of his life outside of Vietnam. He sailed to Europe in 1908, at the age of eighteen, as a cook's helper on a French steamship. He spent the next thirty years studying Communist political ideas in London, Paris, Moscow, Hong Kong, and other major cities. He even spent some time in the United States. He finally returned to Vietnam in 1941, just in time to lead his people in a revolution to overthrow French colonial rule.

- Ho Chi Minh died before he could see his dream of Vietnamese independence come true. North Vietnam captured the South Vietnamese capital of Saigon in 1975—six years after Ho's death in 1969—to win the Vietnam War. Ho's successors then reunited the two parts of the country as an independent nation under Communist rule.

Sources

Buttinger, Joseph. *The Smaller Dragon: A Political History of Vietnam*. New York: Praeger, 1958.

Duiker, William J. *The Communist Road to Power in Vietnam*. 2nd ed. Boulder, CO: Westview Press, 1996.

Fall, Bernard B., ed. *Ho Chi Minh on Revolution: Selected Writings, 1920–1966*. New York: Vintage Books, 1967.

Ho Chi Minh. *Against U.S. Aggression, for National Salvation.* Hanoi, Vietnam: Foreign Languages Publishing House, 1967.

Kamm, Henry. *Dragon Ascending: Vietnam and the Vietnamese.* New York: Arcade, 1996.

Marrin, Albert. *America and Vietnam: The Elephant and the Tiger.* New York: Penguin, 1992.

Wexler, Sanford. *The Vietnam War: An Eyewitness History.* New York: Facts on File, 1992.

Wiegersma, Nancy. *Vietnam: Peasant Land, Peasant Revolution.* New York: St. Martin's Press, 1988.

The War at Home

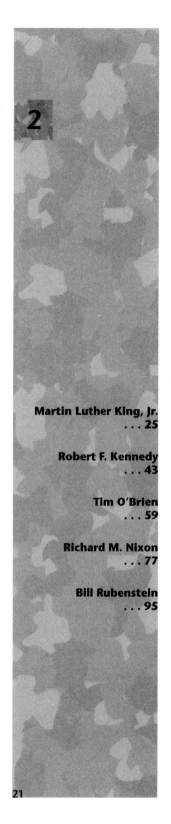

2

U.S. military involvement in the Vietnam War increased dramatically during the 1960s and remained significant until 1973, when American forces were finally withdrawn from the conflict. In the early years of U.S. military involvement in Vietnam, a large majority of Americans supported the government's policies. But as the bloody conflict continued without any end in sight, many Americans declared their opposition to the war in Vietnam. They said that the United States was interfering with the internal affairs of another country. They viewed the war as an immoral campaign that was wasting the lives of American soldiers and destroying the country of Vietnam. By the late 1960s, although many Americans continued to support U.S. involvement, the antiwar movement had become a major force in American politics and society. But as its influence swelled and some of its membership engaged in radical and violent protests, the antiwar movement itself became controversial. People who continued to support U.S. involvement viewed antiwar protestors as uninformed or unpatriotic.

Martin Luther King Jr. (1929–1968) is best known for his leadership in the American civil rights movement during the 1950s and 1960s. As the Vietnam War progressed, he also emerged as a leading critic of U.S. actions and involvement in the conflict. King believed that the Vietnam War was draining money from social programs that might reduce poverty and discrimination in American society. He also believed that African American soldiers were bearing too much of the war's burden and that their absence and losses were causing distress in African American communities. Finally, King charged that the U.S. government's actions in Vietnam violated the American ideals of freedom and equality. King explained many of his objections to the war in his "Beyond Vietnam" speech, delivered in April 1967 at Riverside Church in New York City.

Democratic senator Robert F. Kennedy (1925–1968) from New York was another prominent American political figure who publicly opposed the Vietnam War in the late 1960s. The brother of former president John F. Kennedy (1917–1963; president 1961–63), Robert Kennedy was well known throughout the United States. At first, he supported American involvement in Vietnam. But as the war dragged on, he became alarmed by the growing number of American casualties and the destruction of Vietnam's cities, villages, and farmlands. He also became convinced that South Vietnam's government did not deserve U.S. military support. On March 8, 1968, the powerful senator delivered a speech in which he publicly called for an end to U.S. support for South Vietnam's unpopular government.

As debate about the Vietnam War raged across America, many young men who were eligible for military service in Vietnam and subject to the draft wondered what they should do. Some strongly believed that the American cause was just, and they went to Vietnam willingly. But many others felt that they might be sacrificing their lives for a war that did not have merit. As opposition to the war intensified, millions of young Americans agonized over whether to accept induction (membership in the armed forces) or go to jail or Canada to avoid military service. In his short story "On the Rainy River," Vietnam veteran Tim O'Brien (1946–) explored how one young American struggled with this issue.

When Republican Richard M. Nixon (1913–1994; president 1969–1974) became president of the United States in

A delegate to the
Democratic National
Convention burns his
delegate card protesting
the Democrats' platform
on Vietnam.
*Reproduced by permission of
AP/Wide World Photos.*

January 1969, he decided to withdraw American forces from Vietnam gradually after first strengthening the South Vietnamese government and military. The antiwar movement opposed this strategy, saying that he should immediately withdraw all U.S. troops. But Nixon refused to change his mind. Instead, he decided to appeal to the American public for support. In a nationally televised speech in November 1969, Nixon defended his decision to keep American troops in Vietnam and claimed that immediate withdrawal would be disastrous for the United States.

As the Vietnam War progressed and casualties mounted on both sides, the American antiwar movement gained strength and became increasingly vocal in its protests. The most famous example of American unrest over the Vietnam War took place in the spring of 1970. That April, U.S. and South Vietnamese forces launched a big military operation into Cambodia, a country on the western border of Vietnam. Americans who opposed the war viewed this action as an expansion of the conflict, and antiwar demonstrations erupted on dozens of colleges and universities across the country. One of the strongest student protests against the invasion of Cambodia took place at Kent State University in Kent, Ohio. The campus demonstrations against the war ended in tragedy on May 4, 1970, when National Guardsmen shot and killed four Kent State students. One Kent State student, Bill Rubenstein, recalled the events of that day in his essay "Tragedy at Kent," published in *Middle of the Country*.

Martin Luther King, Jr.

Excerpt from his antiwar speech "Beyond Vietnam"
Delivered April 4, 1967, at Riverside Church in New York City

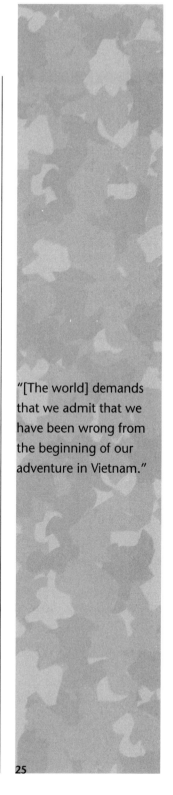

"[The world] demands that we admit that we have been wrong from the beginning of our adventure in Vietnam."

When the United States sent ground troops into Vietnam in 1964, one out of every seven (about 14 percent) of those soldiers was African American. In the time leading up to the Vietnam War, blacks tended to view military service as a very positive thing. Many African Americans joined the armed forces out of high school in order to receive training, career opportunities, and wages that were not readily available to them in civilian (non-military) society due to segregation.

At that time in American history, there were laws that segregated (separated) people by race. For example, white people and people of color were required to use separate restrooms, drinking fountains, schools, theaters, and restaurants. These laws discriminated against blacks and placed them in an inferior position in society. The military was one of the first American institutions to be desegregated. "Military service was for blacks a vehicle for social equality in which rank replaced race as a measure of respect and accomplishment," Clark C. Smith wrote in *Brothers: Black Soldiers in the Nam.*

Black and white soldiers lived and worked side-by-side in the early years of the Vietnam War, and the generally good relations between them were a point of pride for the U.S. military. But this situation soon began to change. As black soldiers faced discrimination in duty assignments and promotions, their resentment toward white officers grew. At the same time, the high number of African Americans who were killed or wounded in combat sounded an alarm through black communities in the United States.

Black leaders of the civil rights movement began speaking out against the war in Vietnam. They claimed that it was just another example of the U.S. government trying to control people of color. Empowered by changes taking place at home, black soldiers became more aggressive in demanding equal treatment in Vietnam. By the late 1960s race relations in the U.S. military had deteriorated significantly, especially in non-combat units.

Black soldiers face discrimination in Vietnam

A number of different factors contributed to the increasing tension between black and white soldiers in Vietnam. One of these factors was a decline in the qualifications of recruits. In mid-1966 the U.S. government came up with a new recruiting program called Project 100,000. It was intended to encourage poor and uneducated blacks to enlist in the armed forces by lowering the standards for induction (admission) and offering special training programs.

Between 1966 and 1968, 340,000 people enlisted in the American military through Project 100,000. More than 40 percent of these new recruits were African Americans from poor urban areas. They hoped to serve a tour of duty in Vietnam and return home with useful skills. But the government soon cut the special training programs from its budget. The Project 100,000 recruits arrived in Vietnam to find that many white officers considered them inferior to other soldiers. As a result, they were often assigned to menial tasks or to dangerous combat duty.

The poor treatment of the Project 100,000 recruits highlighted the discrimination that other African American soldiers faced in Vietnam. Many black soldiers received less desirable housing and duty assignments than white soldiers in the same unit. In addition, blacks often found themselves passed over for promotions. Only 2 percent of officers in the U.S. armed forces were black, even though blacks made up a much larger percentage of all military personnel during the Vietnam War.

The military justice system tended to discriminate against African Americans as well. One study found that black soldiers received harsher sentences than white soldiers for similar crimes committed during active service. In addition, white soldiers were twice as likely to be released without punishment for a first offense. By 1971 more than half of all U.S. soldiers held in military detention facilities were black.

But the most disturbing statistic in the minds of many African Americans was the number of black soldiers who were killed or wounded in combat. A high percentage of blacks and other minorities were assigned to dangerous combat duty in the early years of the Vietnam War. In fact, African Americans made up 20 percent of U.S. combat units in 1965 and 1966. As a result, black soldiers accounted for 25 percent of Americans killed in Vietnam during those years.

The U.S. government noted these statistics and took some steps to shift the ethnic balance in combat units. The government's efforts reduced the percentage of black fatalities (deaths) to 13.5 percent in 1967. This figure was more in line with the percentage of African Americans serving in the U.S. armed forces, but it was not enough to please black leaders in the United States.

Although a much larger percentage of armed service personnel serving in the Vietnam War were African American, only two percent of officers were African American.
Reproduced by permission of Archive Photos.

Civil rights leaders oppose the war

The early years of the Vietnam War were a time of upheaval in the United States, as black people fought to receive

Stokely Carmichael, national head of the Student Nonviolent Coordinating Committee (SNCC), speaking at a rally in 1967 about Black Power and the role of African Americans in the Vietnam War.
Reproduced by permission of AP/Wide World Photos.

equal rights and opportunities in American society. Many leaders of the civil rights movement initially supported the U.S. government's decision to send troops to Vietnam to stop the spread of communism in Asia. Some black leaders were reluctant to criticize President Lyndon Johnson because they believed he supported their call for civil rights. In addition, some African Americans worried that opposing the war would make them seem unpatriotic. But it did not take long for such attitudes to change.

The first civil rights organization to oppose the Vietnam War was the militant Student Nonviolent Coordinating Committee (SNCC). One of its leaders, Stokely Carmichael (1941–1998), denounced the U.S. government's policies as "white people sending black people to make war on yellow people [Asians] in order to defend the land they stole from red people [Native Americans]."

Civil rights leader Martin Luther King, Jr., began speaking out against the war in his church sermons in 1966. He made his feelings public on March 25, 1967, when he led an antiwar demonstration in Chicago that attracted more than 5,000 marchers. But his most notable antiwar statement came a few days later at a meeting of Clergy and Laity Concerned about Vietnam (CALCAV), a group of antiwar religious leaders. At this meeting, held at Riverside Church in New York City, King delivered his historic "Beyond Vietnam" speech.

In this famous and controversial speech, King explains his reasons for opposing the Vietnam War. For example, he says that the war reduces the time and money spent on social programs to reduce poverty and discrimination in American society. He also views the loss of black soldiers in combat as a disaster for the African American community. In addition, he believes that the U.S. government's policies are destroying the ideals of freedom and equality that the nation once stood for. For these reasons, King claims that Americans with moral character have a responsibility to protest against the war.

Things to remember while reading the excerpt from "Beyond Vietnam":

- This speech marked the first time King linked the civil rights movement with the growing antiwar movement. Because the war had a negative effect on blacks both at home and in Vietnam, he felt that the two movements should forge a partnership. But many people disagreed with him. They thought that he was hurting the cause of equal rights for African Americans by speaking out against the government's policies on Vietnam. "As the war in Vietnam intensified, advocates of civil rights wrestled with the question of whether to link opposition to the war in Vietnam with their commitment to domestic justice. On the one hand, the Johnson administration had done more to advance the civil rights of black Americans than had any administration since 1865," Robert D. Schulzinger wrote in *A Time for War.* "On the other hand, proponents of civil rights gradually came to believe that progress stalled because of involvement in Vietnam, and unless the administration reversed course all momentum would be lost. No one felt the dilemma of reconciling support for civil rights and speaking out over Vietnam more

No Room for Racism in Combat

Even as racial tensions erupted into violence on American military bases and in noncombat support units, combat troops found a way to overcome racial barriers and get along. Faced with life-or-death situations on a daily basis, soldiers in the field had to depend on each other for survival. One soldier noted that the only color that mattered in combat was "olive drab," the color of the uniforms worn by all American servicemen.

Harold Bryant, a black Vietnam veteran who was interviewed by journalist Wallace Terry for his book *Bloods: An Oral History of the Vietnam War by Black Veterans,* recalled an incident that occurred when a member of the white supremacist group Ku Klux Klan joined his combat unit: "That [angered] a lot of us," he stated, "'cause we had gotten real tight. We didn't have racial incidents like what was happening in the rear area, 'cause we had to depend on each other. . . . Well, we got out into a fire fight, and Mr. Ku Klux Klan got . . . trapped. . . . So we laid down a base of fire to cover him. But he was just immobile. He froze. And a brother [black soldier] went out there and got him and dragged him back. Later on, he said that action had changed his perception of what black people were about."

keenly than did Martin Luther King, Jr." King addresses these concerns in his speech.

- Throughout the civil rights movement, King was known as a strong supporter of the idea of nonviolent resistance. He sponsored peaceful sit-ins and protest marches for civil rights, and he cautioned African Americans against the use of violence in their fight for equality. But as he explains in his speech, the Vietnam War made it difficult for him to justify this position to his supporters. After all, the U.S. government engaged in violence to achieve its goals in Vietnam. "[Blacks] wonder what kind of nation it is that applauds nonviolence whenever Negroes face white people in the streets of the United States, but then applauds violence and burning and death when these same Negroes are sent to the field of Vietnam," he wrote.

- In his speech King outlines some of the terrible effects American bombing and defoliation (the use of harsh chemicals to kill crops and other vegetation) had on the Vietnamese people and culture. He notes that the U.S. government supposedly became involved in the war in order to free the Vietnamese people from the threat of communism and build a new, democratic Vietnam. But he says that the American forces have done so much damage that the South Vietnamese now consider them the enemy.

Excerpt from Martin Luther King, Jr.'s "Beyond Vietnam" speech:

Since I am a preacher by trade, I suppose it is not surprising that I have seven major reasons for bringing Vietnam into the field of my moral vision. There is at the outset a very obvious and almost **facile** connection between the war in Vietnam and the **struggle** I, and others, have been waging in America. A few years ago there was a shining moment in that struggle. It seemed as if there was a real promise of hope for the poor—both black and white—through the **poverty program.** There were experiments, hopes, new beginnings. Then came the buildup in Vietnam and I watched the program broken and **eviscerated** as if it were some idle political plaything of a society gone mad on war, and I knew that America would never invest the necessary funds or energies in **rehabilitation** of its poor so long as adventures like Vietnam continued to draw men and skills and money like some **demonic** destructive suction tube. So I was increasingly compelled to see the war as an enemy of the poor and to attack it as such.

Perhaps the more tragic recognition of reality took place when it became clear to me that the war was doing far more than devastating the hopes of the poor at home. It was sending their sons and their brothers and their husbands to fight and to die in extraordinarily high proportions relative to the rest of the population. We were taking the black young men who had been crippled by our society and sending them eight thousand miles away to guarantee liberties in Southeast Asia which they had not found in southwest Georgia and East Harlem. So we have been repeatedly faced with the cruel **irony** of watching Negro and white boys on TV screens as they kill and die together for a nation that has been unable to seat them together in

Facile: Too easy.

Struggle: The fight to achieve equal rights and opportunities for African Americans.

Poverty program: A social program enacted by President Lyndon Johnson to help the poor.

Eviscerated: Gutted.

Rehabilitation: Helping to become productive citizens.

Demonic: Evil or fiendish.

Irony: A situation that appears different than it really is.

Solidarity: Unity or togetherness.

Manipulation: Control by unfair means.

Molotov cocktails: Crude explosives made from bottles filled with flammable liquid.

Oppressed: Weighed down by abusive use of power or authority.

Purveyor: Source.

Exclude: Prevent from joining or participating.

Affirmed: Supported or agreed with.

Conviction: Strong belief.

Shackles: Bonds or restraints.

Incandescently: Extremely bright or glowing.

Autopsy: A medical examination to determine the cause of death.

Dissent: A difference of opinion.

Peninsula: The Indochina Peninsula, an area of Southeast Asia that includes Vietnam, Cambodia, and Laos.

Junta: A group of military officers in charge of the government.

Saigon: The capital of South Vietnam.

the same schools. So we watch them in brutal **solidarity** burning the huts of a poor village, but we realize that they would never live on the same block in Detroit. I could not be silent in the face of such cruel **manipulation** of the poor.

My third reason moves to an even deeper level of awareness, for it grows out of my experience in the ghettos of the North over the last three years—especially the last three summers. As I have walked among the desperate, rejected and angry young men I have told them that **Molotov cocktails** and rifles would not solve their problems. I have tried to offer them my deepest compassion while maintaining my conviction that social change comes most meaningfully through nonviolent action. But they asked—and rightly so—what about Vietnam? They asked if our own nation wasn't using massive doses of violence to solve its problems, to bring about the changes it wanted. Their questions hit home, and I knew that I could never again raise my voice against the violence of the **oppressed** in the ghettos without having first spoken clearly to the greatest **purveyor** of violence in the world today—my own government. For the sake of those boys, for the sake of this government, for the sake of the hundreds of thousands trembling under our violence, I cannot be silent.

For those who ask the question, "Aren't you a civil rights leader?" and thereby mean to **exclude** me from the movement for peace, I have this further answer. In 1957 when a group of us formed the Southern Christian Leadership Conference, we chose as our motto: "To save the soul of America." We were convinced that we could not limit our vision to certain rights for black people, but instead **affirmed** the **conviction** that America would never be free or saved from itself unless the descendants of its slaves were loosed completely from the **shackles** they still wear. . . .

Now, it should be **incandescently** clear that no one who has any concern for the integrity and life of America today can ignore the present war. If America's soul becomes totally poisoned, part of the **autopsy** must read Vietnam. It can never be saved so long as it destroys the deepest hopes of men the world over. So it is that those of us who are yet determined that America will be [a land of freedom and opportunity] are led down the path of protest and **dissent**, working for the health of our land. . . .

As I ponder the madness of Vietnam and search within myself for ways to understand and respond to compassion my mind goes constantly to the people of that **peninsula**. I speak now not of the soldiers of each side, not of the **junta** in **Saigon**, but simply of the people who

Martin Luther King, Jr. *Reproduced by permission of AP/Wide World Photos.*

Languish: Suffer and become weak.

Apathetically: Showing little feeling or emotion.

Concentration camps: An area where refugees are confined.

Casualties: People who are killed or wounded in war.

Vietcong: Vietnamese Communist guerilla fighters who worked with the North Vietnamese Army to conquer South Vietnam.

Degraded: Reduced to low standards of behavior.

Soliciting: Searching for customers for a prostitute.

Ally: Form bonds of cooperation and friendship.

Landlords: Wealthy people who own land and control its use.

Germans: The armed forces of Nazi Germany during World War II.

Buddhist: Follower of the religious leader Gautama Buddha who seeks moral purity and spiritual enlightenment.

Liberators: People who try to free others from oppression.

Fortified hamlets: Villages surrounded by walls designed to keep Vietcong guerilas out.

have been living under the curse of war for almost three continuous decades now. I think of them too because it is clear to me that there will be no meaningful solution there until some attempt is made to know them and hear their broken cries. . . .

They **languish** under our bombs and consider us—not their fellow Vietnamese—the real enemy. They move sadly and **apathetically** as we herd them off the land of their fathers into **concentration camps** where minimal social needs are rarely met. They know they must move or be destroyed by our bombs. So they go—primarily women and children and the aged.

They watch as we poison their water, as we kill a million acres of their crops. They must weep as the bulldozers roar through their areas preparing to destroy the precious trees. They wander into the hospitals, with at least twenty **casualties** from American firepower for one "**Vietcong**"-inflicted injury. So far we may have killed a million of them—mostly children. They wander into the towns and see thousands of the children, homeless, without clothes, running in packs on the streets like animals. They see the children **degraded** by our soldiers as they beg for food. They see the children selling their sisters to our soldiers [as prostitutes], **soliciting** for their mothers.

What do the peasants think as we **ally** ourselves with the **landlords** and as we refuse to put any action into our many words concerning land reform? What do they think as we test out our latest weapons on them, just as the **Germans** tested out new medicine and new tortures in the concentration camps of Europe? Where are the roots of the independent Vietnam we claim to be building? Is it among these voiceless ones?

We have destroyed their two most cherished institutions: the family and the village. We have destroyed their land and their crops. We have cooperated in the crushing of the nation's only non-Communist revolutionary political force—the unified **Buddhist** church. We have supported the enemies of the peasants of Saigon. We have corrupted their women and children and killed their men. What **liberators!**

Now there is little left to build on—save [except for] bitterness. Soon the only solid physical foundations remaining will be found at our military bases and in the concrete of the concentration camps we call **fortified hamlets**. The peasants may well wonder if we plan to build our new Vietnam on such grounds as these? Could we blame them for such thoughts? We must speak for them and raise the questions they cannot raise. These too are our brothers. . . .

At this point I should make it clear that while I have tried in these last few minutes to give a voice to the voiceless on Vietnam . . . I am as deeply concerned about our troops there as anything else. For it occurs to me that what we are **submitting** them to in Vietnam is not simply the **brutalizing** process that goes on in any war where armies face each other and seek to destroy. We are adding **cynicism** to the process of death, for they must know after a short period there that none of the things we claim to be fighting for are really involved. Before long they must know that their government has sent them into a struggle among Vietnamese, and the more **sophisticated** surely realize that we are on the side of the wealthy and the secure while we create a hell for the poor.

Somehow this madness must cease. We must stop now. I speak as a child of God and brother to the suffering poor of Vietnam. I speak for those whose land is being laid waste, whose homes are being destroyed, whose culture is being **subverted**. I speak for the poor of America who are paying the double price of smashed hopes at home and death and corruption in Vietnam. I speak as a citizen of the world, for the world as it stands **aghast** at the path we have taken. I speak as an American to the leaders of my own nation. The great **initiative** in this war is ours. The initiative to stop it must be ours.

This is the message of the great Buddhist leaders of Vietnam. Recently one of them wrote these words: Each day the war goes on the hatred increases in the heart of the Vietnamese and in the hearts of those of **humanitarian instinct**. The Americans are forcing even their friends into becoming their enemies. It is curious that the Americans, who calculate so carefully on the possibilities of military victory, do not realize that in the process they are **incurring** deep psychological and political defeat. The image of America will never again be the image of revolution, freedom and democracy, but the image of violence and **militarism**.

If we continue there will be no doubt in my mind and in the mind of the world that we have no honorable intentions in Vietnam. It will become clear that our **minimal expectation** is to occupy it as an American colony and men will not **refrain** from thinking that our maximum hope is to **goad** China into a war so that we may bomb her nuclear installations. If we do not stop our war against the people of Vietnam immediately the world will be left with no other alternative than to see this as some horribly clumsy and deadly game we have decided to play.

The world now demands a maturity of America that we may not be able to achieve. It demands that we admit that we have been

Submitting: Subjecting; causing to endure.

Brutalizing: Extremely harsh or unfeeling.

Cynicism: A feeling of distrust and contempt toward other people and their actions.

Sophisticated: Wise, knowledgeable, or experienced.

Subverted: Corrupted or ruined.

Aghast: With shock and horror.

Initiative: Power or energy to begin.

Humanitarian instinct: An inner desire to help other people or promote human welfare.

Incurring: Bringing down upon themselves.

Militarism: Willingness to use aggressive military power.

Minimal expectation: Simplest or lowest-level goal.

Refrain: Prevent themselves.

Goad: Provoke or force to take action.

Detrimental: Harmful.

Atone: Make up for or repair an offense or injury.

Extricating: Removing from an entanglement or difficulty.

Unilateral: One-sided.

Thailand: A country in Southeast Asia located to the southwest of Vietnam.

Laos: A Southeast Asian nation located on the western border of North Vietnam.

National Liberation Front: A revolutionary group organized to overthrow the South Vietnamese government and reunify Vietnam under Communist rule.

Geneva Accords: The peace treaty that ended the First Indochina War between Vietnam and France; it divided Vietnam into northern and southern sections.

Asylum: Protection or sanctuary.

Reparations: Repairs or payments to make up for a wrong or injury.

Synagogues: Places of worship for people of the Jewish faith.

Disengage: Withdraw or detach from.

Conscientious objection: Opposition to war for religious or moral reasons.

Alma mater: The school or college a person attended.

wrong from the beginning of our adventure in Vietnam, that we have been **detrimental** to the life of the Vietnamese people. The situation is one in which we must be ready to turn sharply from our present ways.

In order to **atone** for our sins and errors in Vietnam, we should take the initiative in bringing a halt to this tragic war. I would like to suggest five concrete things that our government should do immediately to begin the long and difficult process of **extricating** ourselves from this nightmarish conflict:

1. End all bombing in North and South Vietnam.

2. Declare a **unilateral** cease-fire in the hope that such action will create the atmosphere for negotiation.

3. Take immediate steps to prevent other battlegrounds in Southeast Asia by curtailing [reducing] our military buildup in **Thailand** and our interference in **Laos**.

4. Realistically accept the fact that the **National Liberation Front** has substantial support in South Vietnam and must thereby play a role in any meaningful negotiations and in any future Vietnam government.

5. Set a date that we will remove all foreign troops from Vietnam in accordance with the **1954 Geneva agreement**.

Part of our ongoing commitment might well express itself in an offer to grant **asylum** to any Vietnamese who fears for his life under a new regime [government] which included the Liberation Front. Then we must make what **reparations** we can for the damage we have done. We must provide the medical aid that is badly needed, making it available in this country if necessary.

Meanwhile we in the churches and **synagogues** have a continuing task while we urge our government to **disengage** itself from a disgraceful commitment [shameful course or action]. We must continue to raise our voices if our nation persists in its perverse ways in Vietnam. We must be prepared to match actions with words by seeking out every creative means of protest possible.

As we counsel young men concerning military service we must clarify for them our nation's role in Vietnam and challenge them with the alternative of **conscientious objection**. I am pleased to say that this is the path now being chosen by more than seventy students at my own **alma mater**, Morehouse College, and I recommend it to all who find the American course in Vietnam a dishonorable and unjust one. Moreover I would encourage all ministers of draft age to give up

*their **ministerial exemptions** and seek status as conscientious objectors. These are the times for real choices and not false ones. We are
at the moment when our lives must be placed on the line if our nation
is to survive its own **folly**. Tragically foolish behavior.*

*Every man of **humane convictions** must decide on the protest
that best suits his convictions, but we must all protest. . . .*

*We must move past **indecision** to action. We must find new ways
to speak for peace in Vietnam and justice throughout the developing
world—a world that borders on our doors. If we do not act we shall
surely be dragged down the long dark and shameful corridors of time
reserved for those who possess power without compassion, might
without morality, and strength without sight.*

*Now let us begin. Now let us rededicate ourselves to the long and
bitter—but beautiful—struggle for a new world. This is the calling of
the sons of God, and our brothers wait eagerly for our response. Shall
we say the odds are too great? Shall we tell them the struggle is too
hard? Will our message be that the forces of American life **militate**
against their arrival as full men, and we send our deepest regrets? Or
will there be another message, of longing, of hope, of solidarity with
their yearnings, of commitment to their cause, whatever the cost? The
choice is ours, and though we might prefer it otherwise we must
choose in this crucial moment of human history.*

What happened next . . .

At first King's speech created a great deal of controversy. Some of his fellow black leaders criticized him for losing
his focus on civil rights, an issue that they felt was more important than the Vietnam War. Meanwhile, members of the Johnson administration resented him for speaking out against their
policies. "King's speech was immediately criticized, by both
the civil rights movement and White House officials, who
described King as either a fool or a Communist," Albert Marrin
wrote in *America and Vietnam: The Elephant and the Tiger.* But
fellow religious leaders responded more positively to King's
remarks. Within a short time, several Christian groups
endorsed his views of the war.

Ministerial exemptions:
Releases from military service
because of one's position
as a religious leader.

Folly Foolish.

Humane convictions: Deep
feelings of sympathy or
compassion for other people.

Indecision: Wavering among
various courses of action.

Militate: Have a strong effect.

Boxing Great Muhammad Ali Resists the Draft

Like Martin Luther King, Jr., heavyweight boxing champion Muhammad Ali was a leader in the African American community who spoke out against the Vietnam War. Ali was born Cassius Clay on January 18, 1942, in Louisville, Kentucky. Growing up in near-poverty in Louisville, he experienced the racial discrimination that was widespread in the American South during the mid-twentieth century.

Ali took up boxing at a local gym at the age of twelve. He soon launched an impressive career as an amateur boxer, winning 100 of 108 amateur fights and two national Golden Gloves championships. He first came to national attention, however, when he won a gold medal in the 1960 Olympic Games in the light heavyweight division. Shortly after his Olympic glory, Ali moved up to the heavyweight division and announced his decision to fight professionally. He soon became well-known for his intelligence, quickness, and heart as a fighter, as well as for his flamboyant personality outside the boxing ring. He claimed the first of his three career heavyweight championships by beating Sonny Liston in 1964.

The day after he became the heavyweight boxing champion of the world, Ali announced that he was converting to the Islamic religion and changing his name from Cassius Clay to Muhammad Ali. His decision was very controversial. Many people perceived the Nation of Islam to be a racist group that was prejudiced against whites. But Ali defended his new faith: "People brand us a hate group. They say we want to take over the country. That is not true. Followers of Allah [the Islamic God] are the sweetest people in the world. . . . All they want to do is live in peace."

Over the next three years, Ali waged nine successful defenses of his heavyweight title. But then, in 1967, he was drafted by the U.S. Army to fight in Vietnam. Ali was determined not to serve in Vietnam. For one thing, he opposed war because of his Islamic religious beliefs. For another, he believed that the war drew the U.S. government's attention away from programs designed to reduce discrimination against black people in American society. "Why should they ask me to put on a uniform and go 10,000 miles from home and drop bombs and bullets on brown people in Vietnam while so-called Negro people in Louisville are treated like dogs?" he asked. "If I thought going to war would bring freedom and

Over time, antiwar feelings spread through the civil rights movement, and more and more African Americans began to criticize the U.S. involvement in Vietnam. By 1969 equality to 22 million of my people, they wouldn't have to draft me; I'd join tomorrow. But I either have to obey the laws of the land or the laws of Allah. I have nothing to lose by standing up and following my beliefs."

At first, Ali applied for conscientious objector status based upon his religious beliefs. But his application was denied and he was called up into the army. At this point, Ali formally refused to report for military service. This action was a direct violation of the nation's draft laws. He was put on trial and found guilty of violating the Selective Service Act. His punishment was a $10,000 fine and five years in prison, though he was allowed to remain free while the ruling was under appeal. In addition, the World Boxing Association stripped him of his heavyweight title and his boxing license. This action meant that Ali, who was at the peak of his career, was not allowed to box.

Ali thus became one of the most prominent Americans to resist being drafted to serve in Vietnam. Many people questioned his patriotism and turned against him. But many others praised him for standing up for what he thought was right. Over time, as opposition to the war

increased, Ali became a sort of folk hero to the antiwar and civil rights movements. He often spoke on college campuses and at peace rallies around the country. "I think Muhammad's actions contributed enormously to the debate about whether the United States should be in Vietnam and galvanized [stimulated] some of his admirers to join protests against the war for the first time," said Senator Ted Kennedy. "He had a worldwide audience, and naturally, anyone with that wide an audience will have an impact when they take a stand."

In June 1970 the U.S. Supreme Court overturned Ali's conviction for draft resistance. He regained his boxing license that September, three years after it was taken from him. Ali claimed the world heavyweight championship two more times, then retired in 1981 with a career record of 56 wins and 5 losses. Many experts claim that he was the greatest boxer of all time. In 1984 Ali was diagnosed with the degenerative nerve disorder Parkinson's disease. Since then he has struggled with symptoms— including uncontrollable tremors and difficulty walking—but he remains a well-known ambassador of racial harmony and peace.

polls showed that the majority of African Americans opposed the war (it would be several years before a majority of white Americans held the same view). The changing attitudes at home had an effect on the attitudes of black soldiers serving in Vietnam. Many African American servicemen began to question their roles in the conflict. They also began to speak out against discrimination and demand equal treatment in the U.S. armed forces. In the meantime, some white American soldiers grew resentful of blacks for their outspoken opposition to the war. Some whites even blamed King and other civil rights leaders for starting the antiwar movement. As a result, racial tensions increased among some groups of U.S. soldiers in Vietnam.

Racial tensions among U.S. troops

For the most part, race relations remained positive in American combat units. These troops shared experiences in a frightening environment, which often created strong bonds between black and white soldiers. When forced to face danger and the threat of death together, they tended to band together for protection. "When you drink out of the same canteen and eat off the same spoon, you get real tight together," a black paratrooper explained. Still, many soldiers recognized that combat was a unique situation, and that the interracial bonds they formed in the Vietnamese jungle might not last when they returned to the United States. As one wounded black soldier told black journalist Wallace Terry, "The officers, the generals, and whoever came to see you in the hospital, they respected you and pat you on the back. . . . In the States the same officers that pat me on the back wouldn't even speak to me."

In contrast to combat units, non-combat support units and base camps experienced a noticeable deterioration in race relations. In some cases, African American soldiers intentionally segregated themselves from the rest of their unit. They stuck together and often refused to associate with whites. "A year ago most black GI's [soldiers] were grateful for the chance to share a white man's foxhole," Terry stated in 1969. "But today many black GI's have become advocates of black power [a militant movement emphasizing racial pride] and want no part of a white U.S. war. The reason is not that we are losing the war here, but that we are losing the one in the ghettos of America." At the same time, some white soldiers in base camps made racist comments and displayed racially insensitive symbols, like the Confederate flag (the symbol of the slaveholding South during the American Civil War).

In some cases racial tensions exploded into violence. Some of the worst incidents included race riots at an army stockade in Long Binh, Vietnam, in 1967; at a marine base in North Carolina in 1969; and on board the aircraft carrier *Kitty Hawk* on the way to Vietnam in 1972. Some white officers began to fear that black troops would shoot at them instead of the enemy. Many of the documented cases of attacks on officers by their own men, commonly known as "fragging," were racially motivated.

By the mid-1970s race relations began to improve in the American armed forces. This improvement happened partly because the U.S. government recognized the problem and put programs in place to reduce discrimination among troops in Vietnam. Once the American forces withdrew from Vietnam in 1973, the military draft ended. From that point on, the U.S. armed forces were made up of volunteers who chose to serve rather than draftees who were forced to serve. As a result, soldiers tended to share similar views about the military regardless of their race. Over time, many African Americans again began to view the armed services as a good opportunity to receive education, technical training, and career advancement. In fact, black soldiers accounted for 25 percent of the American forces sent to the Persian Gulf in 1991.

Did you know . . .
- Martin Luther King, Jr., delivered his controversial speech at Riverside Church exactly one year before he was assassinated.

Sources

Goff, Stanley, and Robert Sanders. *Brothers: Black Soldiers in the Nam.* Novato, CA: Presidio, 1982.

King, Martin Luther, Jr. *I Have a Dream: Writings and Speeches That Changed the World.* New York: HarperCollins, 1986.

Marrin, Albert. *America and Vietnam: The Elephant and the Tiger.* New York: Viking Penguin, 1992.

Mullen, Robert W. *Blacks and Vietnam*. Washington, D.C.: University Press of America, 1981.

Schulzinger, Robert D. *A Time for War: The United States and Vietnam, 1941–1975*. New York: Oxford University Press, 1997.

Taylor, Clyde, ed. *Vietnam and Black America: An Anthology of Protest and Resistance*. Garden City, NY: Anchor Press, 1973.

Terry, Wallace, ed. *Bloods: An Oral History of the Vietnam War by Black Veterans*. New York: Ballantine, 1984.

Robert F. Kennedy

Excerpt from a speech on the Vietnam War
Delivered on February 8, 1968

Throughout the years of American involvement in Vietnam, U.S. government officials and military leaders became entangled in a great debate about the government of South Vietnam. Some people argued that if the United States continued to provide military and economic support, the South Vietnamese government could eventually build a democratic state that would be popular with the nation's people. But critics disagreed. They charged that the government was hopelessly corrupt and ineffective, and they noted that the South Vietnamese people felt no allegiance to their leaders. Some observers even claimed that the government's flaws were so great that it did not make sense for the United States to support it. This viewpoint became more common as the war dragged on and American opposition to involvement in Vietnam increased.

Doubts about the effectiveness of the South Vietnamese government first arose shortly after the 1954 Geneva Accords. This treaty, which ended the First Indochina War between Vietnam and France, divided the nation of Vietnam into a Communist-ruled North and a U.S.-supported South. South Vietnam's

"Reality is grim and painful. But it is only a remote echo of the anguish toward which a policy [U.S. military policy in Vietnam] founded on illusion is surely taking us."

Diem's family (left to right): Ngo Dinh Nhu, Diem's influential brother; Diem; Archbishop Ngo Dinh Thuc, another brother; Mrs. Nguyen Van Am, Diem's sister; the powerful and ruthless Mrs. Ngo Dinh Nhu known as Madame Nhu; Ngo Dinh Dan, brother who bossed central Vietnam; Ngo Dinh Luyen, brother-in-law and ambassador to Britain; and Nguyen Van Am, brother-in-law. Seated is Diem's mother with the Nhu's children.
Reproduced by permission of AP/Wide World Photos.

first leader was Ngo Dinh Diem, an educated Catholic who opposed communism. At first, most American lawmakers and diplomats saw Diem as a promising leader. As time passed, however, U.S. officials expressed growing concern about his management of the young country.

Diem's government showed little interest or ability to implement democratic reforms, tackle social problems, or work on behalf of ordinary South Vietnamese people. Instead, Diem devoted much of his time and energy to protecting his power. He installed family members in many important government positions and cultivated the support of fellow Catholics and wealthy Vietnamese, who made up only a small percentage of the total population. Many government officials discovered that they did not have to be honest in their dealings, as long as they remained loyal to Diem. In the meantime, Diem made virtually no attempt to expand support for his government among the South's vast populations of non-Catholics, peasants, and working-class city residents.

Over time, corruption emerged as a serious problem in nearly every area of Diem's government. It became particularly troublesome in the military, which was responsible for defending the South from Communist guerrillas known as Viet Cong who wanted to overthrow the government. "President Diem chose commanders for their loyalty to himself, not their fighting skill," wrote Albert Marrin in *America and Vietnam*. "High-ranking officers came from wealthy land-owning or merchant families. . . . The army was merely another business to them, not a way of serving a cause in which they believed. Commanders sold promotions, hired out their troops as laborers, taxed the peasants illegally, and took bribes. With fortunes to be made, fighting was the farthest thing from their minds. They played it safe, stayed close to base, and avoided battle whenever possible."

Not surprisingly, popular opposition to Diem's government increased in South Vietnam throughout the late 1950s. Diem approved brutal crackdowns on his political opponents in the early 1960s. But these efforts failed to halt the rising tide of opposition to his rule. In fact, Diem's attempts at political repression further increased the unhappiness that most South Vietnamese people felt toward his regime.

This trend deeply alarmed the United States, which desperately wanted to keep South Vietnam out of Communist hands. American officials recognized that Diem's policies were alienating his people and increasing the strength of the Viet Cong. The United States urged him to introduce policies that would help the nation's poor, tackle corruption, and show tolerance for Buddhism, the majority religion in South Vietnam. But U.S. efforts to convince Diem to change his ways failed.

In mid-1963 South Vietnam was rocked by nationwide Buddhist protests and a series of Viet Cong military successes. In September 1963 U.S. President John F. Kennedy expressed grave concern about Diem's government. "In the final analysis, it's their war and they are the ones who will either win it or lose it. . . . I don't think that the war [against the Communists] can be won unless the people support the effort and, in my opinion, in the last two months, the government has gotten out of touch with the people." Two months later, a group of South Vietnamese military leaders overthrew the government and executed Diem. The United States did not take an active role in the coup (attempt to overthrow the government). But it did signal its support for the action, for it had come to believe that a change of leadership was necessary to save South Vietnam from collapse. The only part of the coup that reportedly upset U.S. officials was the execution of Diem.

America hoped that the institution of a new government in Saigon (South Vietnam's capital) would stabilize and unite the country. But South Vietnam experienced a succession of governments from 1963 to 1967, as political leaders and military generals maneuvered for control of the nation. During this same period, the United States became much more heavily involved in the bloody conflict between North and South Vietnam. In fact, the United States took control of the war against the Communists of North Vietnam at this time, even as it urged leaders in Saigon to stop fighting each other, implement democratic reforms, and take responsibility for the country's future.

Many observers claim that the United States had no choice but to take a leading role in the Vietnam War. They point out that South Vietnam was in terrible economic, political, and military shape by 1965, when U.S. combat troops first arrived in the country. Indeed, many people believe that South Vietnam would have fallen to the Communists in the North within a period of months without American economic aid and military operations. But deepening U.S. involvement in Vietnam's affairs became a terrible dilemma for both countries. "If the Americans didn't step in and hold the government together, it would collapse," wrote Jonathan Schell in *The Real War.* "But if they did step in, whatever independent strength it [the South Vietnamese government] had was still further weakened and the regime's chances of ever standing on its own were further reduced."

South Vietnamese officials quickly became resentful of the U.S. presence and financial aid, even though it saved their government from falling apart. "American decision makers" showed a "startling attitude" toward South Vietnam, claimed Bui Diem, who served as South Vietnam's ambassador to the U.S. from 1966 to 1972. "At the top levels of the administration, the State Department, and the Pentagon, there is no evidence to suggest that anyone considered the South Vietnamese as partners in the venture to save South Vietnam," he wrote in *In the Jaws of History.* "In a mood that seemed mixed of idealism and naivete [innocence], impatience and overconfidence, the Americans simply came in and took over. It was an attitude that would endure throughout the remainder of the conflict. The message seemed to be that this was an American war, and the best thing the South Vietnamese could do was to keep from rocking the boat and let the Americans get on with their business."

Angry and frustrated about their increased dependence on the United States, South Vietnamese leaders sometimes resisted U.S. strategies to build a stronger nation simply because they wanted to show that they still exercised control over their own existence. "The Communists . . . always treated us as a puppet of America," complained South Vietnamese leader Nguyen Cao Ky. "But then the American people themselves also considered us as a puppet of America, not as true leaders of the Vietnamese people."

The perception that South Vietnam had become a puppet of America contributed to the continued unpopularity of the Saigon government in the late 1960s. But a much bigger factor was the tremendous wave of bloodshed and destruction that enveloped the nation during this period. Indeed, the ongoing war took a crushing toll on the people of South Vietnam. It killed thousands of Vietnamese with each passing month, destroyed huge sections of the countryside with bombings and chemical sprayings, and forced millions of Viet-

U.S. army helicopter picking up dead and wounded U.S. soldiers. *Reproduced by permission of Corbis-Bettmann.*

namese families to flee their traditional homes for wretched refugee camps. This misery severely diminished support for the South Vietnamese government among peasants and city dwellers alike.

In September 1967 Nguyen Van Thieu was elected president of South Vietnam in a rigged election. He quickly moved to strengthen his position, using violence, intimidation, bribery, and political maneuvers to build a powerful political machine in Saigon. At times he also showed sensitivity to the concerns of various ethnic and religious groups in the South. In 1969, for example, he introduced major land ownership reforms that benefitted poor rural Vietnamese. But Thieu approved of violence against political foes and permitted corruption in exchange for loyalty to his government.

Many Americans—both supporters and opponents of the war—expressed grave concerns about Thieu's government. After all, the United States was pouring billions of dollars and millions of soldiers into Vietnam to defend a corrupt and undemocratic regime that remained unpopular with many South Vietnamese citizens. But U.S. political and military leaders continued to support Thieu. They were desperate to win the war, and they believed that South Vietnam might crumble if its government changed hands again. As a result, the United States abandoned its earlier emphasis on cleaning up the South Vietnamese government in favor of efforts to stabilize the Thieu regime.

In early 1968 North Vietnam launched a surprise invasion of the South. This massive invasion, called the Tet Offensive, was eventually turned back by U.S. and South Vietnamese forces. But it stunned the American public, which had been repeatedly assured that the United States was on the verge of victory in Vietnam. The invasion showed that North Vietnam remained a dangerous and defiant foe.

In the weeks following the Tet Offensive, U.S. support for the South Vietnamese government came under renewed attack. These critics, who ranged from antiwar activists to political and religious leaders, charged that the government of South Vietnam was an unreliable ally that did not even enjoy the support of its own people. Without that support, these critics believed that U.S. efforts to win the war were doomed to fail. They then called on President Lyndon Johnson

(1908–1973) to enter into negotiations with North Vietnam to withdraw American troops and end the war.

One of the leading critics of the Johnson administration's Vietnam policies during this period of the war was Democratic Senator Robert F. Kennedy of New York. The brother of former President John F. Kennedy (1917–1963), Robert Kennedy was a respected and powerful figure in the U.S. Senate. An early supporter of American involvement in Vietnam, he emerged as a critic of the war in 1967. Not surprisingly, then, he viewed the Tet Offensive as further evidence that the United States should reconsider its support for the South Vietnamese government. The following excerpt is taken from a February 8, 1968, speech on that subject.

Things to remember while reading Kennedy's speech:

- South Vietnam's political leadership was unpopular throughout the 1960s. The nation had several different rulers during this time, but all of them became known for corruption, brutal repression of political opponents, and resistance to democratic reforms. These characteristics, combined with the terrible toll of the war, made life very difficult for the majority of South Vietnamese people. As a result, many South Vietnamese families and communities did not feel any desire to defend their young nation—and its government—from the Communists. They wanted peace above all else, and were willing to accept any political system that would end the bloodshed in their country.

- As American involvement in the Vietnam War escalated in the mid-1960s, the Democratic Party became divided over the conflict. Many Democratic Congressmen supported the war effort and the Vietnam policies of President Johnson, a fellow Democrat. But a significant number grew to oppose the war. Some critics expressed opposition because they viewed the war as immoral. Others believed that the war distracted America from civil rights issues and other social and economic problems within its own borders. And some expressed doubts about the war on strategic grounds. They charged that the United States would not be able to claim victory without sacrificing thousands of additional lives.

- The Tet Offensive shocked U.S. political and military leaders as well as the American public. By late 1967 the United States thought that its bombing campaigns and other military operations were taking a heavy toll on the Viet Cong and North Vietnamese forces. Many American officials expressed confidence that North Vietnam's leadership would soon give up its efforts to reunite North and South Vietnam under Communist rule. But the Tet invasion destroyed those hopes. It showed that the Americans and their South Vietnamese allies had underestimated the dedication and strength of the Communists.

Excerpt from Senator Robert F. Kennedy's speech:

*Our enemy, savagely striking at will across all of South Vietnam, has finally shattered the mask of official illusion with which we have concealed our true **circumstances**, even from ourselves. But a short time ago we were **serene** in our reports and predictions of progress.*

*The Viet Cong will probably withdraw from the cities, as they were forced to withdraw from the American Embassy [in Saigon, which they temporarily occupied]. Thousands of them will be dead. But they will, nevertheless, have demonstrated that no part or person of South Vietnam is secure from their attacks: neither district capitals nor American bases, neither the peasant in his rice **paddy** nor the commanding general of our own great forces. . . .*

*The events of the last two weeks have taught us something. For the sake of those young Americans who are fighting today, if for no other reason, the time has come to take a new look at the war in Vietnam; not by cursing the past but by using it to **illuminate** the future.*

*And the first and necessary step is to face the facts. It is to seek out the **austere** and painful reality of Vietnam, freed from wishful thinking, false hopes and sentimental dreams. It is to rid ourselves of the "good company" of those illusions which have lured us into the deepening swamp of Vietnam.*

Circumstances: Situation.

Serene: Confident.

Paddy: Wet field where rice is grown.

Illuminate: Explain or make visible.

Austere: Very plain.

We must, first of all, rid ourselves of the illusion that the events of the past two weeks represent some sort of victory. That is not so. It is said the Viet Cong will not be able to hold the cities. This is probably true. But they have demonstrated despite all our reports of progress, of government strength and enemy weakness, that half a million American soldiers with 700,000 Vietnamese allies, with total command of the air, total command of the sea, backed by huge resources and the most modern weapons, are unable to secure even

Robert F. Kennedy, attorney general under his brother former president John F. Kennedy, U.S. Senator, and 1968 Democratic contender for the presidential nomination.
Reproduced by permission of AP/Wide World Photos.

a single city from the attacks of an enemy whose total strength is about 250,000 . . .

For years we have been told that the measure of our success and progress in Vietnam was increasing security and control for the population. Now we have seen that none of the population is secure and no area is under sure control.

*Four years ago, when we only had about 30,000 troops in Vietnam, the Viet Cong were unable to mount the assaults on cities they have now conducted against our enormous forces. At one time a suggestion that we protect **enclaves** was derided. Now there are no protected enclaves.*

*This has not happened because our men are not brave or effective, because they are. It is because we have **misconceived** the nature of the war. It is because we have sought to resolve by military might a conflict whose issue depends upon the will and conviction of the South Vietnamese people. It is like sending a lion to halt an epidemic of **jungle rot**.*

*This **misconception** rests on a second illusion—the illusion that we can win a war which the South Vietnamese cannot win for themselves. You cannot expect people to risk their lives and endure hardship unless they have a stake in their own society. They must have a clear sense of identification with their own government, a belief they are participating in a cause worth fighting for. People will not fight to line the pockets of generals or swell the bank accounts of the wealthy. They are far more likely to close their eyes and shut their doors in the face of the government—even as they did last week.*

More than any election, more than any proud boast, that single fact reveals the truth. We have an ally in name only. We support a government without supporters. Without the efforts of American arms that government would not last a day.

*The third illusion is that the **unswerving** pursuit of military victory, whatever its cost, is in the interest of either ourselves or the people of Vietnam. For the people of Vietnam, the last three years have meant little but horror. Their tiny land has been devastated by a weight of bombs and shells greater than Nazi Germany knew in the Second World War. We have dropped 12 tons of bombs for every square mile in North and South Vietnam. Whole provinces have been substantially destroyed. More than two million South Vietnamese are now homeless refugees.*

Enclaves: Distinct groups within a larger unit.

Misconceived: Misunderstood.

Jungle rot: Skin infection common among soldiers in Vietnam.

Misconception: Mistaken belief.

Unswerving: Steady dedication.

*Imagine the impact in our own country if an equivalent number—over 25 million Americans—were wandering homeless or **interned** in refugee camps, and millions more refugees were being created as New York and Chicago, Washington and Boston, were being destroyed by a war raging in their streets.*

Whatever the outcome of these battles, it is the people we seek to defend who are the greatest losers . . .

*The fourth illusion is that the American national interest is identical with—or should be **subordinated** to—the selfish interest of an **incompetent** military regime. . . . The fifth illusion is that this war can be settled in our own way and in our own time on our own terms. Such a settlement is the privilege of the triumphant: of those who crush their enemies in battle or wear away their will to fight. We have not done this, nor is there any prospect we will achieve such a victory.*

*Unable to defeat our enemy or break his will—at least without a huge, long and ever more costly effort—we must actively seek a peaceful settlement. We can no longer harden our terms every time **Hanoi** indicates it may be prepared to negotiate; and we must be willing to foresee a settlement which will give the Viet Cong a chance to participate in the political life of the country. . . .*

*No war has ever demanded more bravery from our people and our government—not just bravery under fire or the bravery to make sacrifices—but the bravery to **discard** the comfort of illusion—to do away with false hopes and **alluring** promises. Reality is grim and painful. But it is only a remote echo of the **anguish** toward which a policy founded on illusion is surely taking us.*

This is a great nation and a strong people. Any who seek to comfort rather than speak plainly, reassure rather than instruct, promise satisfaction rather than reveal frustration—they deny that greatness and drain that strength. For today as it was in the beginning, it is the truth that makes us free.

Interned: Confined or held.

Subordinated: Given secondary importance.

Incompetent: Not effective or capable.

Hanoi: Capital of North Vietnam.

Discard: Throw away.

Alluring: Attractive.

Anguish: Pain and suffering.

What happened next . . .

On March 16, 1968, Robert Kennedy announced his intention to challenge President Johnson for the Democratic

Party's presidential nomination. Many observers thought that Kennedy's bid might prove successful, for the Vietnam War had greatly weakened Johnson's presidency. Two weeks later Johnson said that the United States was willing to engage in peace talks with North Vietnam. He then stunned the nation by stating that he would not run again for president.

Johnson's decision not to seek re-election made Kennedy a strong contender for the Democratic nomination. On June 5, 1968, however, Kennedy was assassinated by a gunman only hours after winning the California primary (a state election in which party nominees for national office are elected). His murder occurred less than five years after his brother's assassination and mere months after the killing of civil rights leader Martin Luther King, Jr. These killings, combined with domestic turmoil associated with the war and civil rights campaigns, made many Americans feel like their country was being torn apart.

Republican Richard Nixon defeated Democratic nominee Hubert Humphrey in the 1968 presidential election. Upon assuming office in January 1969, Nixon decided to place more responsibility for the war on South Vietnam's government and military. This would allow him to gradually withdraw U.S. troops from the conflict, which had become very unpopular with the American people. This policy came to be known as "Vietnamization."

President Thieu maintained his tight grip on power during this period of "Vietnamization," a policy change that he had no choice but to accept. He continued to treat opponents of his government harshly, using intimidation, violence, and torture as weapons. Fearful of losing power if the war ended with a compromise treaty, Thieu reserved especially harsh treatment for South Vietnamese people who called for negotiations with the North Vietnamese Communists. In July 1970 Thieu declared, "I am ready to smash all movements calling for peace at any price. . . . We will beat to death the people who demand an immediate peace." During this same period South Vietnam's national police chief told his forces to use any measures necessary to break up anti-government demonstrations, including bayonets and bullets.

Despite these repressive tactics, however, internal opposition to the Saigon government remained strong. Some of this resistance was encouraged by Communist agents. But many civilian opponents of Thieu's regime—including student activists, Buddhist groups, labor unions, and community leaders—acted out of a genuine belief in the need for sweeping changes in the government's political, social, and economic policies.

The United States continued to provide massive military and economic assistance to South Vietnam in the early 1970s, but much of this aid was stolen or misused. In the meantime, Thieu's ineffective leadership and the mounting devastation of the war created even more desperate conditions across the country. Conditions became particularly grim in the cities, which were totally unequipped to deal with the millions of homeless refugees who fled their rural homes during the war. By early 1972 there were an estimated 800,000 orphans roaming Saigon and other cities across the South, begging, stealing, and selling themselves as prostitutes in order to survive.

When the last U.S. troops left Vietnam in mid-1972, the Thieu regime felt even more vulnerable to attack from North Vietnam. The United States promised to continue giving economic aid to South Vietnam. The Nixon administration also promised to strike back with full force if the North tried to invade the South again. But Thieu and many other South Vietnamese thought that America might finally be abandoning its longtime ally. These concerns became even more pronounced when the United States and North Vietnam reached an agreement on a peace treaty in early 1973, and when the U.S. Congress began cutting its financial aid packages to Thieu later that year.

The Paris Peace Accords of 1973 called for the formation of a coalition government in South Vietnam that would include Communist representatives. Thieu refused to accept this part of the agreement. Instead, he ordered a series of military offensives in an effort to maintain the South's independence from the Communists. But these military operations failed miserably. His economic programs, meanwhile, triggered widespread hunger in rural areas and economic collapse in Southern cities during 1973 and 1974. By January 1975 one South Vietnamese legislator commented that "the leaders of the Republic of Vietnam [South Vietnam] are now spreading the view that the present deteriorating situation is due to the

Women fleeing a war-torn village in South Vietnam in 1968. Viet Cong lie dead after being killed by American soldiers. Much of the war was fought in the villages.
Reproduced by permission of Corbis Corporation.

lack of aid [from the United States]. But the reality of the situation is that the difficulty is not because of a lack of aid but because of *lack of support of the people.*"

The South Vietnamese government finally collapsed in the spring of 1975, when North Vietnam launched a final invasion. During that time few South Vietnamese military forces or communities offered any resistance to the invaders. The United States, meanwhile, declined to provide any military assistance to the crumbling Thieu regime. Embittered by America's decision to stay on the sidelines, Thieu resigned and fled the country on April 26. A few days later North Vietnamese forces seized control of Saigon.

Many scholars believe that it was only a matter of time until South Vietnam collapsed. After all, the nation's corrupt and ineffective leadership destroyed most popular support for the national government. In fact, the South Vietnamese government probably would have fallen to North Vietnam years earlier, if it had not been for America's massive infusions of military and economic assistance during the 1960s and early 1970s. "Again and again [during the war], the Saigon regime . . . came to the end of its natural life," commented Schell. "But again and again the United States hoisted the cadaver [corpse] to its feet and tried to breathe artificial life into it. Like a ghost that is denied a grave to rest in, this regime stalked the earth posthumously [after its natural life ended]."

Did you know . . .

- In 1967 South Vietnam managed to pass a formal constitution and hold national elections, despite the war. Supporters of the South Vietnamese government hailed these developments as evidence of the nation's great promise. These claims became less convincing, though, when it was discovered that government officials used bribery, intimidation, and other illegal measures to shape the election results.

- Vietnam historians estimate that by 1975 nearly 12 million South Vietnamese citizens—about half the country's population—had been forced to flee their homes because of the war.

- President Thieu settled in the United States after fleeing Vietnam in 1975. He made a fortune as a businessman in Massachusetts. In fact, some people believe that he became a billionaire. He never forgot his homeland, however. Thieu repeatedly expressed pride in his presidency, and in 1992 he declared that he someday wanted to return to Vietnam and lead the country again.

Sources

Bui Diem, and David Chanoff. *In the Jaws of History*. New York: Houghton Mifflin, 1987.

DeBenedetti, Charles. *An American Ordeal: The Antiwar Movement of the Vietnam Era*. Syracuse: Syracuse University Press, 1990.

Fall, Bernard. *The Two Vietnams*. New York: Praeger, 1967.

FitzGerald, Frances. *Fire in the Lake: The Vietnamese and the Americans in Vietnam*. Boston: Little, Brown, 1972.

Kearns, Doris. *Lyndon Johnson and the American Dream*. New York: Harper and Row, 1976.

Schell, Jonathan. *The Real War: The Classic Reporting on the Vietnam War*. New York: Pantheon, 1987.

Schlesinger, Arthur M., Jr. *Robert Kennedy and His Times*. Boston: Houghton Mifflin, 1978.

Van DeMark, Brian. *Into the Quagmire: Lyndon Johnson and the Escalation of the Vietnam War*. New York: Oxford University Press, 1991.

Werner, Jayne, and Luu Doan Huynh, eds. *The Vietnam War: Vietnamese and American Perspectives*. Armonk, NY: M.E. Sharpe, 1993.

Wiegersma, Nancy. *Vietnam: Peasant Land, Peasant Revolution*. New York: St. Martin's Press, 1988.

Tim O'Brien

Excerpt from his story "On the Rainy River"
Published in *The Things They Carried*, 1990

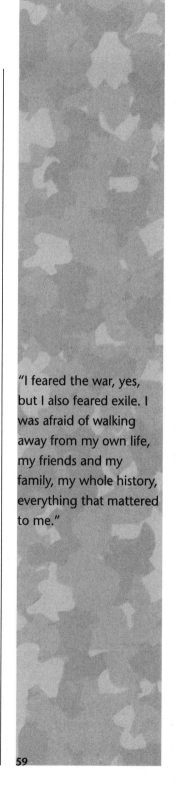

"I feared the war, yes, but I also feared exile. I was afraid of walking away from my own life, my friends and my family, my whole history, everything that mattered to me."

As American involvement in Vietnam deepened, the United States used a military draft system known as the Selective Service to meet its troop needs. But the draft soon became one of the most controversial aspects of the entire war. The antiwar movement condemned it as a terrible system that forced America's sons to fight an immoral war. Some supporters of the war disliked its rules as well. In fact, they joined antiwar activists in charging that draft rules favored young men from middle-class and wealthy families and forced America's poor and working-class families to shoulder most of the burden of the war. As criticism of the draft intensified and opposition to the war increased, millions of young draftees resorted to a variety of strategies to avoid military service in Vietnam. Millions of others decided to obey their draft notices. Either way, reaching a decision on this all-important issue was not easy for most men. Many draftees agonized over whether to accept induction (membership in the armed forces), torn by their conflicted feelings about the war and their responsibilities to family and country.

Originally created in 1948, the Selective Service was a federal agency that had the power to draft male citizens and residents between the ages of eighteen and twenty-six to serve in the U.S. armed forces. This pool of potential draftees was continually replenished over time, because every American male was required to register for the draft when he turned eighteen. During peacetime, the draft was not used very frequently. The armed services were able to meet their troop needs with volunteers. When the U.S. military commitment in Vietnam deepened in the mid-1960s, though, President Lyndon Johnson turned to the draft to meet the increased demand for soldiers.

The foundation of the Selective Service was a national network of draft boards. The boards were made up of volunteer citizens—usually white, financially secure, middle-aged men who were generally supportive of the war. These board members were responsible for reviewing the records of young draftees who lived in the area and deciding whether to approve or deny applications for draft "deferments" or "exemptions." Draftees who were given deferments were allowed to postpone entering the military service, while draftees who received exemptions were permanently excused from military duty. All other draftees—those who either did not request special status or had their requests turned down by the board—entered the military, provided they passed their medical exams.

The Selective Service process was very simple. Once a month, every draft board in the United States received instructions from the federal government to select a set number of draftees for conscription (enlistment) in the armed services. The boards then contacted eligible draftees to arrange medical exams. Those who failed were classified "4-F," which means ineligible for military service. Those who passed (and were not granted deferments or exemptions) usually were assigned to the U.S. Army. The Army was the largest branch of the military, and the other branches of the armed forces usually received enough volunteers to meet their needs.

At first glance, only a small percentage of American men appeared to be directly impacted by the draft. After all, of the approximately 26.8 million American men who became eligible for the draft during the war, only 2.2 million were actually inducted into the Selective Service. But the threat of the draft changed the lives of millions of other young men, and it became one of the most widely criticized aspects of the entire war.

Avoiding military induction

During the course of the war, millions of young American males became "draft dodgers" in order to avoid serving in Vietnam. Some evaded the draft because they feared for their lives. Others objected to military service because of a genuine belief that the war was immoral and unjust. And many men resisted the draft because they believed that the U.S. effort in Vietnam was doomed to fail. Most draftees who worked to avoid induction were probably motivated by a combination of all of these reasons.

Draftees used a variety of strategies to evade induction, many of which were legally allowed. In fact, approximately 16 million men—about 60 percent of the total number of draftable men who became eligible during the war—avoided military service by legal means. But men from middle- and upper-class families had much greater success in using these strategies than did young draftees from poor and working-class families. This fact gave rise to a slogan that became very well known during the war: "If you got the dough, you don't have to go."

Student deferments. The most popular strategy for evading the draft was to gain a student deferment. Under Selective Service rules of the mid-1960s, full-time college students were automatically excused from military service for as long as they remained in school. They could also preserve their draft immunity by going on to graduate school. Millions of young men took advantage of these rules to avoid induction into the armed forces. But this protection did not extend to part-time students, who often had to work their way through college because their families could not cover college expenses. Critics charged that this arrangement was blatantly unfair because it made young men from working-class or poor backgrounds much more vulnerable to the draft than their wealthier peers.

Medical exemptions. Another 3.5 million Americans were excused from the draft for medical reasons. This exemption also benefitted men from economically prosperous backgrounds more than draftees who came from poor and working-class communities. "One might expect men from disadvantaged backgrounds, with poorer nutrition and less access to decent health care, to receive most of these exemptions," wrote Christian Appy in *Working-Class War.* "In practice, however, most physical exemptions were assigned to men who had the knowledge and resources to claim an exemption." These draftees used cooperative family doctors to secure medical excuses and thus avoid military service.

Men from poor and working-class backgrounds, on the other hand, generally took their medical exams at government-run military induction centers. Exemptions were much more difficult to obtain at these centers. "Even very minor disabilities were grounds for medical disqualification," noted Appy. "Skin rashes, flat feet, asthma, trick knees—such ailments were easily missed or ignored by military doctors, but they were legal exemptions that were frequently granted when attested to by a family physician."

Many draftees were excused from military service for valid medical reasons. But some otherwise healthy young men purposely mistreated their bodies in order to gain a medical exemption. Some took large quantities of drugs in hopes of flunking the medical exam. Others starved themselves or fattened themselves up in order to get outside the military's weight requirements. Finally, some draftees pretended that they were insane or homosexual in an effort to avoid induction. Generally, young men from good economic backgrounds were more likely to know about these strategies. In fact, antiwar organizations often held meetings on college campuses to inform potential draftees about their options.

Guard or reserve duty. Another popular option for young men who wanted to avoid going to Vietnam was to enlist in the National Guard or Army Reserves. These part-time volunteer military organizations, based in the United States, were regarded as a relatively safe form of military service during the war. Consequently, competition to gain admittance into these organizations was fierce. By 1968, for example, the National Guard had a waiting list of 100,000 men.

During the course of the war, both the Guard and the Reserves became notorious for unfair admission policies. The rosters of both groups became dominated by young men from wealthy or politically connected families who were able to

make special arrangements for inclusion. Sons of poor and working-class families, meanwhile, often were left on the outside. Black men found it almost impossible to obtain a place in the Guard or Reserves.

Over one million Americans served in the National Guard and Army Reserves during the war. Occasionally, the safety of this type of military duty came into doubt. During the mid-1960s, for example, U.S. military leaders repeatedly asked President Lyndon Johnson to make greater use of these men in the war effort. But Johnson rejected these requests because of fears that America's middle-class and wealthy communities would turn against the war. President Richard Nixon adopted the same basic position when he assumed office in 1969. As a result, only 37,000 men from these organizations were mobilized (actively operated) during the conflict, and only 15,000 were sent to Vietnam.

Conscientious objectors. Another 170,000 Americans received "conscientious objector" (CO) deferments during the

Military police confront peace protestors outside the Pentagon in Washington, D.C., in 1967.
Reproduced by permission of Corbis Corporation.

A young man burning his draft card.

Reproduced by permission of AP/Wide World Photos.

Vietnam War. Conscientious objectors are people who refuse to fight in the military because of their religious and moral beliefs. Some COs asked to be excused from all military duties. Others volunteered to serve as combat medics or in other capacities in which they would not be asked to kill.

Conscientious objectors were actively supported by many local church groups and antiwar groups, but CO applications remained light in the war's early years. CO applications became much more popular as the war progressed and as the legal definition of conscientious objection changed. Initially, CO exemptions were given only to those who opposed all wars because of their belief in a Supreme Being. But the Supreme Court changed the definition in 1967 so that men could make CO applications based on general religious and moral objections to war. In 1970 the Supreme Court further ruled that the basic requirement for a CO deferment was a conviction that participation in the military violated one's "religious or moral" beliefs.

Not all CO requests were approved. In fact, local draft boards turned down more than 300,000 applications for CO deferments during the war. But many young men whose CO applications were denied mounted legal challenges to board rulings. The challenges delayed their induction into the military. They also overwhelmed the Selective Service System and created a huge backlog of cases in many of the nation's courtrooms.

Leaving the country. Some young Americans who became eligible for the draft during the war left the country rather than submit to military service. The most popular destination for these draftees was Canada, America's neighbor to the north. U.S. officials estimate that 50,000-75,000 draftees fled to Canada during the war (the Canadian government puts the figure lower, at about 30,000). Another 20,000 men relocated to Sweden, Mexico, and other countries.

Avoiding the Draft in North Vietnam

Some North Vietnamese men tried to evade their own country's military draft during the Vietnam War. Many families supported their sons in this effort. Important officials in the government often arranged to keep their sons out of the military by sending them overseas to study. Ordinary families, meanwhile, hid their sons or bribed doctors to disqualify them from service.

"Many parents tried to keep their sons out of the army," recalled one North Vietnamese man in *Vietnam: A Portrait of Its People at War.* "They would hide them when they were called up by the recruiting center. Anyone who didn't show up automatically had his rice ration cut off. But families would buy food on the black market or just get along by sharing whatever they had. They would survive that way while they tried to scrape up

enough to bribe a recruiting official to fix up the files. Other draftees mutilated themselves or managed to find other ways to fail the physical. People with money were able to pay doctors to disqualify their children. These kinds of things were easier to do in the three big cities—Hanoi, Haiphong, and Nam Dinh . . . where the government officials and Party leaders lived. Many of them were looking for ways to keep their children out too. . . . And people had more money in these places, so corruption was more a normal thing. Also, it was simply easier to hide in the cities and there was more information about how to stay out. The result was that the big majority of the Northern army was made up of young people from the countryside. They were just more naive. They believed the propaganda more easily. They didn't have the same chances to get out of it."

Although tens of thousands of young men relocated to Canada and elsewhere to avoid military service, this strategy was commonly seen as a last resort. It was usually chosen only after other possible "draft dodging" alternatives had been exhausted. After all, men who fled to Canada knew that they might never be able to return home to America to see their family and friends without risking arrest.

Draft resisters. Another popular strategy for avoiding military induction was outright defiance. Hundreds of thousands of young American men openly resisted the Selective Service System during the war. Some refused to register for the

Draft card burning in New York City's **Central Park.** *Reproduced by permission of AP/Wide World Photos.*

draft. Others burned their draft cards to protest the war. "Hell no, we won't go!" became a popular rallying cry within the antiwar movement.

Active resistance to the draft became particularly commonplace during the mid- and late 1960s, when the American public became divided about supporting the war. "The growth in public opposition to the war . . . enhanced draft resistance's appeal," confirmed Tom Wells in *The War Within*. "Resisters also maintained that noncooperation would increase protestors' credibility with the public. By challenging the government to send them to jail, resisters asserted, they were demonstrating that their opposition to the war sprang not from cowardice or youthful frivolity [silliness]—as supporters of the war often alleged—but from unyielding moral convictions."

David Harris, a draft resister who received a three-year jail sentence for his stance, agreed that active defiance of the Selective Service was a good way to show the American public that the antiwar movement was serious about its beliefs. "One of the first things that opponents of the antiwar movement pointed to was, 'Hey, look, our young men are over in Vietnam dying, and these guys are sitting around smoking dope.'" Harris told Wells. "I felt that in order for the antiwar movement to be effective speaking to that larger audience, it had to pay its own prices and make its own sacrifices and put itself in a position of vulnerability. Because I thought they were right, the critics were."

Between 1965 and 1975, approximately 200,000 Americans were formally accused of draft offenses. But most of these draftees never actually went to trial because the nation's court system was so heavily clogged with draft-related cases. Only 22,000 resisters were actually charged with draft law violations. Of these, 8,756 were convicted of crimes and 4,000 received prison sentences. The percentage of resisters who went to jail, then, was actually quite low. But Wells noted that their *willingness* to risk imprisonment had a noticeable impact on American society. "Resisters' personal courage increased the peace movement's credibility with some Americans," he wrote in *The War Within*. "Their sheer numbers nourished public questioning of the war as well. Perhaps most important, the Resistance inspired greater dedication and resolve among other antiwar activists."

Volunteering for service. Approximately 8.7 million men volunteered to join the U.S. military during the Vietnam War, four times the number of troops who were inducted through the Selective Service System. Many of these soldiers enlisted out of a genuine desire to answer America's military call to arms. But millions of the young men who voluntarily enlisted in the armed forces did so in an effort to exercise some control over their fate.

These volunteers recognized that they were exposing themselves to possible combat duty in Vietnam by enlisting. But many of them did so anyway for two major reasons. First, many enlistees came from poor and working-class communities, where knowledge of draft evasion strategies was weak and pressure to serve one's country was strong. Second, many enlistees believed that by volunteering for military service before being drafted, they were more likely to draw relatively safe assignments in Vietnam or at other U.S. bases around the world. Upon enlisting, however, many of these young soldiers still found themselves assigned to combat units in Vietnam.

In 1990 Vietnam veteran Tim O'Brien published "On the Rainy River," a short story that gives a dramatic account of one young man's feelings after being drafted. The story was published in a short story collection called *The Things They Carried,* a classic work of Vietnam War literature.

Like the other stories in *The Things They Carried,* "On the Rainy River" is narrated by a character who has the same name as the author. In addition, many of the incidents and places that are described in the short story collection are based on O'Brien's own life. For example, the author actually received a draft notice shortly after graduating from Macalester College in Minnesota, just as the narrator does in "On the Rainy River." But even though many of the people, places, and events described in *The Things They Carried* closely mirror O'Brien's actual experiences in Vietnam, he describes the story collection as a work of fiction.

Things to remember while reading "On the Rainy River":

- O'Brien was drafted after graduating from Macalester College in Minnesota in 1968. In 1969 he began his tour of duty in Vietnam, where he served in an army infantry unit. When he left Vietnam a year later, he had earned a Purple Heart for being wounded and had been promoted to sergeant. Upon returning to the United States, O'Brien became one of America's leading writers on the Vietnam War and its impact on U.S. soldiers who served there.

- Canada remained officially neutral throughout the Vietnam War, although it provided $9 million to South Vietnam for medical supplies and training. Canada's political leaders did not openly criticize U.S. involvement in the war. But they also made little effort to stop draft evaders from settling within the country's borders, and most Canadian communities welcomed the American exiles.

Tim O'Brien.
Photograph by Jerry Bauer.
Reproduced by permission.

Excerpt from Tim O'Brien's short story "On the Rainy River":

*In June of 1968, a month after graduating from Macalester College, I was drafted to fight a war I hated. I was twenty-one years old. Young, yes, and politically **naive**, but even so the American war in Vietnam seemed to me wrong. Certain blood was being shed for uncertain reasons. I saw no unity of purpose, no consensus on matters of philosophy or history or law. . . .*

The draft notice arrived on June 17, 1968. It was a humid afternoon, I remember, cloudy and very quiet, and I'd just come in from a round of golf. My mother and father were having lunch out in the kitchen. I remember opening up the letter, scanning the first few lines, feeling the blood go thick behind my eyes. I remember a sound in my

Naive: Innocent.

head. It wasn't thinking, just a silent howl. A million things all at once—I was too good for this war. Too smart, too compassionate, too everything. . . . I was no soldier. I hated Boy Scouts. I hated camping out. I hated dirt and tents and mosquitos. The sight of blood made me queasy, and I couldn't tolerate authority, and I didn't know a rifle from a slingshot. . . . I remember the rage in my stomach. Later it burned down to a smoldering self-pity, then to numbness. At dinner that night my father asked what my plans were. "Nothing," I said. "Wait."

*[He spent the summer working in a meat-packing plant in Minnesota.] In the evenings I'd sometimes borrow my father's car and drive aimlessly around town, feeling sorry for myself, thinking about the war and the pig factory and how my life seemed to be collapsing toward slaughter. I felt paralyzed. All around me the options seemed to be narrowing, as if I were hurtling down a huge black funnel, the whole world squeezing in tight. There was no happy way out. The government had ended most graduate school deferments; the waiting lists for the National Guard and Reserves were impossibly long; my health was solid; I didn't qualify for **CO** status—no religious grounds, no history as a **pacifist**. Moreover, I could not claim to be opposed to war as a matter of general principle. There were occasions, I believed, when a nation was justified in using military force to achieve its ends, to stop a **Hitler** or some comparable evil, and I told myself that in such circumstances I would've willingly marched off to the battle. The problem, though, was that a draft board did not let you choose your war. Beyond all this, or at the very center, was the raw fact of terror. I did not want to die. . . .*

*At some point in mid-July I began thinking seriously about Canada. The border lay a few hundred miles north, an eight-hour drive. Both my conscience and my instincts were telling me to make a break for it, just take off and run like hell and never stop. . . . I couldn't make up my mind. I feared the war, yes, but I also feared **exile**.*

*I was afraid of walking away from my own life, my friends and my family, my whole history, everything that mattered to me. I feared losing the respect of my parents. I feared the law. I feared ridicule and **censure**. My hometown was a conservative little spot on the prairie, a place where tradition counted, and it was easy to imagine people sitting around a table down at the old Gobbler Cafe on Main Street, coffee cups poised, the conversation slowly zeroing in on the young O'Brien kid, how the damned sissy had taken off for Canada. . . .*

[After weeks of agonizing, he makes a sudden decision to run for Canada. He packs a suitcase and drives north toward the Canadian

CO: Conscientious objector.

Pacifist: One who opposes all wars and acts of violence.

Hitler: Adolf Hitler, the leader of Germany's Nazi party during World War II.

Exile: Forced absence from one's family or country.

Censure: Disapproval or blame.

border.] It was pure flight, fast and mindless. I had no plan. Just hit the border at high speed and crash through and keep on running. . . . I spent the night in the car behind a closed-down gas station a half mile from the border. In the morning, after gassing up, I headed straight west along the Rainy River, which separates Minnesota from Canada, and which for me separated one life from another. The land was mostly wilderness. Here and there I passed a motel or bait shop, but otherwise the country unfolded in great sweeps of pine and birch and sumac. . . .

[Tired and confused, he rents a room at an old fishing lodge just south of the border. The lodge is owned by a quiet, elderly man named Elroy Berdahl. The two spend the next several days together, sharing meals, hiking through the woods, playing Scrabble, and reading in front of the fireplace.] We spent six days together at the Tip Top Lodge. Just the two of us. Tourist season was over, and there were no boats on the river, and the wilderness seemed to withdraw into a great perma-nent stillness. . . . One thing for certain, he knew I was in desperate trouble. And he knew I couldn't talk about it. The wrong word—or even the right word—and I would've disappeared. I was wired and jittery. My skin felt too tight. . . . I went through whole days feeling dizzy with sorrow. I couldn't sleep; I couldn't lie still. At night I'd toss around in bed, half awake, half dreaming, imagining how I'd sneak down to the beach and quietly push one of the old man's boats out into the river and start paddling my way toward Canada. . . . It all seemed crazy and impossible. Twenty-one years old, an ordinary kid with all the ordinary dreams and ambitions, and all I wanted was to live the life I was born to—a mainstream life—I loved baseball and hamburgers and cherry Cokes—and now I was off on the margins of exile, leaving my country forever, and it seemed so impossible and terrible and sad.

[He enjoys Elroy's quiet company but remains tormented by the thought of entering Canada to evade the draft.] During that long sum-mer I'd been over and over the various arguments, all the pros and cons, and it was no longer a question that could be decided by an act of pure reason. Intellect had come up against emotion. My conscience told me to run, but some **irrational** and powerful force was resisting, like a weight pushing me toward the war. What it came down to, stu-pidly, was a sense of shame. Hot, stupid shame. I did not want people to think badly of me. Not my parents, not my brother and sister, not even the folks down at the Gobbler Cafe. I was ashamed to be there at the Tip Top Lodge. I was ashamed of my conscience, ashamed to be doing the right thing. Some of this Elroy must've understood. Not the details, of course, but the plain fact of crisis.

Irrational: Not logical.

*On my last full day, the sixth day, the old man took me out fishing on the Rainy River. The afternoon was sunny and cold. . . . All around us, I remember, there was a vastness to the world, an unpeopled rawness, just the trees and the sky and the water reaching out toward nowhere. The air had the brittle scent of October. . . . For a time I didn't pay attention to anything, just feeling the cold spray against my face, but then it occurred to me that at some point we must've passed into Canadian waters, across that dotted line between two different worlds, and I remember a certain tightness in my chest as I looked up and watched the far shore come at me. This wasn't a daydream. It was **tangible** and real. As we came in toward land, Elroy cut the engine, letting the boat fishtail lightly about twenty yards off shore. The old man didn't look at me or speak. Bending down, he opened up his tackle box and busied himself with a bobber and a piece of wire leader, humming to himself, his eyes down.*

*It struck me then that he must've planned it. I'll never be certain, of course, but I think he meant to bring me up against the realities, to guide me across the river and to take me to the edge and to stand a kind of **vigil** as I chose a life for myself.*

I remember staring at the old man, then at my hands, then at Canada. . . . Twenty yards. I could've done it. I could've jumped and started swimming for my life. Inside me, in my chest, I felt a terrible squeezing pressure. Even now, as I write this, I can still feel that tightness. And I want you to feel it—the wind coming off the river, the waves, the silence, the wooded frontier. You're at the bow of a boat on the Rainy River. You're twenty-one years old, you're scared, and there's a hard squeezing pressure in your chest.

What would you do?

Would you jump? Would you feel pity for yourself? Would you think about your family and your childhood and your dreams and all you're leaving behind? Would it hurt? Would it feel like dying? Would you cry, as I did?

I tried to swallow it back. I tried to smile, except I was crying. . . .

*At the rear of the boat Elroy Berdahl pretended not to notice. He held a fishing rod in his hands, his head bowed to hide his eyes. He kept humming a soft, **monotonous** little tune. Everywhere, it seemed, in the trees and water and sky, a great worldwide sadness came pressing down on me, a crushing sorrow, sorrow like I had never known it before. And what was so sad, I realized, was that Canada had*

Tangible: Something that can be touched.

Vigil: Watch.

Monotonous: Dull or unchanging.

become a pitiful fantasy. Silly and hopeless. It was no longer a possibility. Right then, with the shore so close, I understood that I would not do what I should do. I would not swim away from my hometown and my country and my life. . . . All those eyes on me—the town, the whole universe—and I couldn't risk the embarrassment. It was as if there were an audience to my life, that swirl of faces along the river, and in my head I could hear people screaming at me. Traitor! They yelled. **Turncoat!**. . . . I felt myself blush. I couldn't tolerate it. I couldn't endure the mockery, or the disgrace, or the patriotic ridicule. Even in my imagination, the shore just twenty yards away, I couldn't make myself be brave. It had nothing to do with morality. Embarrassment, that's all it was.

And right then I **submitted.**

I would go to the war—I would kill and maybe die—because I was embarrassed not to.

That was the sad thing. And so I sat in the bow of the boat and cried. . . . Elroy Berdahl remained quiet. He kept fishing. He worked his line with the tips of his fingers, patiently, squinting out at his red and white bobber on the Rainy River. . . . Then after a time the old man pulled in his line and turned the boat back toward Minnesota.

I don't remember saying goodbye. That last night we had dinner together, and I went to bed early, and in the morning Elroy fixed breakfast for me. When I told him I'd be leaving, the old man nodded as if he already knew. He looked down at the table and smiled.

At some point later in the morning it's possible that we shook hands—I just don't remember—but I do know that by the time I'd finished packing the old man had disappeared. Around noon, when I took my suitcase out to the car, I noticed that his old black pickup truck was no longer parked in front of the house. I went inside and waited for a while, but I felt a bone certainty that he wouldn't be back. . . . I washed up the breakfast dishes. . . . got into the car, and drove south toward home.

The day was cloudy. I passed through towns with familiar names, through the pine forests and down to the prairie, and then to Vietnam, where I was a soldier, and then home again. I survived, but it's not a happy ending. I was a coward. I went to the war.

Turncoat: Traitor.

Submitted: Gave up.

What happened next . . .

Throughout the course of the Vietnam War, the U.S. government and the legal system made changes to the Selective Service system. Many of these changes were designed to address the charges that the draft rules placed an unfair burden on America's less economically and politically powerful families. But the draft remained controversial, and legal challenges to Selective Service policies made the system increasingly ineffective.

In 1967 deferments for graduate school were eliminated, although students currently enrolled were usually permitted to keep their deferments. Two years later, the government placed additional restrictions on deferments. At the same time, it introduced a random draft lottery in an effort to draw troops more equally from all American communities. But draft evasion remained widespread, overwhelming federal efforts to enforce the Selective Service laws.

Finally, in 1971, President Nixon eliminated student deferments altogether. But by this time the American withdrawal of troops was well underway, so the move did not have a major impact. On January 27, 1973, Nixon formally shut down the Vietnam-era draft for good.

Nixon's decision to end the draft delighted the many Americans who had opposed the war. But it did not end the legal problems of those Americans who had illegally resisted the Selective Service system in one way or another. Approximately 280,000 civilians remained in trouble with the law for their actions. These included convicted draft resisters and men who had moved to Canada or other foreign countries to avoid induction.

Many Americans thought that the federal government should dismiss the charges that these civilians faced and let them resume their lives. Some argued that they should be "pardoned"—forgiven for crimes committed against the government. Others, including many of the draft resisters and evaders, argued that they should receive an "amnesty." Under an amnesty, all legal charges would be dropped, just as with a pardon. But an amnesty was viewed as an admission that the government had been wrong to prosecute the resisters and evaders for following their beliefs.

Not all Americans believed that amnesties or pardons should be granted, however. In fact, political conservatives, veterans groups, and many other Americans thought that the men who had disobeyed their draft orders should be prosecuted to the full extent of the law. This issue became yet another point of division in American society until 1977, when President Jimmy Carter approved an unconditional amnesty to those who had gotten in legal trouble for their peaceful opposition to the war.

Since Nixon ended the military draft in 1973, the United States has only used volunteers in its armed forces. Since 1980, however, young men have been required to register with the federal government when they turn 18 years old. This law ensures that the government can renew the military draft at any time if necessary.

Did you know . . .

- A 1966 study revealed that only 1.3 percent of draft board members in American communities were black. Women, meanwhile, were prohibited from serving on draft boards altogether until 1967, when Congress changed the rules.

- Approximately 1.4 million young men who were eligible for the draft were excused from serving because they failed intelligence exams.

- College students who posted poor grades ran the danger of losing their deferments and becoming eligible for the draft. This factor made many male students devote more time to their classes. It also put extra pressure on some college professors. They knew that if they gave a student a failing grade, the student might lose his deferment and eventually end up in Vietnam.

Sources

Appy, Christian G. *Working-Class War: American Combat Soldiers and Vietnam.* Chapel Hill, NC: University of North Carolina Press, 1993.

Baskir, Lawrence, and William A. Strauss. *Chance and Circumstance: The Draft, the War, and the Vietnam Generation.* New York: Alfred A. Knopf, 1978.

Gottlieb, Sherry Gershon. *Hell No, We Won't Go: Resisting the Draft during the Vietnam War.* New York: Viking, 1991.

Hall, Mitchell. *Because of Their Faith: CALCAV and Religious Opposition to the Vietnam War.* New York: Columbia University Press, 1990.

Levy, David W. *The Debate Over Vietnam.* 2nd ed. Baltimore: Johns Hopkins University Press, 1995.

Marrin, Albert. *America and Vietnam: The Elephant and the Tiger.* New York: Viking, 1992.

O'Brien, Tim. *The Things They Carried.* Boston: Houghton Mifflin, 1990.

Tollefson, James W. *The Strength Not to Fight: An Oral History of Conscientious Objectors of the Vietnam War.* Boston: Little, Brown and Company, 1993.

Wells, Tom. *The War Within: America's Battle Over Vietnam.* Berkeley: University of California Press, 1994.

Williams, Roger N. *The New Exiles: American War Resisters in Canada.* New York: Liveright, 1971.

Richard M. Nixon

Excerpt from the "Silent Majority" speech
Delivered on national television, November 24, 1969

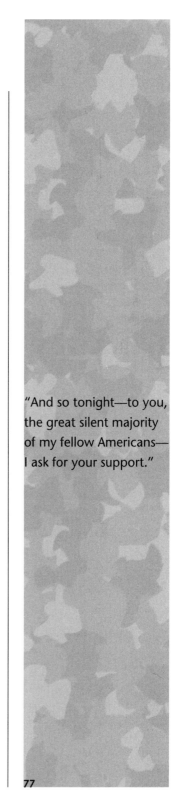

"And so tonight—to you, the great silent majority of my fellow Americans— I ask for your support."

By the time Richard M. Nixon was elected president of the United States in November 1968, the majority of the American people had grown tired and frustrated with the war in Vietnam. Polls showed that 60 percent of Americans thought that becoming involved in the war had been a mistake, while 20 percent favored an immediate withdrawal of U.S. combat troops. Many people began to question whether Vietnam was important enough to U.S. interests to justify the loss of more American lives. In addition, some people began to worry about the effects the war was having on American society. "Controversy over the war in Vietnam brought vast changes to the United States in the 1960s," Robert D. Schulzinger wrote in *A Time for War.* "The war affected every institution in American life: universities, Congress, the presidency, the Democratic Party, the armed forces, labor unions, religious organizations, and the mass media."

Historians have noted that the Vietnam War divided the American people more than any other event since the Civil War (1861–65) a century earlier. Some people believed that the war was immoral and opposed it strongly. They wanted the

President Nixon and U.S. tank personnel in Vietnam. *Reproduced by permission of Corbis Corporation.*

United States to reduce its role and negotiate a peace agreement with North Vietnam. They resented war supporters, whom they considered ignorant or heartless. Meanwhile, other people felt just as strongly that they had a responsibility to support the U.S. government and American military forces. While they might agree that the war was dragging on too long, they believed that only intensifying American military action would bring a quick end to the conflict. They resented antiwar activists, and many viewed them as cowards or traitors.

The strong feelings on both sides of the issue made it almost impossible for Americans to engage in a constructive debate over Vietnam. Over time, the controversy ripped apart families, friends, and communities. "It is important to understand the terribly difficult nature of the choice being forced upon many citizens by this war. Americans traded harsh charges amongst themselves during these troubled years, and they frequently did so in very strident [loud] tones," David W. Levy wrote in *The Debate over Vietnam*. "When we remember that inflated rhetoric [language] and extreme gestures of animosity [hostility] are often signs of serious social strain, we can begin to gauge the extent to which Vietnam tore at the nation as a whole."

The deep and dangerous divisions among the American people became clear at the Democratic Presidential Convention in Chicago during the summer of 1968. Inside the convention hall, the Democrats struggled to agree on the Vietnam policy they would present in their campaign. Meanwhile, the streets of Chicago outside the convention hall became the site of a raucous antiwar protest. Chicago Mayor Richard Daley sent his police force to control the protesters, and the situation quickly turned into a riot. Scenes of fights between antiwar activists and police officers dominated television newscasts and overshadowed the convention. More than one thousand protesters and two hundred police officers were injured in the fighting.

The violence and controversy surrounding the Democratic convention disgusted many Americans and made them worry that the whole country was falling apart. It also convinced some voters that the Democrats could not lead the country out of the situation in Vietnam. Such doubts helped Republican candidate Richard Nixon defeat

Democratic candidate Hubert Humphrey in the 1968 election to become president of the United States. During his campaign, Nixon promised that he had a "secret plan" to end the Vietnam War.

After taking office in January 1969, Nixon began outlining his plan to achieve "peace with honor" in Vietnam. "The administration was committed to getting out of Vietnam as quickly as was practicable, but to doing it with dignity, without seeming to flee, and without appearing to abandon . . . the dream of a stable and independent South Vietnam," Levy explained. Nixon promised to withdraw American combat forces gradually over time, while also taking steps to strengthen the South Vietnamese government and military. He noted that this plan—which became known as "Vietnamization"—would enable the United States to end its involvement without allowing South Vietnam to fall to communism. He began implementing this plan in June 1969, when he withdrew the first 25,000 American troops from Vietnam. Nixon also opened peace talks in Paris with North Vietnamese officials.

For the first six months that Nixon was in office, the antiwar movement remained relatively quiet. For one thing, many people had turned away from antiwar protests after the trauma of the Chicago convention. The scenes of violence on TV convinced many Americans that "antiwar activity was largely the work of ill-kempt troublemakers who burned American flags and abused policemen," Levy noted. In addition, some people were encouraged by the steps Nixon had taken to begin peace negotiations and troop withdrawals.

But the antiwar movement began gaining strength again by the middle of 1969. As the number of American soldiers killed in combat continued to increase, some people argued that Nixon was moving too slowly toward peace. One example of the resurgence of the antiwar movement was the Moratorium Day demonstrations, held on October 15. In this nationwide peaceful protest, hundreds of thousands of people gave speeches, took part in marches, and held candlelight vigils in cities and towns across the country. These demonstrations worried and angered Nixon, even though they were less violent and confrontational than the protests of earlier years.

Realizing that opposition to the war remained strong, in November Nixon decided to outline his plans to the American public in a nationally televised speech. In the following excerpt from his "Silent Majority" speech, Nixon defends his decision to keep American troops in Vietnam. He argues that an immediate withdrawal would hurt the South Vietnamese people, America's reputation as a world power, and the chances of achieving world peace. He claims that his Vietnamization plan will allow the United States to "win the peace."

Nixon also uses this speech to make a direct appeal to the American people to support his plans. He expresses his resolve not to let the antiwar movement—which he calls a "vocal minority"—dictate his actions. He also criticizes antiwar protesters, saying that they humiliate the United States and increase the North Vietnamese will to fight. Finally, he asks the patriotic "silent majority" of Americans to come forward and support him.

Military police observe an antiwar demonstration. They are wearing masks to protect themselves in case they use tear gas against the demonstrators.
Reproduced by permission of AP/Wide World Photos.

Things to remember while reading the excerpt from Nixon's "Silent Majority" speech:

- In his speech Nixon says that he wants to tell the American people the truth about the situation in Vietnam. But Nixon was not always truthful about his actions during the war. For example, in the spring of 1969 he approved a series of bombing raids over Cambodia, a neutral country located on Vietnam's western border. Fearing a new round of protests, he kept the bombing of Cambodia secret. He did not inform the American people or even members of Congress.

- Nixon did not consult with South Vietnamese President Nguyen Van Thieu before announcing his Vietnamization program. Some South Vietnamese government and military leaders resented the plan. For one thing, it made it seem as if South Vietnamese forces had not been involved in the fighting up to that point. In addition, it made people in both North and South Vietnam question the American commitment to winning the war. To some, Vietnamization clearly indicated that the main priority of U.S. strategy was to reduce American involvement in Vietnam rather than to achieve peace there.

- Nixon mentions the violence that took place when Communist forces took control of North Vietnam in the mid-1950s. After the Geneva Accords of 1954 divided the country, Ho Chi Minh and other Communist leaders concentrated on building a socialist society in the North (socialism is a political doctrine that calls for state ownership and control of industry, agriculture, and distribution of wealth). For example, they instituted a land reform campaign to distribute privately owned land to poor and landless people. But the land reform campaign soon turned vicious. Thousands of people who had previously owned land or were thought to be unfriendly to communism were put in prison or executed. Estimates of Vietnamese killed during this period range from 30,000 to as many as 100,000. Throughout the Vietnam War, American officials pointed to this violence as evidence that the Communists would treat the people of South Vietnam harshly if they won the war.

- Even Americans who opposed the Vietnam War did not always agree on what steps the U.S. government should

take to end it. Some people favored immediate withdrawal of American troops, some wanted a gradual withdrawal like the one Nixon proposed, and others wanted to increase American troop commitments in hopes of achieving a quick military victory. Such differences of opinion made it more difficult for the Nixon administration to develop popular policies.

A flag bearing a peace symbol flown from a U.S. tank in South Vietnam during the war.
Reproduced by permission of Corbis-Bettmann.

- Nixon struggled with the antiwar movement throughout his time in office. He viewed antiwar protesters with hostility and suspicion. After all, they made it more difficult for him to conduct the war. He also believed that the vocal antiwar demonstrations in the United States encouraged the North Vietnamese and kept them from negotiating a settlement. Nixon used a variety of means to keep an eye on the antiwar groups and make them look bad. For example, he used government agencies like the Federal Bureau of Investigation (FBI) and the Central Intelligence Agency (CIA) to investigate or harass their leaders. He also sent spies into various organizations. "No one at an antiwar meeting could ever be sure that the person in the next chair was not an FBI spy, sent either to report on the meeting or, in some well-documented cases, even to propose outrageous and illegal actions leading to embarrassment of the participants or to their arrest," Levy noted.

Excerpt from Richard M. Nixon's "Silent Majority" speech:

Good evening, my fellow Americans. Tonight I want to talk to you on a subject of deep concern to all Americans and to many people in all parts of the world—the war in Vietnam.

*I believe that one of the reasons for the deep division about Vietnam is that many Americans have lost confidence in what their Government has told them about our policy. The American people cannot and should not be asked to support a policy which involves the **overriding** issues of war and peace unless they know the truth about that policy.*

*Tonight, therefore, I would like to answer some of the questions that I know are on the minds of many of you listening to me: How and why did America get involved in Vietnam in the first place? How has this **administration** changed the policy of the previous administration? What has really happened in the negotiations in Paris and on the battlefront in Vietnam? What choices do we have to end the war? What are the prospects for peace?*

*Let me begin by describing the situation I found when I was **inaugurated** on January 20. The war had been going on for four years. 31,000 Americans had been killed in action. The training program for the South Vietnamese was behind schedule. 540,000 Americans were in Vietnam, with no plans to reduce that number. No progress had been made at the negotiations in Paris and the United States had not put forth a comprehensive peace proposal. The war was causing deep division at home and criticism from many of our friends, as well as our enemies, abroad.*

In view of these circumstances there were some who urged that I end the war at once by ordering the immediate withdrawal of all

Overriding: Most important or pressing.

Administration: The group of people who run a government, including a president and his or her advisors; also refers to their term of office.

Inaugurated: Sworn in as president.

American forces. From a political standpoint this would have been a popular and easy course to follow. After all, we became involved in the war while my **predecessor** was in office. I could blame the defeat which would be the result of my action on him and come out as the peacemaker. Some put it to me quite bluntly: this was the only way to avoid allowing Johnson's war to become Nixon's war.

But I had a greater obligation than to think only of the years of my administration and the next election. I had to think of the effect of my decision on the next generation and on the future of peace and freedom in America and in the world.

Let us all understand that the question before us is not whether some Americans are for peace and some Americans are against peace. The question at issue is not whether Johnson's war becomes Nixon's war. The great question is: How can we win America's peace?

Let us turn now to the fundamental issue. Why and how did the United States become involved in Vietnam in the first place? Fifteen years ago North Vietnam, with the **logistical** support of Communist China and the Soviet Union, launched a campaign to impose a Communist government on South Vietnam by **instigating** and supporting a revolution.

In response to the request of the Government of South Vietnam, President Eisenhower sent economic aid and military equipment to assist the people of South Vietnam in their efforts to prevent a Communist takeover. Seven years ago President Kennedy sent 16,000 military personnel to Vietnam as combat advisers. Four years ago President Johnson sent American combat forces to South Vietnam.

Now, many believe that President Johnson's decision to send American combat forces to South Vietnam was wrong. And many others, I among them, have been strongly critical of the way the war has been conducted. But the question facing us today is: Now that we are in the war, what is the best way to end it?

In January I could only conclude that the **precipitate** withdrawal of American forces from Vietnam would be a disaster not only for South Vietnam but for the United States and for the cause of peace.

For the South Vietnamese, our precipitate withdrawal would **inevitably** allow the Communists to repeat massacres which followed their takeover in the North fifteen years before. They murdered more than 50,000 people, and hundreds of thousands more died in slave labor camps. We saw a preview of what would happen in South Vietnam when the Communists entered the city of **Hue** last year. During

Predecessor: The person who previously occupied an office; in this case, President Lyndon B. Johnson.

Logistical: Relating to the details of a military operation, such as supplies and transportation.

Instigating: Provoking or causing to happen.

Precipitate: Sudden or abrupt; proceeding with unwise speed.

Inevitably: Certainly or without a doubt; unable to be avoided.

Hue: A major city in South Vietnam that was captured by North Vietnamese forces during the 1968 Tet Offensive.

Pro-War "Hard Hats" Clash Violently with Antiwar Protesters

Throughout the late 1960s and early 1970s, disputes over the Vietnam War threatened to tear the United States apart. Some of the most intense antiwar demonstrations took place in May 1970, in response to Nixon's invasion of Cambodia and the killing of four student activists on the campus of Kent State University in Ohio. By this time, however, many Americans had grown angry and disgusted with the radical antiwar movement. They resented college students and other activists who taunted police officers, caused riots, destroyed property, expressed support for the enemy, and displayed the North Vietnamese flag. "The public had not only lost patience with the war, but with those who protested against it," Albert Marrin noted in *America and Vietnam*.

These feelings erupted into violence in New York City. A week after the Kent State tragedy, a funeral was held for one of the students in Manhattan. The flag on top of city hall was lowered to half-mast as a symbol of mourning for the dead students, and antiwar demonstrators gathered outside the building. Meanwhile, members of labor unions who supported the war organized counter-protests. At one point, 200 angry construction workers, or "hard hats," marched on city hall and attacked the antiwar protesters. They used their fists, crowbars, hammers, and metal wrenches to beat the antiwar demonstrators. When police arrived, they were unable to stop the violence. Some observers claimed that police officers even cheered on the construction workers. Seventy antiwar protesters were injured, some seriously. At the end of their rampage, the hard hats forced the mayor's office to raise the flag to its normal position.

Some people claimed that the Nixon administration had secretly arranged the attack on antiwar demonstrators during meetings with union leaders. Although there is no evidence that he was involved in planning the New York City incident, Nixon did tell union leaders afterward that he found their expressions of support "very meaningful." Three weeks later the leader of a construction workers' union presented Nixon with a hard hat as a gift.

their brief rule there, there was a bloody reign of terror in which 3,000 civilians were clubbed, shot to death, and buried in mass graves. With the sudden collapse of our support, these atrocities of Hue would become the nightmare of the entire nation—and particularly for the million and a half Catholic refugees who fled to South Vietnam when the Communists took over in the North.

Civilians: People not involved in the military.

For the United States, this first defeat in our nation's history would result in a collapse of confidence in American leadership not only in Asia but throughout the world. . . .

For the future of peace, precipitate withdrawal would thus be a disaster of immense magnitude. A nation cannot remain great if it betrays its allies and lets down its friends. Our defeat and humiliation in South Vietnam without question would promote recklessness in the councils of those **great powers** who have not yet abandoned their goals of world **conquest**. This would spark violence wherever our commitments help maintain the peace—in the Middle East, in Berlin, eventually even in the Western Hemisphere. Ultimately, this would cost more lives. It would not bring peace; it would bring more war.

For these reasons I rejected the recommendation that I should end the war by immediately withdrawing all our forces. I chose instead to change American policy on both the negotiating front and the battlefront. . . .

At the time we launched our search for peace, I recognized we might not succeed in bringing an end to the war through negotiation. I therefore put into effect another plan to bring peace—a plan which will bring the war to an end regardless of what happens on the negotiating front. It is in line with a major shift in U.S. foreign policy which I described in my press conference at **Guam** on July 25.

Let me briefly explain what has been described as the Nixon doctrine—a policy which not only will help end the war in Vietnam but which is an essential element of our program to prevent future Vietnams.

We Americans are a do-it-yourself people. We are an impatient people. Instead of teaching someone else to do a job, we like to do it ourselves. And this trait has been carried over into our foreign policy. In **Korea** and again in Vietnam, the United States furnished most of the money, most of the arms, and most of the men to help the people of those countries defend their freedom against Communist aggression.

Before any American troops were committed to Vietnam, a leader of another Asian country expressed this opinion to me when I was traveling in Asia as a private citizen. He said: "When you are trying to assist another nation defend its freedom, U.S. policy should be to help them fight the war, but not to fight the war for them."

Great powers: A reference to Communist countries like China and the Soviet Union.

Conquest: Takeover by force.

Guam: An island in the western Pacific that is a territory of the United States.

Korea: A country in Southeast Asia where the United States engaged in a war 1950–53.

In 1954, while vice president under President Dwight Eisenhower, Nixon had visited Vietnam. Here he greets a South Vietnamese soldier. *Reproduced by permission of AP/Wide World Photos.*

Accordance: Agreement or recognition.

Furnish: Supply or provide.

*Well, in **accordance** with this wise counsel, I laid down in Guam three principles as guidelines for future American policy toward Asia: First, the United States will keep all of its treaty commitments. Second, we shall provide a shield if a nuclear power threatens the freedom of a nation allied with us or of a nation whose survival we consider vital to our security. Third, in cases involving other types of aggression, we shall **furnish** military and economic assistance when requested in accordance with our treaty commitments. But we shall look to the nation directly threatened to assume the primary responsibility of providing the manpower for its defense. . . .*

The defense of freedom is everybody's business—not just America's business. And it is particularly the responsibility of the people whose freedom is threatened. In the previous administration we Americanized the war in Vietnam. In this administration we are Vietnamizing the search for peace.

The policy of the previous administration not only resulted in our assuming the primary responsibility for fighting the war, but even more significantly did not adequately stress the goal of strengthening the South Vietnamese so that they could defend themselves when we left.

The Vietnamization plan was launched following **Secretary Laird**'s visit to Vietnam in March. Under the plan, I ordered first a substantial increase in the training and equipment of South Vietnamese forces. In July, on my visit to Vietnam, I changed **General Abrams'** orders so that they were consistent with the **objectives** of our new policies. Under the new orders, the primary mission of our troops is to enable the South Vietnamese forces to assume the full responsibility for the security of South Vietnam. . . .

We have adopted a plan which we have worked out in cooperation with the South Vietnamese for the complete withdrawal of all U.S. combat ground forces and their replacement by South Vietnamese forces on an orderly scheduled timetable. This withdrawal will be made from strength and not from weakness. As South Vietnamese forces become stronger, the rate of American withdrawal can become greater. . . .

My fellow Americans, I am sure you can recognize from what I have said that we really only have two choices open to us if we want to end this war: I can order an immediate, precipitate withdrawal of all Americans from Vietnam without regard to the effects of that action. Or we can **persist** in our search for a just peace, through a negotiated settlement if possible or through continued implementation of our plan for Vietnamization if necessary—a plan in which we will withdraw all of our forces from Vietnam on a schedule in accordance with our program, as the South Vietnamese become strong enough to defend their own freedom.

I have chosen this second course. It is not the easy way. It is the right way. It is a plan which will end the war and serve the cause of peace, not just in Vietnam but in the Pacific and in the world.

In speaking of the consequences of a precipitate withdrawal, I mentioned that our allies would lose confidence in America. Far more dangerous, we would lose confidence in ourselves. Oh, the immediate reaction would be a sense of relief that our men were coming home. But as we saw the consequences of what we had done, inevitable **remorse** and divisive **recrimination** would scar our spirit as a people.

We have faced other crises in our history and have become stronger by rejecting the easy way out and taking the right way in meeting our challenges. Our greatness as a nation has been our capacity to do what had to be done when we knew our course was

Secretary Laird: Melvin R. Laird (1922–), who served in Nixon's cabinet as secretary of defense, 1969–73.

General Abrams: Creighton Abrams (1914–1974), who was in charge of implementing the Vietnamization program.

Objectives: Goals.

Persist: Continue.

Remorse: Sadness and regret.

Recrimination: Bitter arguments over blame.

right. I recognize that some of my fellow citizens disagree with the plan for peace I have chosen. Honest and patriotic Americans have reached different conclusions as to how peace should be achieved.

*In San Francisco a few weeks ago, I saw demonstrators carrying signs reading: "Lose in Vietnam, bring the boys home." Well, one of the strengths of our free society is that any American has a right to reach that conclusion and to **advocate** that point of view. But as president of the United States, I would be untrue to my oath of office if I allowed the policy of this nation to be **dictated** by the minority who hold that point of view and who try to **impose** it on the nation by mounting demonstrations in the street.*

*For almost 200 years, the policy of this nation has been made under our Constitution by those leaders in the Congress and the White House elected by all of the people. If a vocal minority, however **fervent** its cause, **prevails** over reason and the will of the majority, this nation has no future as a free society.*

*And now I would like to address a word, if I may, to the young people of this nation who are particularly concerned, and I understand why they are concerned, about this war. I respect your **idealism**. I share your concern for peace. I want peace as much as you do. There are powerful personal reasons I want to end this war. This week I will have to sign 83 letters to mothers, fathers, wives and loved ones of men who have given their lives for America in Vietnam. It is very little satisfaction to me that this is only one-third as many letters as I signed the first week in office. There is nothing I want more than to see the day come when I do not have to write any of those letters.*

I want to end the war to save the lives of those brave young men in Vietnam. But I want to end it in a way which will increase the chance that their younger brothers and their sons will not have to fight in some future Vietnam someplace in the world.

And I want to end the war for another reason. I want to end it so that the energy and dedication of you, our young people, now too often directed into bitter hatred against those responsible for the war, can be turned to the great challenges of peace, a better life for all Americans, a better life for all people on this Earth.

I have chosen a plan for peace. I believe it will succeed. If it does succeed, what the critics say now won't matter. If it does not succeed, anything I say then won't matter.

Advocate: Support or argue in favor of.

Dictated: Decided or commanded.

Impose: Force upon.

Fervent: Intense.

Prevails: Wins or overcomes.

Idealism: Belief in the possibility of building a perfect society.

*I know it may not be fashionable to speak of **patriotism** or national destiny these days. But I feel it is appropriate to do so on this occasion. Two hundred years ago this nation was weak and poor. But even then, America was the hope of millions in the world. Today we have become the strongest and richest nation in the world. And the wheel of destiny has turned so that any hope the world has for the survival of peace and freedom will be determined by whether the American people have the moral stamina and the courage to meet the challenge of free world leadership.*

*Let historians not record that when America was the most powerful nation in the world we passed on the other side of the road and allowed the last hopes for peace and freedom of millions of people to be suffocated by the forces of **totalitarianism.***

And so tonight—to you, the great silent majority of my fellow Americans—I ask for your support.

*I pledged in my campaign for the presidency to end the war in a way that we could win the peace. I have initiated a plan of action which will enable me to keep that pledge. The more support I can have from the American people, the sooner that pledge can be **redeemed**; for the more divided we are at home, the less likely the enemy is to negotiate at Paris.*

Let us be united for peace. Let us also be united against defeat. Because let us understand: North Vietnam cannot defeat or humiliate the United States. Only Americans can do that.

Patriotism: Deep feelings of love and devotion to a country.

Totalitarianism: A political system in which everything is controlled by the central government and individuals have few rights.

Redeemed: Fulfilled or made good.

What happened next . . .

Just as Nixon had hoped, the "Silent Majority" speech increased public support for his policies and quieted the antiwar movement—at least temporarily. Shortly afterward, polls showed that 48 percent of Americans approved of his handling of Vietnam, while 41 percent disapproved. In addition, his remarks seemed to shift people's attention away from the war and increase public criticism of antiwar activists.

But this situation changed dramatically a few months later. In the spring of 1970 Nixon sent U.S. ground troops into

Demonstrators holding a sign that recalls the killing of four Kent State University students by National Guardsmen during a peace demonstration. It objects to Nixon's claim that the "Silent Majority" of Americans support his policies.
Kent State University.
Public Domain.

Cambodia. He explained that this "incursion" would destroy enemy supply lines, force the North Vietnamese into serious negotiations, and reduce the pressure on South Vietnam so that the Vietnamization program would have time to work. But many Americans viewed the invasion of neutral Cambodia as an escalation of the war. They felt that Nixon had broken his promise to bring American troops home and end the war.

The antiwar movement reacted to the invasion of Cambodia by launching protests across the country. Many of these antiwar demonstrations took place on college campuses, including the campus of Kent State University in Ohio. Beginning on May 1, hundreds of Kent State students gathered to protest the invasion of Cambodia. Some of the demonstrations turned violent. On May 2 the protesters burned down a campus building that had been used for military training of the Reserve Officers Training Corps (ROTC). In response, Ohio Governor James Rhodes called out the National Guard to restore order. But the demonstrations continued, resulting in several angry confrontations between students and guardsmen. During one of these confrontations on May 4, members of the National Guard fired their guns into a crowd of demonstrators, killing four students and injuring nine others.

Many Americans were shocked and outraged at the tragedy that had taken place on the Kent State campus. Angry demonstrations against the killing of the students broke out on many other college campuses. In fact, many colleges decided to close for the year and send students home early in order to prevent violent protests.

But some people had grown so tired of the unrest in American society—and felt so much resentment toward the antiwar movement—that they claimed the Kent State protesters had gotten what they deserved. In fact, a *Newsweek* poll showed that six out of seven Americans blamed the students rather than the national guard for the Kent State tragedy. "Millions of Americans had no regrets about Kent State; some actually welcomed it," Albert Marrin wrote in *America and Vietnam*. "For five years they had watched student protests, seen students carrying Viet Cong flags, heard students insulting the nation. Those privileged youngsters were attacking their most cherished values: steady work, patriotism, the flag." Once again, the nation seemed to be on the verge of falling apart over the war in Vietnam.

Did you know . . .

- Nixon had retired from politics before he became the Republican presidential nominee in 1968. After serving as vice president under Dwight Eisenhower, he had run for president in 1960 but was defeated by John F. Kennedy. He then ran for governor of California in 1962, but he lost again. At that point he retired from politics, telling the media that "You won't have Nixon to kick around anymore." But he made a remarkable political comeback from these defeats, ran for president again in 1968, and finally won.

- Nixon gave his "Silent Majority" speech exactly one year after he was elected president.

Sources

Ambrose, Stephen E. *Nixon.* 3 vols. New York: Simon and Schuster, 1987–1991.

Kimball, Jeffrey. *Nixon's Vietnam War.* Lawrence, KS: University Press of Kansas, 1998.

Levy, David. *The Debate over Vietnam.* Baltimore: Johns Hopkins University Press, 1991.

Marrin, Albert. *America and Vietnam: The Elephant and the Tiger.* New York: Viking Penguin, 1992.

Nixon, Richard. *No More Vietnams.* New York: Arbor House, 1985.

Schulzinger, Robert D. *A Time for War: The United States and Vietnam, 1941–1975.* New York: Oxford University Press, 1997.

Small, Melvin, and William D. Hoover, eds. *Give Peace a Chance: Exploring the Vietnam Antiwar Movement.* Syracuse, NY: Syracuse University Press, 1992.

Wells, Tom. *The War Within: America's Battle over Vietnam.* Berkeley: University of California Press, 1994.

Wicker, Tom. *One of Us: Richard Nixon and the American Dream.* New York: Random House, 1991.

Bill Rubenstein

Excerpt from his essay "Tragedy at Kent"
Published in *Middle of the Country*, edited by Bill Warren, 1970

In November 1968 Republican nominee Richard M. Nixon was elected president of the United States, defeating Democratic nominee Hubert Humphrey. One important factor in Nixon's successful campaign to win the presidency was his repeated promise to end the war in Vietnam if elected. Upon assuming office in early 1969, Nixon did take some steps to decrease U.S. involvement in the war. For example, he devised a military strategy that allowed him to begin withdrawing American troops from the conflict. This withdrawal was interpreted by most Americans as a sign that the war might finally be drawing to a close. Even American antiwar activists expressed hope that an end to U.S. military involvement in Vietnam was in sight, although they grumbled about the slow pace of the troop withdrawal.

In late April of 1970, however, Nixon approved a massive military operation into Cambodia, a country on the western border of Vietnam. Nixon explained that the invasion was intended to wipe out Communist military bases that threatened both the Cambodian government and South Vietnam. But news of the invasion of Cambodia sparked tremendous

"This is a "national tragedy," one that will, when history is written, be one of the hallmarks of a leadership distinterested in and unconcerned with the pulse of its people."

anger across the United States. Only weeks earlier, Nixon had promised the American people that peace was near. Many people, ranging from antiwar activists to ordinary citizens, believed that the president's expansion of U.S. military operations into Cambodia was a betrayal of that promise.

When the American people were informed of the incursion (raid) into Cambodia, fierce and angry debates about Nixon's decision erupted in communities all over the country. At the same time, antiwar demonstrations flared up on dozens of college campuses. The protests infuriated Nixon, who called the student protestors "bums" who were "blowing up" the nation's campuses.

One of the strongest student protests against the invasion of Cambodia took place at Kent State University in Kent, Ohio. In previous years divisions over the war in Vietnam had created a tense atmosphere on the Kent State campus and its surrounding community. In fact, hostility between student peace activists and supporters of the war (both in the student body and in the larger community) had actually escalated into violence on several occasions. Despite this troubled history, however, no one anticipated that the demonstrations that erupted on the Kent State campus after the invasion of Cambodia would ultimately end in tragedy.

The sequence of events on campus

The first Kent State student protests took place on May 1, one day after Nixon announced the U.S. invasion into Cambodia. An antiwar rally was held at noon on the Commons, a grassy area that was regularly used for various types of campus events and demonstrations. During the course of this rally, antiwar leaders called for a second antiwar demonstration to be held at noon on Monday, May 4.

Later in the evening of May 1, a large number of young people rampaged through downtown Kent, breaking windows, setting small fires, and committing other destructive acts of vandalism. Most observers—and many members of the Kent business community—identified the rioters as primarily Kent State students. But others claimed that the vandals were mostly "radicals" or non-students from outside the community who took advantage of campus demonstrations as an excuse to

Antiwar demonstration in Washington, D.C. *Reproduced by permission of Corbis Corporation.*

make trouble. Several witnesses, for example, claimed that members of a motorcycle gang were prominent participants in the disturbance. In any case, the angry crowd roamed throughout the downtown area until the Kent police force received reinforcements from other nearby communities. At that point, police used tear gas to push the crowd out of the business district and back to the campus, where they dispersed.

The next day, Kent Mayor Leroy Satrom declared a state of emergency in the town. He was worried about the possibility of new disturbances and concerned about rumors that radical revolutionaries planned to use antiwar demonstrators to create violent chaos throughout the community. Later that day, Ohio Governor James Rhodes approved Satrom's request for assistance from the Ohio National Guard. (The National Guard is a volunteer military organization whose membership can be mobilized to serve during wars, natural disasters, and other emergencies. Many young Americans joined the National Guard to avoid serving in Vietnam during the war.)

Ohio National Guard troops arrived at Kent State on the evening of May 2. That same evening, the campus ROTC (Reserve Officer Training Corps) building went up in flames as demonstrators cheered. This building served as the training center for students who planned to pursue military careers. The identity of the arsonists was never fully determined. But radical demonstrators were widely blamed for the fire because of the antiwar movement's hostility toward the military training program. As the evening wore on, the atmosphere on the campus continued to deteriorate. Some demonstrators sliced fire hoses and threw rocks at firemen who tried unsuccessfully to save the building. Other protestors clashed with policemen, guardsmen, and other students who supported U.S. involvement in Vietnam. These angry confrontations did not end until late in the night.

On May 3 the Kent State campus was quiet for most of the day, as National Guard units took up positions all over the campus. All in all, nearly one thousand Ohio National Guardsmen were stationed around the university. Some students expressed anger and concern about the heavy military presence. But the afternoon remained peaceful, and many students and National Guardsmen actually chatted quietly and respectfully with one another. Governor Rhodes, meanwhile, traveled

to Kent to hold a press conference about the disturbances. He warned that he was prepared to use force to stop the demonstrators, who he called "the worst type of people that we harbor in America." Rhodes also indicated that he would seek a court order declaring a state of emergency in the community. The governor never actually made this request, but both National Guard and university officials interpreted his statement as a signal that the Guard was responsible for maintaining control of the campus.

Later that evening, the peaceful atmosphere on campus gave way to a new round of clashes between protestors and law enforcement personnel. Students and other antiwar activists expressed anger about efforts to impose a curfew on the campus. They claimed that the curfew was a transparent attempt to silence their protests against the war. Guardsmen, meanwhile, heard rumors that radical snipers (riflemen who shoot from concealed positions) might be lurking atop campus buildings. As anger and tension mounted on both sides, violence broke

National Guardsment preparing to challenge demonstrators on the Kent State University campus in Ohio.
Reproduced by permission of Corbis Corporation.

out once again. Demonstrators threw rocks and insulted Guardsmen, who responded with tear gas and mass arrests.

On the morning of May 4, students began gathering around the campus Commons area for the noon antiwar rally that had been planned three days earlier. University officials had tried to ban the rally, but their efforts were ineffective. By noon the Commons area contained about 3,000 people. The students in attendance ranged from avid antiwar demonstrators to curious spectators. At the other end of the Commons, meanwhile, stood approximately one hundred Ohio National Guardsmen, each armed with M-1 rifles and riot gear. The rest of the Guardsmen were dispersed elsewhere on campus.

Just before noon, the commander of the National Guard, General Robert Canterbury, ordered the demonstrators to end the rally and disperse. Authorities announced Canterbury's order using a bullhorn, but the students ignored the directive. A group of police officers and Guardsmen then tried to drive across the Commons to end the rally, but their jeep was driven back by rock-throwing protestors. Canterbury then ordered his men to load their weapons and fire tear gas canisters into the growing crowd.

Over the next several minutes, National Guardsmen and crowds of demonstrators maneuvered against one another. Dividing into smaller groups, the Guardsmen repeatedly used tear gas and the threat of force to push protestors off one area of the Commons, only to have another group of protestors move back into another area. Many of these demonstrators shouted insults at the Guardsmen or pelted them with rocks. After about ten minutes, one large group of frustrated and angry Guardsmen turned their backs on the demonstrators and moved up Beacon Hill, near the ruins of the ROTC building.

Near the top of the hill twenty-eight of the Guardsmen suddenly turned without warning and fired their weapons in the direction of a group of students. Many of the Guardsmen fired into the air or into the ground. But some of the soldiers shot directly into the crowd of unarmed students. Altogether, more than sixty shots were fired in a thirteen-second period. Four students were killed and another nine were wounded in the barrage of gunfire. Several of the victims had not even been part of the demonstrations; they were shot while walking to and from their classes.

Bill Rubenstein was an eighteen-year-old history major at Kent State when the shootings occurred. In the following essay he recalls the events that led up to this tragic event. He also offers eyewitness testimony about the shootings, which stunned the American people and threw colleges and universities across the nation into even greater turmoil.

Things to remember while reading the excerpt from Bill Rubenstein's essay "Tragedy at Kent" . . .

- Rubenstein sympathized with the antiwar demonstrators, so he is not an impartial source of information on the events that took place at Kent State in May 1970. Nonetheless, his account of the facts surrounding the shooting incident closely matches those offered by historians.

- Most people who lived in the town of Kent reacted to the arrival of the National Guard at Kent State with "great relief and thankfulness," recalled one Kent resident in *Kent State/May 4.* They viewed the downtown riot of May 1 as evidence that the campus demonstrations against the war were spinning out of control.

- Many scholars believe that the National Guard crackdown on Kent State protestors during the first few days of May 1970 actually increased support for the demonstrators among the rest of the school's student body. Many students who had not actively protested against the war resented the presence of the Guard on campus, especially after the violent clashes that took place on the evenings of May 2 and 3.

- Most members of the American antiwar movement strongly disliked the presence of ROTC (Reserve Officer Training Corps) programs on college campuses. They charged that these programs trained young men to serve as military officers in Vietnam, thus contributing to an immoral war. As protests against the war increased in America, a number of ROTC facilities were burned or vandalized on college and university campuses around the nation. Nonetheless, large numbers of people who opposed the war disapproved of attacks on ROTC build-

Tear gas being used by National Guardsmen on Kent State University students.
Reproduced by permission of AP/Wide World Photos.

ings, vandalism of area businesses, and other acts of destruction committed by radical antiwar activists. Many believed that such acts of destruction were themselves immoral, no matter what the target was. Others claimed that attacks on ROTC facilities and other radical actions were stupid because they eroded public support for the antiwar movement.

• The National Guardsmen who were assigned to the Kent State campus were relatively young and inexperienced. Their repeated clashes with student demonstrators undoubtedly made many of them angry and frustrated. In addition, persistent rumors that radical snipers might be prowling the area made some Guardsmen uneasy. But the lives of the Guardsmen, all of whom were heavily armed and equipped with protective gear, were never in any danger from the protestors. As a result, many people agree with the findings of President Nixon's Commission on Campus Unrest, which was formed after the shooting. This commission, chaired by former Pennsylvania Governor William Scranton, concluded in 1970 that "the indiscriminate [random or careless] firing of rifles into a crowd of students [by the Guardsmen] and the deaths that followed were unnecessary, unwarranted, and inexcusable."

- Many students who attended Kent State University in 1970 did not actively participate in the furious debate over the Vietnam War. They neither protested with the antiwar movement nor spoke out in favor of the war. Instead, they simply pursued ordinary college activities like studying and dating. The shootings at Kent State, though, turned their lives upside-down.

Excerpt from "Tragedy at Kent":

*It was Monday morning, May 4, 1970. The sun was shining and the temperature was rising. An armored personnel carrier was parked at the southwest corner of the campus and armed sentries stood around it. I had an uneasy feeling. As I slowly passed by the patrols of National Guard and State Police, my uneasiness increased. I could not help but think of the past two days, of the curfew, and the **bayonets**, and the tear gas.*

*I went directly to the **student union** to have lunch and to wait for my 12:05 class. . . . When I reached the union, I stopped to look at the ruins of the **adjacent** ROTC building which had been burned down two nights before by students protesting its presence on campus. The National Guard surrounded it. In front of the union, students were discussing the rally of the night before and were reading the **distorted** news stories published in the local papers. Sitting on the lawn in front of the union, I began to read Governor Rhodes' statement in the Plain Dealer (a Cleveland newspaper) that the demonstrators were worse than "**fascists** and **vigilantes**," and that the National Guard was necessary to maintain order. The Guard had been here for two nights now and its presence sickened me.*

*At 11:55, the Victory Bell, the traditional rallying call on campus, began to ring, **beckoning** the students to a rally on the **commons**. By*

Bayonets: Long knives fitted to the ends of rifles.

Student union: Building that serves as center of student activities.

Adjacent: Next to.

Distorted: Twisted or misleading.

Fascists: In this context, people who use violence and intimidation to silence other viewpoints; this is also a term used for repressive dictatorships like the governments of Italy and Germany during World War II.

Vigilantes: People who take the law into their own hands without legal authority.

Beckoning: Calling.

Commons: Large grassy area in the middle of the campus.

the time we reached the commons, there were already over a thousand students amassed on the hill. [A few people then spoke at the rally, calling for a halt to the ROTC program on campus and the removal of the National Guard.] When we heard a voice through a bullhorn ordering us to disperse, the . . . resentful crowd became defiant. It was our opinion that we had a right to demonstrate on our own campus and we refused to move. We hurled some unpleasant **verbiage** *back and were ordered to disperse again. We remained* **adamant** *and became more defiant. Ten or fifteen minutes had now gone by.*

A jeep with guardsmen started to advance toward us. It was halfway between us and the guardsmen at the ROTC building when the first stones were thrown by the students. The jeep fell back. As it turned around, about four tear gas grenades were launched into the crowd. . . . We began to feel the effects of the gas. Our eyes teared and our faces burned.

We began to move slowly up the hill and by the time we got to the top of the hill, more gas had been launched. Passing over the crest of the hill, we lost sight of the guardsmen, but as we descended, some more grenades went off. We covered our mouths and noses with handkerchiefs to protect ourselves as much as possible from the **pungent** *gas.*

Just then, I saw the National Guard in line formation coming up over the hill. They were in full gear and their bayonets were **fixed.** *My friend and I made a short detour into the lobby of Dunbar Hall (a dorm) to find some water to relieve our stinging eyes. When we came out, the guardsmen were lined up on the football practice field at the bottom of the hill. Most of the students were outside the dormitory where I was, or outside the practice field fence below the guard. . . .*

While the guardsmen were on the football practice field, another crowd gathered at the top of the hill. The Guard turned and . . . they began to march up the hill [Beacon Hill]. The students at the top of the hill immediately and totally dispersed from view. The Guard continued to march up the hill. The students at the practice field at the bottom of the hill, thoroughly **embittered** *by the Guard's bullying actions, started to follow them back up the hill to regain their position on the commons. Some began to throw stones again. Given the fact that there was considerable distance between the guardsmen and the students, and given the fact that the guardsmen were in full gear, including helmets and* **field jackets***, . . . these stones were of little threat to the Guard.*

Verbiage: Remarks or statements.

Adamant: Stubborn or unyielding.

Pungent: Bitterly strong.

Fixed: Attached.

Embittered: Bitter and angry.

Field jackets: Protective jackets.

The Guard reached the summit and paused with their backs still to us. And then, I witnessed the most horrifying event of my life. Without any warning, the guardsmen turned and began to fire ammunition aimlessly into the crowd. I was horror-struck. Amidst screams and gunfire, I turned and ran for cover in Dunbar Hall. The windows of the dorm lobby allow a complete view of the practice field and the hill from which the guardsmen were firing down on the students. I saw people fall to the ground. I saw others stop to help. And then the firing stopped.

*My first reaction was that the Guard had been using blanks to frighten the students and that the tactic had worked well, for as soon as the shots began, the students turned to run. I stood in amazement. But when my friend Robby Stamps was dragged into the dorm by two fellow-students with a bullet in his buttock, I knew it was no **hoax**. I just stood in disbelief.*

*I looked out of the window and I saw people standing around. And then I saw some lying on the ground. I just stood there **gaping**. From Victory Bell to murder took a half hour. Ambulances arrived. Two fellows brought Robby out. An attendant approached them with a stretcher and Robby told them to use it for someone who needed it more. Then he hobbled into the ambulance. . . . As I walked outside, I saw the pools of blood on the parking lot. It made me sick. I went inside. Inside and outside, I saw the same disbelief on everyone else's face.*

We were requested by loudspeaker to return to our dorms, but I live off campus and went to the dorm where my friends live. We sat around to wait for even more horrible news. I already knew of Robby's injury because I had seen it. But I was not prepared for what came next. They told us that Sandy Sheuer was dead. Then they told us that Allison Krause was dead. It was not until 6:00 p.m. that we learned that Jeff Miller was dead. In all, four were killed. I don't know how many were wounded.

*I shall never forget the **spectre** of my friends lying dead on the field. I shall never forget that shooting without warning. No one can really believe that it happened there. No one can really believe that it happened at all. It all seems like some sort of **macabre** trick that my mind is playing. And yet I know that it did happen because I saw the blood. I saw the distorted faces of my dead friends. I saw the shock and disbelief as the shots rang out. I heard the **volley** and the screams and didn't believe my ears. I saw the murder and didn't believe my eyes.*

Hoax: Trick.

Gaping: Staring in disbelief

Spectre: Ghostly vision or memory.

Macabre: Weird or grotesque.

Volley: Simultaneous gunfire.

Bill Rubenstein   105

*What I do believe, though, is that this is a "national tragedy," one that will, when history is written, be one of the **hallmarks** of a leadership distinterested in and unconcerned with the pulse of its people.*

What happened next . . .

After the shooting, the Guardsmen retreated back to the Commons area. Some of the demonstrators rushed to provide assistance to the shooting victims who lay bleeding on the ground, while others wandered around in stunned disbelief. Many of the students, however, gathered together in a large and vengeful crowd that advanced on the Guardsmen. At this point, violence could have easily exploded again. Some of the demonstrators were so angry about the shootings that they were reportedly willing to risk their own lives to attack the Guardsmen. If such an attack had been launched, the Guardsmen almost certainly would have opened fire again on the gathered crowd.

Further tragedy was averted, however, by university faculty members and student leaders. They convinced the crowd to disperse and leave the Commons area, even as ambulances roared onto the campus to pick up the dead and wounded students. A short time later, Kent State University President Robert White ordered the school to be shut down. By early evening the entire university had been sealed off with roadblocks. The student body—by this time nearly paralyzed with grief and rage—received a court order to leave the campus. Within hours of the shooting, the entire campus was deserted except for National Guardsmen, investigators, and university officials.

When the townspeople of Kent heard about the shootings and the deaths of the four students—Jeffrey Miller, Allison Krause, William Schroeder, and Sandra Lee Scheuer—reaction was mixed. Some community members expressed shock and sadness about the incident. But many others held the demonstrators responsible for the deaths. Sick of the unrest that had rocked their community and nation in recent years, many

Reaction to the Kent State killings was intense. Here a University of California-Berkeley student hurls tear gas at police.
Reproduced by permission of Corbis Corporation (Bellevue).

Ohio National Guard Releases a Declaration of Regret

In 1980 the Ohio National Guard agreed to issue a declaration of regret about the 1970 shootings at Kent State. This declaration was part of a legal settlement of a lawsuit filed by surviving victims and the families of slain students. Following is the full text of that declaration:

In retrospect, the tragedy of May 4, 1970, should not have occurred. The students may have believed that they were right in continuing their mass protest in response to the Cambodian invasion, even though this protest followed the posting and reading by the university of an order to ban rallies and an order to disperse. These orders have since been determined by the Sixth Circuit Court of Appeals to have been lawful.

Some of the Guardsmen on Blanket Hill, fearful and anxious from prior events, may have believed in their own minds that their lives were in danger. Hindsight suggests that another method would have resolved the confrontation. Better ways must be found to deal with such a confrontation.

We devoutly wish that a means had been found to avoid the May 4th events culminating in the Guard shootings and the irreversible deaths and injuries. We deeply regret those events and are profoundly saddened by the deaths of four students and the wounding of nine others which resulted. We hope that the agreement to end the litigation will help to assuage [heal] the tragic memories regarding that sad day.

Kent residents viewed student protestors as unpatriotic and immoral troublemakers. In addition, many of the townspeople supported U.S. military involvement in Vietnam. As a result, many members of the community felt that the protestors got what they deserved. In fact, some townpeople expressed regret that the Guard had not killed *more* demonstrators.

Outside of Kent, meanwhile, news of the shootings stunned the nation. Many Americans saw the violence at Kent State as the surest sign yet that the country was ripping itself apart over the Vietnam War. Reaction to the shootings was particularly strong on the nation's campuses. In the days following the tragedy at Kent State, an estimated 4.3 million students mounted antiwar and anti-government protests at 1,350 universities and colleges across the United States. Significantly, many of the protestors who took part in these rallies were participating in antiwar activities for the very first time. "The overflow of emotion seemed barely containable," said the

Washington Post on May 6. "The nation [is] witnessing what amounted to a virtual general and uncoordinated strike by its college youth." As the demonstrations continued, more than five hundred campuses were temporarily closed, including the entire state university system in California. Fifty-one of these schools remained closed for the rest of the academic year.

The Nixon administration was alarmed by the widespread campus unrest. But Nixon continued to believe that the Cambodian incursion had been a wise move, and his hostility to the antiwar movement made it hard for him to feel sympathy for the protestors. In fact, the White House issued a statement after the shooting that seemed to blame the demonstrators for the tragedy: "This should remind us all once again that when dissent turns to violence, it invites tragedy." In the meantime, Vice President Spiro Agnew called the killings "predictable" and refused to criticize the National Guard. Instead, he suggested that the tragedy should be placed at the feet of the antiwar movement, which he characterized as a collection of "traitors and thieves and perverts and irrational and illogical people in our midst."

The Nixon administration's attitude toward the Kent State tragedy infuriated many Americans, including the father of Sandy Krause, one of the slain students. "My daughter was not a bum," he tearfully declared in a television interview. "She resented being called a bum because she disagreed with someone else's opinion. She felt that war in Cambodia was wrong. Is this dissent a crime? Is this a reason for killing her? Have we come to such a state in this country that a young girl has to be shot because she disagrees deeply with the actions of her government?"

A variety of state and federal investigations were launched in the weeks following the shootings, but none of the Guardsmen involved in the Kent State shooting were ever punished for their actions. The inquiries did result in federal criminal and civil charges against several of the Guardsmen. But they were not convicted. A judge dismissed the criminal charges against the Guardsmen, indicating that the prosecution did not have enough evidence to gain convictions. In a 1975 civil trial, meanwhile, a jury voted nine to three that none of the Guardsmen were legally responsible for the shootings. A new trial was ordered, however, when the Court of

Appeals ruled that the first trial had been tainted by a threat against a member of the jury.

Legal action associated with the Kent State shootings finally came to an end in January 1980. At that time, a settlement was reached between the National Guardsmen and the wounded students and parents of the students who had been killed. Under the terms of this settlement, the state of Ohio agreed to pay $675,000, which would be shared by the wounded students and the parents of the slain students. The Guardsmen were not required to make any financial payment. They did agree to sign a statement of "regret" over the shootings. But the Guardsmen and their supporters were quick to note that the statement was not an apology or an admission of wrongdoing.

Did you know . . .

- In the days following the Kent State tragedy, vicious and baseless rumors about all of the dead students were spread by people who opposed the antiwar movement. These rumors ranged from statements that they had been violent radicals to gossip about their personal appearance and lives. Even high-ranking government officials joined in this character assassination of the slain students. FBI director J. Edgar Hoover, for instance, dismissed one of the women who was killed as "nothing more than a whore."

- One of the students who was killed in the Kent State shootings—William Schroeder—had himself been enrolled in the university's ROTC program.

- The most famous photograph from the Kent State shootings showed a young woman screaming over the body of one of the slain students (Jeffrey Miller). Kent State student John Filo, a photography major who took the picture, won a Pulitzer Prize for the photograph. It appeared on the front pages of newspapers all across the country, and it continues to be one of the best-known images of the entire Vietnam War era. When the photograph was first published, everyone assumed that the young woman crying over the body was a Kent State student. In reality, however, she was Mary Vecchio, a fourteen-year-old runaway who became trapped in the chaos on campus.

- Two days after the Kent State shootings, police officers in Mississippi opened fire on a crowd of unarmed black students at Jackson State College. The attack killed two students—Phillip Gibbs and James Green—and wounded twelve others. These shootings added to the wave of outraged protests that washed across the country during the spring of 1970.

- Kent State University remained closed for six weeks after the shootings. During that time, school faculty held off-campus meetings and sent assignments through the mail so that students could receive credit for the semester. The university opened for classes again in the summer of 1970.

Sources

Bills, Scott. *Kent State/May 4: Echoes through a Decade*. Kent, OH: Kent State University Press, 1988.

Davies, Peter. *The Truth about Kent State: A Challenge to the American Conscience*. New York: Farrar, Straus and Giroux, 1973.

Grant, Edward J., and Michael Hill. *I Was There: What Really Went On at Kent State*. Lima, OH: CSS Publishing, 1974.

Heineman, Kenneth J. "'Look Out Kid, You're Gonna Get Hit!': Kent State and the Vietnam Antiwar Movement." In *Give Peace a Chance: Exploring the Vietnam Antiwar Movement*. edited by Melvin Small and William D. Hoover. Syracuse, NY: Syracuse University Press, 1992.

Michener, James. *Kent State: What Happened and Why*. New York: Random House, 1971.

Report of the President's Commission on Campus Unrest. Washington, DC: U.S. Government Printing Office, 1970.

Taylor, Stuart, et al. *Violence at Kent State, May 1 to May 4, 1970: The Students' Perspective*. New York: College Notes and Texts, 1971.

Warren, Bill, ed. *The Middle of the Country: The Events of May 4th as Seen by Students and Faculty at Kent State University*. New York: Avon, 1970.

The War in Vietnam

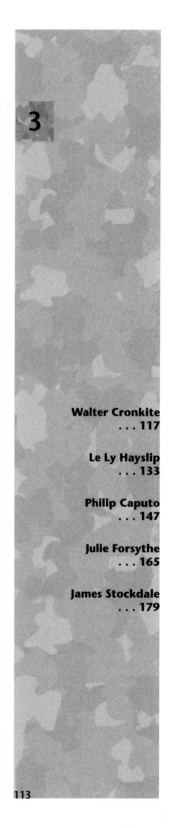

3

T he Vietnam War was a brutal and bloody conflict that took the lives of more than fifty-eight thousand American soldiers and an estimated two million Vietnamese soldiers and civilians. In addition, air bombings, mortar attacks, and gun battles destroyed countless forests, farmlands, villages, and city neighborhoods in both North and South Vietnam. As the war progressed, it also took a great emotional toll on its American and Vietnamese participants as they struggled to keep themselves, their comrades, and—in the case of Vietnamese civilians—their families alive.

Most of the battles that were waged in Vietnam were fierce gunfights between small bands of opposing soldiers. But both sides occasionally launched larger military campaigns. The greatest and most important of these major campaigns was called the Tet Offensive. This massive surprise attack by the North Vietnamese Army and its Viet Cong (South Vietnamese Communists) allies hit targets all across South Vietnam. American and South Vietnamese troops eventually pushed back the Communist assault, delivering heavy casualties to the enemy in the process, but the huge scale of the offensive convinced many disillusioned Americans that the war might drag on for several more years. Following the Tet Offensive, on February 27, 1968, CBS newsman Walter Cronkite (1916–) delivered an editorial from Vietnam in which he described the war as a bloody stalemate.

Throughout the Vietnam War, South Vietnamese farming families and other civilians became caught in the middle of the battle for control of the country. Both the Communists (North Vietnam and the Viet Cong) and the Americans and their South Vietnamese allies used threats and violence against the peasants in order to gain the advantage. This situation caused terrible fear and suffering for countless Vietnamese families, many of whom just wanted the war to end so they could return to their simple lives. In her memoir *When Heaven and Earth Changed Places,* a Vietnamese woman named Le Ly Hayslip (1949–) recalls what it felt like to grow up in such a dangerous environment.

Upon arriving in Vietnam, American combat soldiers found themselves in a strange land of swamps and dense jungles. The hot jungles and unfamiliar mountains of the Vietnamese countryside hid many dangers, from booby traps to snipers to bands of Viet Cong guerrillas (small groups of fighters who launch surprise attacks). In addition, U.S. troops could never be sure whether the Vietnamese civilians they encountered were friendly to them or allied with the Communists who were trying to kill them. Many American soldiers became demoralized and convinced that they were risking their lives for a doomed cause. In *A Rumor of War,* Vietnam veteran Philip Caputo recalled the dangers of the war and the sorrow of losing friends in battle.

Thousands of American women also went to Vietnam during the conflict to care for wounded soldiers and devastated peasant families. These women included civilian aid workers who helped run schools, orphanages, and hospitals in South Vietnam and U.S. nurses who treated wounded soldiers. In a collection of stories called *In the Combat Zone: An Oral History of American Women in Vietnam,* an American relief worker named Julie Forsythe remembered the terrible toll that the war took on rural Vietnamese families.

During the course of the Vietnam War, thousands of soldiers on both sides of the conflict were captured by enemy forces. Most of the Americans who were taken prisoner of war (POWs) were pilots who were shot down in air raids. According to international rules of warfare, POWs are supposed to be treated humanely and given adequate food and medical care. But many American prisoners suffered torture and near starvation at the hands of their captors. In his book *In Love and War,* former POW James Stockdale (1923–) recalled his experiences in a North Vietnamese prison.

Walter Cronkite

Excerpt from an editorial about the Vietnam War
Broadcast on CBS Television, February 27, 1968

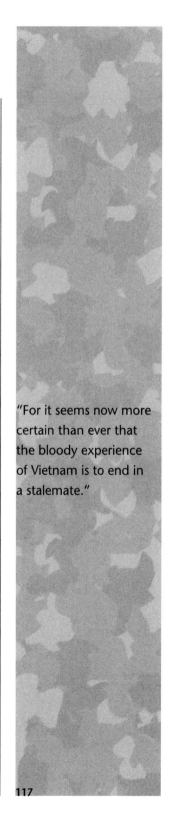

"For it seems now more certain than ever that the bloody experience of Vietnam is to end in a stalemate."

It is generally agreed that American media coverage of the Vietnam War had a major impact on public attitudes toward the conflict. But historians, military leaders, lawmakers, community leaders, and ordinary Americans have different opinions about the nature and quality of coverage provided by U.S. television and print journalists in Vietnam. Defenders of the American press in Vietnam claim that the journalists informed the American people about the true nature of the war at a time when their political and military leaders repeatedly deceived them. But critics in the government, the military, and elsewhere claim that the media was dominated by antiwar journalists who poisoned the American public against the war by delivering superficial and negative coverage of the conflict. Three decades later, the fairness and accuracy of American journalism in Vietnam remains a subject of fierce debate.

When the United States first became involved in Vietnam in the late 1950s and early 1960s, the relationship between America's press and its military and governmental leaders was fairly positive. This cordial relationship is generally attributed both to America's triumph in World War II and the economic prosperity the nation enjoyed in the late 1940s and 1950s. These events gave the American people great confidence in their government and their way of life. Not surprisingly, most U.S. newspaper and magazine news coverage reflected this perspective.

During the early 1960s, however, events in Vietnam put a strain on the generally positive relationship that existed between the press and U.S. governmental and military institutions. The journalists passed along official assurances about the South Vietnamese government's abilities to build popular support and eliminate the threat of the Communist Viet Cong guerrillas. But some members of the American and international press corps stationed in South Vietnam recognized that the country was more unstable than government officials wanted to admit. These reporters filed critical reports about the political and military situation in the country stating that the national government was actually quite corrupt and unpopular. They also noted that Viet Cong guerrillas controlled many of the country's rural regions. These blunt reports embarrassed and angered many American and South Vietnamese officials, and their relationship with the independent-minded journalists began to sour.

Still, most of the journalists who filed critical reports from South Vietnam during the war's early years actually supported American involvement in Indochina. They shared the U.S. government's belief that communism was a dangerous threat to the region. "At the beginning of the war," noted William Hammond, author of *Reporting Vietnam*, "correspondents . . . disagreed at times with official policy, but their reporting never questioned the ends [goals] of the war. Instead, placing great confidence in the American soldier, they argued in favor of more effective tactics and less official obfuscation [attempts to hide information]. The military, for their part, reciprocated [returned the favor], rejecting censorship of the press in favor of a system of voluntary guidelines that respected the willingness of reporters to avoid releasing information of value to the enemy."

American media coverage of the war increased dramatically in the mid-1960s, when U.S. troop commitments soared. "American news organizations cared little about Vietnam while it was primarily a fight between Vietnamese," con-

Journalists and media crews risked their lives covering the war. A television cameraman (left) films Marines in pursuit of a sniper. A soundman (center) works while lying on the ground. *Reproduced by permission of AP/Wide World Photos.*

firmed Clarence Wyatt in *Paper Soldiers*. "But when American soldiers began to fight and die with regularity, journalistic interest and investment increased." As media coverage of the conflict expanded, President Lyndon Johnson, administration officials, and other supporters of the war all expressed concern that it might erode popular support for the U.S. commitment in Indochina.

By the late 1960s American society had become bitterly divided over the Vietnam War. The internal turmoil over the conflict was due in no small part to the contradictory information that the American people received from government officials, military leaders, and journalists. Many of America's leaders contended that the United States was steadily progressing toward meeting its goals of defeating North Vietnam and establishing a democratic government in South Vietnam. But many other people charged that the war had actually deteriorated into a wasteful stalemate that was destroying thousands of American and Vietnamese lives. Distrustful of government assurances that the Communists were being slowly crushed by U.S. firepower and strategy, critics of the war came to see independent American television and press journalists as a more reliable source of information on the conflict.

During this same period, press coverage of the growing antiwar movement also became a topic of heated debate. Supporters of U.S. involvement in Vietnam complained that American newspapers, magazines, and television programs slanted their coverage in favor of the antiwar demonstrators. Antiwar activists, on the other hand, charged that the press ridiculed their concerns and misrepresented their actions. In reality, American newspapers, magazines, and other media were divided on the issue of antiwar protest. Some voices were sympathetic to the antiwar movement, while others expressed great hostility toward the demonstrators.

The Tet Offensive

In early 1968 North Vietnam launched a surprise invasion of the South. The Communists hoped that this attack—known as the Tet Offensive—would overwhelm South Vietnam and its American allies and trigger a nationwide revolt against the Saigon government. The massive assault stunned the American public, which had been repeatedly assured by President Lyndon Johnson (1908–1973) and other U.S. officials that victory was near.

As the Tet Offensive unfolded, hundreds of American journalists rushed to cover the event. The best known of these reporters was Walter Cronkite. Cronkite was a respected World War II correspondent who had served as anchorman of the *CBS Evening News* since 1962. By the time of the Tet Offensive, he had become one of America's most popular public figures. Indeed, he had built a reputation across the country as a level-headed, trustworthy, and patriotic journalist.

When Cronkite traveled to Vietnam to cover the Tet Offensive in February 1968, he was shocked by the military and political situation in the South. He had long held private doubts about the progress of the war, but he had hoped that official U.S. assurances that victory was near were true. As he toured the war-ravaged cities of Saigon and Hue, however, Cronkite realized that North Vietnam remained a strong and

dangerous foe. Armed with this knowledge, the trusted broadcast journalist decided to air a grim editorial detailing his own impressions of the war in Vietnam.

Things to remember while reading the excerpt from Cronkite's editorial:

- As the Vietnam War dragged on and American casualties mounted, journalists and ordinary citizens began questioning official versions of events with greater frequency. Some supporters of the war claimed that this shift in attitude was unfair. But other historians and government officials have expressed amazement that the American press and public remained as supportive as they did for so long. Clarence Wyatt, author of *Paper Soldiers*, recalled that when Vice President Hubert Humphrey (1911–1978) visited South Vietnam in the fall of 1967, he asked a group of journalists to "give the benefit of the doubt to our side."

"Benefit of the doubt?," replied one reporter. "Hell, what do you think we've been doing for the last six years?"

- Few Americans believed that North Vietnam was capable of defeating U.S. forces in direct combat on a regular basis. They recognized that the United States enjoyed big advantages over the enemy in areas such as military firepower, transportation capability, and resources. But the Communists used surprise attacks, guerrilla tactics, and America's unfamiliarity with Vietnam's mountains, jungles, and climate to neutralize the United States' military superiority throughout the war.

- Cronkite's remarks make it clear that he is uncertain whether either side managed to gain a military victory in the Tet Offensive. At one point he suggests that "the referees of history may make [the invasion] a draw." But Cronkite contends that whatever the outcome, the offensive showed that North Vietnam remained a dedicated and potent enemy. He also claims that Tet was a clear indication that U.S. and Vietnamese political leaders had been far too optimistic about their progress in defeating the Communists. "We have been too often disappointed by the optimism of the American leaders, both in Vietnam and Washington, to have faith any longer in the silver linings they find in the darkest clouds," declared Cronkite.

Excerpt from Walter Cronkite's Editorial on the Vietnam War:

*There are doubts about the measure of success or setback, but even more, there are doubts about the exact measure of the disaster itself. All that is known with certainty is that on the first two nights of the Tet Lunar New Year, the **Viet Cong** and North Vietnamese Regular Forces, violating the truce agreed on for that holiday, struck across the entire length of South Vietnam, hitting the largest thirty-five cities, towns, and provincial capitals. How many died and how much damage was done, however, are still but **approximations**, despite the official figures.*

Viet Cong: Communist guerrillas in South Vietnam.

Approximations: Estimates.

The very **preciseness** of the figures brings them under suspicion. Anyone who has wandered through these ruins knows that an exact count is impossible. Why, just a short while ago a little old man came and told us that two **VC** were buried in a hastily dug grave up at the end of the block. Had they been counted? And what about these ruins? Have they gone through all of them for buried **civilians** and soldiers? And what about those 14 VC we found in the courtyard behind the post office at Hue? Had they been counted and **tabulated**? They certainly hadn't been buried.

We came to Vietnam to try to determine what all this means to the future of the war here. We talked to officials, top officials, civilian and military, Vietnamese and American. We toured damaged areas like this, and refugee centers. We paid a visit to the Battle at Hue, and to the men manning the northernmost provinces, where the next big Communist offensive is expected. . . .

We'd like to sum up our findings in Vietnam, an analysis that must be speculative, personal, **subjective**. Who won and who lost in the great Tet Offensive against the cities? I'm not sure. The Viet Cong did not win by a knockout, but neither did we. The referees of history may make it a draw. Another stand-off may be coming in the big battles expected south of the **Demilitarized Zone**. **Khe Sanh** could well fall, with a terrible loss in American lives, prestige, and morale, and this is a tragedy of our stubbornness there; but the **bastion** no longer is a key to the rest of the northern regions, and it is doubtful that the American forces can be defeated across the breadth of the **DMZ** with any substantial loss of ground. Another stand-off. On the political front, past performance gives no confidence that the Vietnamese government can cope with its problems, now compounded by the attack on the cities. It may not fall, it may hold on, but it probably won't show the dynamic qualities demanded of this young nation. Another stand-off.

We have been too often disappointed by the optimism of the American leaders, both in Vietnam and Washington, to have faith any longer in the silver linings they find in the darkest clouds. They may be right, that Hanoi's winter-spring offensive had been forced by the Communist realization that they could not win the longer war of **attrition**, and that the Communists hope that any success in the offensive will improve their position for eventual negotiations. It would improve their position, and it would also require our realization, that we should have had all along, that any negotiations must be that—negotiations, not the **dictation** of peace terms. For it seems now more certain than ever that the bloody experience of Vietnam is to end in a **stalemate**.

Preciseness: Detailed or specific.

VC: Viet Cong.

Civilians: Non-military people.

Tabulated: Calculated or counted.

Subjective: Based on personal impressions.

Demilitarized Zone: Border area between North and South Vietnam.

Khe Sanh: U.S. Marine Corps base that faced constant enemy attack in early 1968.

Bastion: Fortress or stronghold.

DMZ: Demilitarized Zone.

Attrition: Strategy of wearing down an opponent with superior resources.

Dictation: Commanding.

Stalemate: Deadlock between two opponents, so that neither side can gain victory.

Walter Cronkite (1916–)

Walter Cronkite ranks as one of the most influential journalists in American history. Born in St. Joseph, Missouri, Cronkite worked as a newspaper and radio reporter until 1939, when he became a correspondent for United Press International (UPI). He covered many of Europe's major battles during World War II (1939–1945). In 1946 he began a three-year stint as UPI's bureau chief in Moscow in the Soviet Union.

In 1950 Cronkite was hired by the CBS television network, and over the next decade he emerged as one of its leading broadcast journalists. In 1962 he was chosen to anchor the *CBS Evening News,* a position he held until 1981. He became a trusted father-figure to many Americans during this period. As a result, his critical comments on the Vietnam War had a significant influence on public opinion. After retiring from the *CBS Evening News* in 1981, Cronkite continued to pursue his interest in U.S. and world affairs. He worked as a special correspondent for CBS, and he hosted a variety of public affairs programs on PBS and other networks during the 1980s and early 1990s.

In 1996 Cronkite published an autobiography called *A Reporter's Life,* in which he provided additional commentary on the Vietnam War. He claimed that the Johnson administration (which occupied the White House from late 1963 to early 1969) mishandled the war in two basic areas. First, Cronkite charged that Johnson's efforts to "shield the American economy from the consequences of the war" created serious economic and social problems for the country. Second, Cronkite stated that "Johnson never leveled with the American people about the nature or likely extent of the war."

Cronkite's own "disillusionment" with American military involvement in Vietnam developed gradually, as the United States invested ever greater resources and soldiers in the conflict. With each passing month, Cronkite became concerned with what he called "the increasing reports from the military and the political foxholes of Vietnam that neither the battle to subjugate [defeat and bring under control] the Vietcong nor that to win over the Vietnamese villagers was meeting with any tangible success. Additionally, there was something distinctly uncomfortable about a war in which it was impossible for even the most optimistic military spokesmen to claim that we were liberating and holding any sizable parts of the territory of South Vietnam. The criterion [measurement] for success that our military adopted was the body count. The only way to measure victory, it seemed, was in terms of how many Vietcong we could kill. That was scarcely uplifting, scarcely inspiring, scarcely calculated to build the morale of either the fighting forces or the home front. It became increasingly difficult to justify the war as the terrible cost to ourselves in blood and material grew and the supply of Vietcong needing to be killed appeared inexhaustible."

Cronkite also expressed anger about accusations that the antiwar movement opposition to the conflict was a betrayal of the United States. "Patriotism simply cannot be defined," he said. "Many of those against the war protested with the most dedicated patriotism—in the total conviction that the war was not a just one and was besmirching [staining or ruining] the image of a nation they loved."

In 1975—two years after the last American combat troops left Vietnam—North Vietnam finally defeated South Vietnam to end the war. Cronkite anchored CBS's coverage of the fall of Saigon, South Vietnam's capital city, despite being troubled by a painful back injury. In fact, Cronkite rode to the CBS television studio in an ambulance, with a doctor by his side. Outfitted in a back brace, he reported on South Vietnam's final hours of existence while literally strapped to his anchor chair.

Years later, Cronkite continued to claim that he and the other CBS reporters offered fair and objective coverage of the war in Vietnam. He also points out that his famous commentary during the Tet Offensive was clearly labeled as an editorial. "I was proud of the degree to which we had kept our evening newscast free of bias, although on a subject as controversial as the war, we did not get credit from either side for doing so," he said. "A generation of officers later, there still lurks in the Pentagon [the headquarters of the Department of Defense] the belief that the media lost the war. We could have won, they insist, if the press had not shown those pictures of naked, napalmed Vietnamese girls fleeing our bombing, of prisoners being shot in the head, of burning hooches [huts], of wounded GIs [American soldiers]. Television brought the war into our living rooms at home and destroyed our will to fight, their theory goes."

Cronkite, though, argues that television and print journalists provided the American public with valuable information about Vietnam at a time when the U.S. government and military was not being truthful. "Let's be clear," he said. "There must be military censorship in time of war. Strategy, tactics, size of forces, success of operations are all legitimate secrets that the military must not disclose. [But] our government simply must not shy away from sharing with the people the unpleasant results of war. All aspects of such foreign adventures must be exposed, and discussed, in a free society."

*This summer's almost certain stand-off will either end in real give-and-take negotiations or terrible **escalation**; and for every means we have to escalate, the enemy can match us, and that applies to invasion of the North, the use of nuclear weapons, or the mere commitment of 100-, or 200-, or 300,000 more American troops to the battle. And with each escalation, the world comes closer to the brink of cosmic disaster.*

*To say that we are closer to victory today is to believe, in the face of the evidence, the optimists who have been wrong in the past. To suggest we are on the edge of defeat is to yield to unreasonable **pessimism**. To say that we are **mired** in stalemate seems the only realistic, yet unsatisfactory, conclusion. On the off chance that military and political analysts are right, in the next few months we must test the enemy's intentions, in case this is indeed his last gasp before negotiations. But it is increasingly clear to this reporter that the only **rational** way out then will be to negotiate, not as victors, but as an honorable people who lived up to their pledge to defend democracy, and did the best they could.*

Escalation: Increase in military activity.

Pessimism: Depression or gloomy predictions.

Mired: Stuck.

Rational: Sensible.

What happened next . . .

Many of South Vietnam's cities and towns became war zones during the Tet Offensive. But the invasion failed to spark a general uprising against the South Vietnamese government, and the Communist forces suffered tremendous losses at the hands of U.S. and South Vietnamese military forces. North Vietnam eventually was forced to call a general retreat. Their massive invasion had been a military failure.

Nonetheless, Tet proved disastrous for the Johnson administration. In the months prior to the invasion, the president and America's military leadership had repeatedly told the American people that they were on the verge of victory in Vietnam. The scale of the Communist invasion, however, made it clear that defeating the North would require significant new commitments of troops, weapons, and money. As a result, Tet destroyed the credibility of the Johnson administration among large segments of the American public. Many historians believe that this collapse in confidence was best symbolized by journalist Walter Cronkite's post-Tet description of Vietnam as a "stalemate." In fact, Johnson reportedly watched Cronkite's commentary, then flipped off the television and said, "If I've lost Cronkite, I've lost middle America."

American press coverage of the Vietnam War continued to draw criticism from lawmakers and military leaders throughout the remainder of the conflict. President Richard Nixon (1913–1994), who succeeded Johnson in January 1969, expressed frustration with U.S. news coverage on numerous occasions. In 1971 he even stated that aside from the Communists, "our worst enemy seems to be the press." This comment, which was echoed by many of Nixon's pro-war allies, reflected a genuine belief that the press reported events in Vietnam with a negative slant. But the American media, antiwar lawmakers, and other observers dismissed these complaints. They charged that Nixon and other government officials disliked the press coverage because it exposed their flawed policies to the world. In any case, day-to-day coverage of the war declined dramatically in American newspapers and network news programs in the early 1970s, as the U.S. withdrawal from Vietnam accelerated.

Walter Cronkite reporting from Vietnam in 1968.
Reproduced by permission of Archive Photos.

Criticisms of American media coverage of the war

Since the Vietnam War ended in 1975 with a Communist victory, the debate over American media coverage of the conflict has remained a bitter one. The most common complaint heard from critics of the U.S. media performance in

Vietnam is that the majority of America's television, newspaper, and magazine journalists were personally opposed to the war. They claim that these reporters provided negative and misleading coverage of the war, and that their slanted coverage turned American public opinion against U.S. involvement.

Some lawmakers, military leaders, and historians also contend that American journalists did not do a good job of explaining or interpreting events in Vietnam. Nixon, for example, argued that the media did not provide any sense of the "underlying purpose" of the battles and maneuvers that Americans saw, heard, and read about. "Eventually this contributed to the impression that we were fighting in military and moral quicksand, rather than toward an important and worthwhile objective," he claimed. Other critics claim that some journalists simply jumped to the wrong conclusions when reporting events in Vietnam. The most commonly cited example of this phenomenon is the Tet Offensive, which some American reporters initially—and mistakenly—interpreted as a military defeat for the United States.

Other critics complained that the rivalry among news organizations created superficial and incomplete coverage, as reporters competed to submit the most dramatic stories. In addition, journalists were widely criticized for emphasizing coverage of American combat troops at the expense of less glamorous but nonetheless important issues. "An intense focus on spot reporting of day-to-day combat activity, to the detriment of coverage of less dramatic . . . but equally important social and political stories . . . typified American journalism in Vietnam," commented Wyatt. "During the height of American military involvement, even the most interested, diligent [dedicated] news consumer could conclude that the war in Vietnam was primarily an American effort in which nonmilitary issues were either nonexistent or unimportant."

Finally, many observers believe that television coverage of Vietnam had a tremendously negative impact on American attitudes toward the war. Supporters of this theory claim that when the grim imagery of the Vietnam War—including fierce bombing raids, wounded American soldiers, and crying refugees—appeared on America's television screens, the footage gradually eroded public support for the war. As Daniel C. Hallin noted in The "Uncensored" War, "television shows the raw horror of war in a way print cannot." One Marine officer even claimed in *Military Review* magazine that "the power and impact of television was *the* deciding factor in turning American public opinion from one of supporting the U.S. defense of South Vietnam to one of opposing it."

American media coverage defended

Criticism of the American press in Vietnam has remained strong over the years. But many of the journalists who covered the war defend their performance, and they are supported by a wide range of historians, lawmakers, and members of the U.S. military. As Vietnam reporter Don Oberdorfer noted in *The Bad War,* "coverage of Vietnam was a complicated subject, most of which is conveniently forgotten by one side or the other in the debate. For the American press, Vietnam was a learning experience—much as it was for the rest of the country and the government. We knew very little at the beginning, but as the war progressed people in the press, along with people in the government, who were our sources after all, began to get this very hazy, fuzzy situation into focus. And this picture was not the same picture that was being portrayed in the official reports."

Historians and Vietnam-era reporters agree that the coverage of the war was sometimes superficial. Many also believe that journalists sometimes focused too much on American wartime experiences at the expense of informing readers and viewers about Vietnamese perspectives on the conflict. But they strongly object to the charge that they slanted their coverage because of personal opposition to the war. "Republicans in Washington were questioning [Democratic President Lyndon Johnson's] credibility on the war long before most television correspondents were," stated Hallin. "At least a year before Cronkite called the war a 'bloody stalemate' and urged negotiation, the secretary of defense [Robert McNamara] had reached essentially the same conclusion."

Moreover, many observers believe that the American press corps provided a much more objective account of the war than the U.S. government, which repeatedly distorted events to suit its war aims. "Press coverage of the Vietnam War . . . often conveyed more of the truth than official pronouncements on such significant matters as drug abuse, race relations, the state of military morale, combat operations, and conditions within the South Vietnamese government and armed forces," declared historian William Hammond of the U.S. Army Center of Military History.

Some people also believe that the impact of television on American support for the war has been overstated. They agree that some violent television footage shocked and disturbed the American public. But studies indicate that most television coverage of the conflict in Vietnam did not feature scenes of outright warfare. "Television covered Vietnam nearly every day for more than seven years, producing hours of reporting on the war," wrote Hallin. "Some of that reporting concerned events of great immediate significance. But the majority did not: it was taken up with routine battle coverage . . . ; reports on technology; human-interest vignettes about the troops; occasional 'light' stories about such trivia as what it is like to parachute out of an airplane; and many speeches and press conferences." In addition, much of the television coverage—especially prior to Tet—emphasized the bravery and patriotism of the American soldiers. Some observers believe that this emphasis actually increased public support for the war (one 1967 *Newsweek* poll, for instance, reported that 64 percent of American citizens believed that television coverage *heightened* their support for the war effort).

Many journalists who reported on the war in Vietnam confirm that the tone of coverage became more critical in the war's latter stages, as American hopes for outright victory faded. But they insist that the tone of press coverage simply reflected the changing public view of the war. "The American news media both reflected and reinforced the trend [of support for the government], replaying official statements on the value of the war and supporting the soldier in the field, if not always his generals," wrote Hammond. "With time, under the influence of many deaths and contradictions, American society moved to repudiate [reject] that earlier decision. . . . The press followed along, becoming more and more critical of events in South Vietnam as withdrawals continued and the war gradually lost whatever purpose it had held."

Finally, defenders of American press coverage of Vietnam claim that the strongest criticism of the media came from

U.S. lawmakers, government officials, and generals who wanted to shift the blame for the failed war away from themselves. "The press didn't lose the war for us," commented diplomat Richard Holbrooke—a former Johnson administration official—in *The Bad War.* "The war was lost because the strategy was wrong. The military lost the war; the political leadership of this country lost the war. Lyndon Johnson . . . and Richard Nixon and [Secretary of State] Henry Kissinger are the men who cost us this thing. Not the Case-Church Amendment [a law that placed restrictions on presidential war powers], not David Halberstam and Walter Cronkite, and not the antiwar demonstrators. . . . The war was not lost, as Nixon always likes to write, in the halls of Congress and on the pages of the *New York Times;* it was lost in the rice paddies of Indochina."

Did you know . . .

- According to media historian Lawrence Lichty, less than 5 percent of television news film reports from Vietnam between 1965 and 1970 showed scenes of "close-up" combat.

- During President Nixon's first term of office from 1969 to 1973, Vice President Spiro Agnew became well known for his attacks on American television and print journalists who questioned the administration's Vietnam policies. His description of reporters as "nattering nabobs of negativism" drew particular applause from supporters of the war.

- Since the Vietnam War, American officials have imposed greater restrictions on journalists assigned to report on conflicts in which U.S. troops are involved. In the 1991 Persian Gulf War, for example, the U.S. military and civilian officials limited media access to soldiers and prevented reporters from visiting some regions in which military operations took place.

Sources

Braestrup, Peter. *Big Story: How the American Press and Television Reported and Interpreted the Crisis of Tet 1968 in Vietnam and Washington.* Boulder, CO: Westview Press, 1977.

Cronkite, Walter. *A Reporter's Life*. New York: Alfred A. Knopf, 1997.

Dougan, Clark, and Stephen Weiss. *The American Experience in Vietnam.* New York: W. W. Norton, 1988.

Elegant, Robert. "How to Lose a War." *Encounter,* August 1981.

Hallin, Daniel C. *The "Uncensored War": The Media and Vietnam.* New York: Oxford University Press, 1986.

Hammond, William M. *Reporting Vietnam: Media and Military at War.* Lawrence: University Press of Kansas, 1998.

Mandelbaum, Michael. "Vietnam: The Television War." *Daedalus,* Fall 1982.

Porter, William E. *Assault on the Media: The Nixon Years.* Ann Arbor: University of Michigan Press, 1976.

Turner, Kathleen J. *Lyndon Johnson's Dual War: Vietnam and the Press.* Chicago: University of Chicago Press, 1985.

Willenson, Kim, et al. *The Bad War: An Oral History of the Vietnam War.* New York: New American Library, 1987.

Wyatt, Clarence. *Paper Soldiers: The American Press and the Vietnam War.* New York: W. W. Norton, 1993.

Le Ly Hayslip

Excerpt from her memoir **When Heaven and Earth Changed Places**

Published in 1989

In many ways the Vietnam War was a fight to control the countryside of South Vietnam and the loyalty of its people. Before the war most of the people in South Vietnam lived in small, rural villages and supported their families by farming. They tended to be quite poor, and few of them could read or write. They lived simple lives that emphasized the importance of family ties and cultural traditions. They did not know or care much about politics. But when the war began, the South Vietnamese peasants were caught in the middle.

The Geneva Accords of 1954, which ended the war between France and Communist-led Viet Minh forces, divided Vietnam into two sections. The northern section, which was led by a Communist government under Ho Chi Minh, was officially known as the Democratic Republic of Vietnam but was usually called North Vietnam. The southern section, which was led by a U.S.-supported government under Ngo Dinh Diem, was known as the Republic of South Vietnam.

The peace agreement also provided for nationwide free elections to be held in 1956, with a goal of reuniting the two sections of Vietnam under one government. But the South

"I had a terrible dream of ghosts floating through the village and into our house and into my mouth and nose and I couldn't breathe. I woke up to find my father's hand over my face and his voice whispering to me to lie still."

Vietnamese government refused to hold elections. North Vietnamese leaders remained determined to reunite the country, by force if necessary. Within a short time a new war began between the two sections of Vietnam. In 1965 the United States sent troops to join the fight on the side of South Vietnam.

The war for the people's support

One of the Communists' main weapons in the Vietnam War was a group of guerilla fighters known as the Viet Cong that operated in the South Vietnamese countryside. The Viet Cong mingled with the villagers and tried to convince them to support the Communist efforts to overthrow Diem's government. They used several methods to gain the support of the peasants in South Vietnam. One of these methods was propaganda, or spreading information in order to promote their cause and reduce support for the opposing cause. For example, they told the villagers that Diem was just a puppet of the United States. They claimed that Ho Chi Minh would bring freedom and independence to the Vietnamese people. They also taught the villagers patriotic songs and sayings.

But the Viet Cong also used violence to convince the rural people to support their efforts to take over South Vietnam. "Viet Cong efforts were always supported by terror. *Terror* is defined as the deliberate use of murder, torture, and fear, mainly against the defenseless, to gain a political objective. For the Viet Cong, terrorism was 'education by violence,'" Albert Marrin wrote in *America and Vietnam: The Elephant and the Tiger*. "Terrorism provided a daily reminder that Saigon [the South Vietnamese government] could not protect the people. This was important for two reasons. First, it kept citizens in fear. A Viet Cong threat had to be taken seriously, since its agents could strike anyone whenever it pleased. Second, it kept the Viet Cong's own followers in line."

On the other side was the Army of the Republic of South Vietnam, or ARVN. These forces, with the help of American weapons and equipment, tried to prevent the Viet Cong from taking control of the countryside. One method used by the ARVN was to turn rural villages into fortified hamlets. They surrounded the villages with trenches, stakes, barbed wire, and armed guards in order to prevent the Viet Cong from entering.

But this strategy was not very effective. The Viet Cong still found ways to make contact with the people. In addition, the fortifications often disrupted the lives of the peasants and caused them to resent the government.

In many cases the rural people of South Vietnam became trapped in the middle of the dispute between the Viet Cong and the ARVN. Both sides competed for their loyalty and were willing to use intimidation and violence to keep it. This situation created terrible fear and suffering for the peasants. "We had to appease [go along with] the allied forces [of South Vietnam and the United States] by day and were terrorized by the Viet Cong at night," Le Ly Hayslip recalled in *When Heaven and Earth Changed Places*. "We obeyed both sides and wound up pleasing neither. We were people in the middle."

Some of the rural people in South Vietnam continued to support the government. But many others were influenced by the ideas that the Viet Cong spread among them. The Viet Cong claimed that they were fighting to liberate the country from foreign control and reunite the Vietnamese people under one government. These ideas appealed to the villagers. "*Freedom* meant a Vietnam free of colonial domination," Hayslip noted. "*Independence* meant one Vietnamese people— not two countries, North and South— determining its own destiny."

Some of the South Vietnamese villagers became convinced that the United States was just another in a long line of foreign powers that wanted to control Vietnam. "Because we peasants

Vietnamese peasants in the Mekong delta take cover.
Reproduced by permission of Corbis-Bettmann.

knew nothing about the United States, we could not stop to think how absurd it would be for so large and wealthy a nation to covet [wish to possess] our poor little country with its rice fields, swamps, and pagodas [temples]. Because our only exposure to politics had been through the French colonial government (and before that, the rule of Vietnamese kings), we had no concept of democracy," Hayslip explained. "What for [Americans] was normal—a life of peace and plenty—was for us a hazy dream known only in our legends."

In the following excerpt Hayslip recalls a series of incidents that took place around 1961. At that time she was twelve years old and lived in a small village called Ky La near Danang in central Vietnam. The war between Communist-led North Vietnam and U.S.-supported South Vietnam was just beginning. Like many other South Vietnamese villagers, she became caught in the middle of the dispute between the Viet Cong guerilla fighters and the ARVN forces.

Things to remember while reading the excerpt from Le Ly Hayslip's memoir *When Heaven and Earth Changed Places*:

- As North Vietnam and South Vietnam competed for the loyalty of the rural people during the war, villages and even families were divided over which side to support. In fact, Hayslip's family was divided by the war. One of her brothers, Bon Nghe, went to North Vietnam to join the Communist rebels. But one of her sisters, Ba Xuan, was married to a policeman who worked for the South Vietnamese government in Danang. This situation made it even more difficult for Hayslip and her parents to choose between the Viet Cong and the ARVN when these forces came to their village.

- The ARVN built fortifications around Hayslip's village to protect the people from the Viet Cong. But as soon as the soldiers left, the Viet Cong returned and tore down the fortifications. At this point the Viet Cong leader spoke to the villagers. His speech showed the combination of propaganda and intimidation that the Viet Cong typically used to maintain control over the South Vietnamese villages.

- Like many other South Vietnamese peasants, the people of Ky La were torn between cooperating with the ARVN sol-

diers and helping the Viet Cong. In the beginning they feared and distrusted both sides. They cautiously supported whichever side was present. Over time, however, it became clear that the South Vietnamese army could not protect them from the Viet Cong. In addition, Hayslip and many others in her village began to believe the Viet Cong propaganda. They eventually began resisting the government forces and actively supporting the Viet Cong.

Excerpt from When Heaven and Earth Changed Places:

Before I was twelve and I knew better, I played war games with the children in my village. . . . Some of us pretended to be **Republican**

An elderly Vietnamese woman carrying a boy leaves Tan Uyen, South Vietnam, after a Viet Cong attack in 1968. *Reproduced by permission of Corbis-Bettmann.*

Republican: Forces representing the South Vietnamese government; also known as the Army of the Republic of South Vietnam, or ARVN.

Le Ly Hayslip   137

soldiers (who were just like **surly** policemen), while others would be *Viet Cong*, who we supposed were only gangsters. When one force was too badly outnumbered, some of us switched sides, although others refused to play the game at all unless a certain person was "the enemy" or was "on my side"—whichever side that happened to be on that day. The **old war** between the **Viet Minh** and the French seemed a lifetime away (it had been many years since **Ky La** had seen fighting and the village, in fact, had been renamed "Binh Ky" by the new Republic as part of its total break with the past), and armies of this **new war**, the Viet Cong and the Republic, were both filled with Vietnamese. "How bad can this be?" we asked ourselves during rests between mock battles. "A family feud? A spat between brothers?" We had seen plenty of those in our own families. We could not imagine such a war to be real.

Still, I never enjoyed the game. When I played a Republican, I always imagined that the laughing face at the end of my stick-rifle was my brother Bon Nghe, who had gone to **Hanoi** and who might one day come back to fight around Ky La. When I played a Viet Cong, I could think only of my sister Ba in **Danang**, who, being married to a policeman, locked her door every night out of fear of "those terrorists" who blew up power stations and cars and took potshots at the officials for whom her husband worked. I could not accept the idea that either my brother or my sister must somehow become my enemy.

In school, the pressure to take sides was enormous. Our teacher, a villager named Manh, who was paid by the government, asked us, "What will you do if you see a Viet Cong, or hear about someone who's helping them?" We answered in chorus, "Turn him in to the soldiers!" Manh praised us for our answer and told us that the Republicans would pay our families big rewards for every Viet Cong we helped them capture. Still, when we played among ourselves, there was no shortage of Viet Cong fighters, and the children who pretended to be Republicans usually did so halfheartedly. . . .

Republican soldiers were now a familiar sight in our village. Unlike the French, they tried to be kind and often helped us in the fields. Although I was just a flat-chested girl of twelve, I liked the way these handsome young men looked at me and teased me and shared their **rations** when it was time to eat. My mother warned me away from them, though, telling me I would endanger the family if I talked too much. "What business is it of theirs," she would say, "about who married who, or whose relatives worked where and for how long?" I had yet to learn that in the war that was about to begin, many peo-

Surly: Irritable or threatening.

Viet Cong: Vietnamese Communist guerilla fighters who worked with the North Vietnamese Army to conquer South Vietnam.

Old war: The First Indochina War, which took place between France and Communist-led Viet Minh forces in Vietnam, 1946–1954.

Viet Minh: A Communist-led nationalist group that worked to gain Vietnam's independence from French colonial rule.

Ky La: A small village in central Vietnam.

New war: The Vietnam War, between Communist-led North Vietnam and U.S.-supported South Vietnam.

Hanoi: The capital city of North Vietnam.

Danang: A coastal city in central Vietnam.

Rations: Food for one meal.

ple would be killed simply because they were related by birth or by marriage to the wrong person—someone who was an enemy to the person who held the gun. . . .

The first time I saw a Viet Cong fighter up close it was just about dark and I was cleaning up our kitchen. I happened to gaze out the window to the house next door, which (although it was owned by Manh, who had been my teacher) was often used by villagers for gambling. Without a sound, a half-dozen strangers scampered into Manh's house and then shouted "Nobody move!" The oil lamp in Manh's window went out and people began running from the house. At first I thought it was Republican soldiers raiding the gamblers, as they had done several times before, but it soon became obvious that this was not that kind of raid.

Manh was the last one out, led at gunpoint with his hands atop his head. I could hear his familiar voice arguing with the strangers: "But—I don't know what you're talking about!" and "Why? Who told you that?" I leaned into the window to get a better view when I saw one of the strangers standing just outside. He wore black garments, like everyone else, and had on a **conical** sun hat, even though it was already dark. His sandals were made from old tires and his **weapon** had a queer, curved ammunition clip that jutted down from the stock like a banana. He seemed to be keeping an eye on the dusty road that ran by Manh's house and he was so close to me that I was afraid to run away or even duck down for fear that he would hear me.

Suddenly one of the strangers barked out an order in an odd, **clipped** accent (I found out later this was how everyone talked in the **North**) and two of his **comrades** prodded Manh to the edge of the road. I could still hear Manh begging for his life when two rifle shots cut him short. The strangers then ran a Viet Cong flag up the pole that stood outside our schoolhouse and left as quickly as they had come. The leader shouted over his shoulder: "Anyone who touches that flag will get the same thing as that traitor!"

The guard who was standing by my window glanced over and gave me a wink, showing he knew I had been there all along and had learned the lesson he had come to teach; he then followed his troops into the night. . . .

[Hayslip is shocked by what she has seen. She protests to her father that her teacher was a nice man. Her father calms her down and explains that Manh's careless words had gotten him in trouble. Her father then warns her never to talk to the South Vietnamese soldiers.]

Conical: Shaped like a cone.

Weapon: The Viet Cong soldier carried a gun made in the Soviet Union, which was different from the American weapons used by the South Vietnamese troops.

Clipped: Shortened or abbreviated.

North: Communist-led North Vietnam.

Comrades: Fellow soldiers, especially Communists.

An American Reporter Witnesses the Peasants' Terror

While traveling through Vietnam in 1962, David Halberstam of the *New York Times* saw firsthand the terror that many peasants felt at being caught in the middle of the war between the South Vietnamese armed forces and the Viet Cong. The following is an excerpt from a report that was reprinted in his book *The Making of a Quagmire*:

> About a hundred yards away we came upon a dead peasant lying in the yard of his hut with a poncho spread over him. Two huts further on, a desperately frightened old man of eighty was genuflecting [kneeling in respect or worship] in front of the American and Vietnamese officers and telling them that he had never heard of the Viet Cong. How many times had this old man had to tell Government troops that he knew no Viet Cong? How many times had he had to tell the Viet Minh [Communist-led nationalist

David Halberstam. *Reproduced by permission of AP/Wide World Photos.*

> group that worked to gain Vietnam's independence from French colonial rule] or Viet Cong that he knew no Government troops? "The war," a young Vietnamese said to me bitterly later, "only lasts a lifetime."

On the very next day, the Republicans came back to Ky La— more than we'd ever seen—with trucks full of steel **girders** and cement and barbed wire. They chopped down the Viet Cong flag and told the farmers to build defenses around the village. The ditches left over from the French occupation, now overgrown with weeds, were made deeper and bamboo trees were cut down to make spikes and watchtowers. During the weeks of construction, the soldiers told us to stay indoors and keep our houses dark at night. As soon as the sun went down, the Republicans set up **ambushes**

Girders: Materials used as structural supports for buildings.

Ambushes: Traps in which hidden people wait to attack.

around the village and waited for the dogs to bark—a sure sign that intruders were lurking outside.

But nothing happened. After a while, the Republican troops pulled out and left us in the hands of the "Popular Force"—the Dan De—local villagers who had been given small arms and a little training in how to use them. Because the war seemed to leave with the soldiers, the **PF** officials declared peace and Ky La, despite its new necklace of stakes and barbed wire, tried very hard to believe them.

Unfortunately, the peace didn't last very long. A few days later, my father awakened me in the middle of the night and took us to the place where the Republicans had left their biggest **cache** of materials, including some long metal poles. Within a few minutes, we were joined by most of our neighbors. One PF officer said, "Here—take these poles and hide them so that the Republicans won't find them. Our **fighters** need them for protection against enemy tanks."

Without further discussion, we took as many poles as we could carry and hurried off to bury them outside our house. "Oh yes," the PF officer added. "If you have a watchdog, give him to a relative out of town or boil him up for supper. We can't have any dogs barking the next time our freedom fighters come to the village!"

Although I wanted badly to ask my father what was happening, I obediently helped him carry some twenty poles to our house. By the time we finished burying them, a huge bonfire had been started in a clearing behind our house, with most of the villagers—including the children—collected around it. In the light of the dancing flames, I recognized the handsome Viet Cong soldier who had winked at me on the night my teacher Manh had been killed. He just strolled around, cradling his weapon, wearing the amused smile I'd seen many young men wear when they eyed pretty girls at the market. The Viet Cong **cadre**, and many of the villagers, piled onto the fire everything the Republicans had given them to defend the village. . . .

[Then the Viet Cong leader speaks to the villagers.] "We are the soldiers of **liberation!** That is how you will call us. We are here to fight for our land, and our country! Help us stop the **foreign aggression** and you will have peace. Help us win and you will keep your property and everything else you love. Ky La is our village now—and yours. We have given it back to you. . . ." [When the Viet Cong soldiers finish tearing down and burning all of the fortifications built by the Republicans, they prepare to leave the village. Then the leader speaks again.] "Down the road you will find two traitors. I trust they are the last we will see in Ky La. We must leave now, but you will see us again."

PF: Popular Force.

Cache: Storage of food or supplies.

Fighters: The Viet Cong.

Cadre: Core group of trained personnel.

Liberation: Freeing the country from foreign rule.

Foreign aggression: A reference to U.S. military involvement in Vietnam.

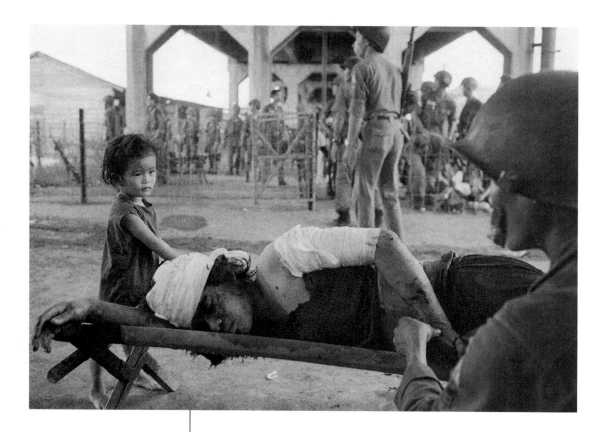

A soldier helps an injured woman while her daughter watches at an aid station in Cholon, a Chinese suburb of Saigon.
Reproduced by permission of Corbis Corporation.

Informer: Someone who supplies information to others.

Vengeance: Punishment given to make up for an injury or offense.

Everyone in the crowd looked at everyone else, wondering which two had been taken. When the Viet Cong were out of sight, a few men began putting out the fire, afraid it might spread to the houses, but most simply went back to their homes. A few minutes later, we heard gunshots on the road to Danang. My father and some others went out to bring back the bodies but as we had already guessed, one was the younger brother of Manh—a victim because of his family connections. The other was a village busybody—a veteran of the Viet Minh, who, after a long imprisonment, had become a government **informer.** He came to our house often and asked my mother about my brother Bon, making her—and all the other mothers who had sons in the North—worry for their lives. Now the informer himself had been informed against and I felt, deep in my young girl's heart, that he, like Manh, had gotten what he deserved. It was my first taste of **vengeance** and I found that revenge, like the blood that once ran from my nose during our war games on the playground, tasted sweeter than I expected. It made even a puny little farm girl feel like someone important.

Kit Carson Scouts

During the Vietnam War hundreds of former Vietnamese Communists defected from the North and became valuable agents for the American side. In October 1966 the U.S. military created an official program to recruit and train former Viet Cong guerillas and North Vietnamese Army (NVA) soldiers. General Herman Nickerson, a Marine commander and history buff, called the former Communist agents Kit Carson Scouts after Kit Carson, a famous soldier and frontier guide of the American West.

The Kit Carson Scouts were particularly useful during combat patrols. They led U.S. military units to enemy camps, food supplies, weapons, tunnels, trails, and booby-traps on many occasions. They also served as interpreters, helping the American soldiers to communicate with the South Vietnamese. In some cases Kit Carson Scouts were sent into South Vietnamese villages to talk with peasants and encourage them to cooperate with U.S. forces.

When the U.S. military withdrew from Vietnam in 1973, most Kit Carson Scouts became soldiers in the South Vietnamese Army. After NVA troops captured the South Vietnamese capital of Saigon in 1975 to win the Vietnam War, most of the former Communists who had helped the Americans were sent to prison.

*The next morning, as we buried the two victims, the Republican troops returned. This time they came into our houses and searched for evidence that might link us to the enemy. The soldiers drafted some workers and made them clean up the remains of the bonfire the Viet Cong had left. They **interrogated** everyone, separately and together, to find out what had happened and, more importantly, what was going to happen next. They were especially displeased with the PF officers and arrested one of them—the wrong one, we noticed—and drove him away in a jeep. Like everyone else, I said nothing. The man was never seen in Ky La again. . . .*

That night, I slept with my mother while my father and brother Sau Ban and several Republican soldiers slept by the door. I had a terrible dream of ghosts floating through the village and into our house and into my mouth and nose and I couldn't breathe. I woke up to find my father's hand over my face and his voice whispering for me to lie still. He held me for a long time—not for comfort, but to keep me from moving—and I went back to sleep. In the morning, the soldiers were

Interrogated: Questioned.

gone and word passed quickly that a half-dozen Republicans had been murdered in their sleep—throats cut from ear to ear. "The dogs—where are the dogs?" I heard a Republican officer cry in dis-
may. *He wondered what had happened to the watchdogs of Ky La.*

The ***infiltration*** *and midnight murders seemed to* ***unnerve*** *the Republicans, and thereafter they stayed in the village only during the day. As soon as they were gone and the sun had set, the Viet Cong came back. . . .*

What happened next . . .

As it became clear that the ARVN soldiers could not protect the peasants from the Viet Cong, more and more South Vietnamese villages came under Communist control. Even villages that seemed peaceful during the day, like Hayslip's, were often taken over by the Viet Cong at night. By 1964 U.S. Secretary of Defense Robert McNamara reported that about 40 percent of the South Vietnamese countryside was under Viet Cong "control or predominant influence."

In Ky La the Viet Cong began organizing the villagers to dig tunnels, carry information, and stand guard for them. They even enlisted the help of Hayslip and other children in stealing weapons, first aid kits, and other supplies from the ARVN troops. They gave the children little awards and placed their names on honorary lists in recognition of their help.

Hayslip was often selected to help the Viet Cong set booby traps for ARVN soldiers. "Surprisingly enough, although we knew how deadly these traps could be, we kids had no second thoughts about helping the Viet Cong make them or put them into place," she recalled. "To us, war was still a game, and our 'enemy,' we were assured, deserved everything bad that happened to them."

When the United States sent combat troops to Vietnam in 1965, they lived under the constant threat of terrorism by the Viet Cong. American foot soldiers patrolling the South Vietnamese countryside fell victim to booby traps and sneak attacks on a regular basis. The U.S. forces took a number of

A man showing reporters his son's mutilated hand after an attack on their village by American troops. He tells newsmen that 370 civilians were slain in the hamlet of Tu Cung on March 16, 1968.
Reproduced by permission of AP/Wide World Photos.

steps to fight the Viet Cong. For example, they launched bombing missions in the countryside, conducted search-and-destroy operations in the villages, and sprayed poisonous chemicals over the land to destroy the enemy's jungle hide-outs. But these tactics failed to wipe out the Viet Cong and caused even more suffering for the South Vietnamese people.

By the late 1960s the North Vietnamese Army (NVA) took over more of the responsibility for fighting against the ARVN and the Americans. Although the Viet Cong lost some of its visibility in the later years of the war, many people in South Vietnam continued to support the Communists. "The government came after the Viet Cong with boats, planes, tanks, trucks, artillery, flamethrowers, and poisons, and still the Viet Cong fought back with what they had, which was mostly cleverness, courage, terror, and the patience of stones," Hayslip wrote. "Even when things were at their worst—when the allied forces devastated the countryside and the Viet Cong themselves resorted to terror to make us act the way they wanted—the villagers clung to the vision the Communists had drummed into us."

Did you know . . .

- In 1993 Hayslip continued telling her life story in a sequel to *When Heaven and Earth Changed Places* called *Child of War/Woman of Peace*. She wrote this second book with the help of her oldest son, James Hayslip. It focuses on her life after she left Vietnam and settled in the United States in 1970.

- Director Oliver Stone turned Hayslip's two books into a movie, *Heaven and Earth,* released in 1993. The film stars Heip Thi Le as Le Ly Hayslip, Tommy Lee Jones as her American husband Steve Butler, Joan Chen as her mother, and Cambodian refugee Haing S. Ngor as her father.

- Hayslip founded the East Meets West Foundation, a humanitarian relief organization with the motto "Working Together to Heal the Wounds of War." The foundation helps both American veterans and the Vietnamese people. One of its programs encourages American veterans to overcome their feelings of guilt about the war by returning to Vietnam and building schools and hospitals to help the Vietnamese people.

Sources

Chanoff, David, and Doan Van Toai. *Portrait of the Enemy.* New York: Random House, 1986.

FitzGerald, Frances. *Fire in the Lake: The Vietnamese and the Americans in Vietnam.* Boston: Little, Brown, 1987.

Hayslip, Le Ly, with Jay Wurts. *When Heaven and Earth Changed Places: A Vietnamese Woman's Journey from War to Peace.* New York: Doubleday, 1989.

Marrin, Albert. *America and Vietnam: The Elephant and the Tiger.* New York: Penguin, 1992.

Pike, Douglas. *War, Peace, and the Viet Cong.* Cambridge, MA: MIT Press, 1969.

Wiegersma, Nancy. *Vietnam: Peasant Land, Peasant Revolution.* New York: St. Martin's Press, 1988.

Philip Caputo

Excerpt from a memoir of his experiences in Vietnam as a U.S. Marine, 1965

Published in his book *A Rumor of War,* 1977

War has always been a terrible experience for American soldiers to endure. This is true even when soldiers go to war to fight for a cause in which they believe, such as defending U.S. liberty or saving another nation or people in danger. Indeed, accounts of major American wars like the Civil War and World War II are filled with stories of the death, pain, sorrow, and cruelty that American soldiers experienced while serving their country.

But many historians and soldiers who participated in the Vietnam War believe that the conflict took an even greater emotional toll on the American soldiers than had earlier wars. They argue that when U.S. troops went to Vietnam, they became trapped in a uniquely nightmarish war that placed a tremendous strain on their emotional well-being.

Combat duty in Vietnam was frustrating for U.S. troops for many reasons. For one thing, traveling through the region's dense mix of wet lowlands, thick jungle, and rugged mountains was a great challenge. With very few passable roads, this rugged terrain seemed strange and threatening to the American troops who slogged through it. In addition, the

"Everything rotted and corroded there [in Vietnam]: bodies, boot leather, canvas, metal, morals. Scorched by the sun, wracked by the wind and rain of the monsoon, fighting in alien swamps and jungles, our humanity rubbed off of us as the protective bluing rubbed off the barrels of our rifles."

soldiers had difficulty adjusting to Vietnam's hot and humid weather and its annual "monsoon season," when high winds and heavy rains lashed the countryside for weeks at a time. "The monsoon had a way of beating down a man's morale," confirmed Vietnam veteran Dale Reich in *Good Soldiers Don't Go to Heaven*. "Fighting the monsoons . . . was pure futility. . . . With every step a man's boots were sucked several inches into the ground, and the weight of his rucksack increased steadily as it took on the water. The enemy now became the weather . . . and there was no way to fight back. There was nothing to do but bear it, and to do that it took as much resolve as it did to pursue the VC [Viet Cong Communist guerrilla fighters] in the jungle."

Another great source of frustration for American soldiers was the type of warfare that the Communist forces favored. Because U.S. forces usually enjoyed sizable advantages in firepower and other resources, the Viet Cong guerrillas and their North Vietnamese Army (NVA) allies rarely engaged in big battles with American military units. Instead, the Communists used quick ambushes, sniper attacks, landmines, and concealed explosives or other deadly devices known as "booby traps" to attack the enemy. The guerrillas would then disappear into the jungle, only to pop up again and attack somewhere else. "The Vietcong are just like ghosts," said one U.S. Marine infantryman in *U.S. News and World Report* (April 4, 1966). "You see them—and you see them fade away right before your eyes."

The U.S. military responded to the Communist "hit-and-run" strategy by sending small patrols of American combat troops out into the countryside. Sometimes these patrols would set out on foot from a U.S. base camp. On other occasions they were transported by helicopters to remote or dangerous locations with orders to find and wipe out the enemy. Many of these patrols marched for days or weeks at a time, carrying heavy packs full of food, clothing, weapons, ammunition, and medicine. During the time they spent on patrol, soldiers rarely had an opportunity to bathe or enjoy a hot meal. On some occasions they were led into the jungle by inexperienced or poor officers (this was especially true in the late 1960s and early 1970s, when greater numbers of inexperienced officers served in the conflict).

American infantry patrols had to remain very alert as they slogged through the jungles and rice fields of Vietnam. They never knew when a sniper might suddenly shoot at a soldier as he drank from his canteen, or when a Viet Cong ambush might explode into a furious "firefight" (gun battle). In addition, the U.S. soldiers had to scan their surroundings continually for signs of hidden landmines or booby traps like the deadly punji pit (a deep, hidden pit with sharp stakes at the

American soldiers rescue wounded comrades during a five-day patrol near Hue, South Vietnam.
Reproduced by permission of AP/Wide World Photos.

bottom). Over time, the constant threat of death took a heavy emotional toll on the exhausted American troops.

Another factor that increased the danger faced by American patrols operating in the Vietnamese countryside was the fact that U.S. soldiers could not trust the Vietnamese villagers that they encountered. The Americans knew that some South Vietnamese opposed communism and wanted to see the United States succeed. But other South Vietnamese peasants either supported the Viet Cong or remained neutral. The Viet Cong used many villages as sources of food and young soldiers. They also sometimes recruited old farmers, young women, and even children to spy on the American patrols or set traps for them.

As a result, the American soldiers viewed the peasants they encountered with great suspicion. In fact, GIs (general infantrymen; another name for U.S. soldiers) came to view all Vietnamese as potential enemies and all villages as potential centers of Viet Cong guerrilla activity. Critics claim that this viewpoint was reinforced by the U.S. military leadership, which automatically classified all dead Vietnamese peasants as Viet Cong unless they had evidence to the contrary. Not surprisingly, racial prejudice against the South Vietnamese people flourished in this tense environment. This hatred, combined with the strategic need to eliminate villages as bases of Viet Cong activity, triggered a pattern of American mistreatment of the South Vietnamese that steadily worsened in the war's later years.

Soldiers form close bonds under stressful conditions

As American casualties (killed or wounded soldiers) mounted, many GIs became convinced that their lives were being wasted in a bloody stalemate. Opposition to the war back in the United States sometimes increased their feelings of being abandoned in a savage war. Frightened, angry, and disillusioned, many of these soldiers came to see their fellow GIs as their only source of support and comfort. As Vietnam veteran William Broyles, Jr., wrote in *Newsweek* in 1982, "Vietnam combat veterans drew this lesson [during the war]: you are alone, no one else shares your experience or cares about you— no one except your buddies."

Veterans agree that the feeling of unity that developed within American combat platoons helped many young men survive their ordeal in Vietnam. The emotional bond among members of infantry battalions (large groups of military troops) could not "be broken by a word, by boredom or divorce, or by anything other than death," wrote Vietnam veteran Philip Caputo in his memoir *A Rumor of War.* "Sometimes even [death] is not strong enough [to break that bond]. Two friends of mine died trying to save the corpses of their men from the battlefield. Such devotion, simple and selfless, the sentiment of belonging to each other, was the one decent thing we found in a conflict otherwise notable for its monstrosities [horrible events and characteristics]. . . . The battlefields of Vietnam were a crucible [a severe test or trial] in which a generation of American soldiers were fused together by a common confrontation with death and a sharing of hardships, dangers, and fears. The very ugliness of the war, the sordidness [foul nature] of our daily lives, the degradation of having to take part in body counts [the U.S. policy of measuring war's progress by totaling the number of enemy killed] made us draw still closer to one another. It was as if in comradeship we found an affirmation of life and the means to preserve at least a vestige [portion] of our humanity."

The friendships that developed among the members of American combat units helped individual soldiers maintain their will to go on. But as these relationships increased in importance, the loss of men to enemy landmines or snipers became a terrible blow to the morale of survivors. In some cases soldiers' desires to gain revenge for their friends' deaths led them to engage in savage acts of violence against enemy soldiers or Vietnamese civilians. "For the most part nobody is particularly wild with patriotic feeling for the war," admitted one army lieutenant in 1968. "Most people generate their enthusiasm for two reasons: one is self-preservation—if I don't shoot him, he'll eventually shoot me—and the other is revenge. It's apparently quite something to see a good friend blown apart by a VC booby trap, and you want to retaliate in kind."

War crimes in Vietnam

As American involvement in the Vietnam War deepened, atrocities (extremely cruel or brutal acts) or war crimes

"Dear John" Letters

Soldiers serving in wars usually loved receiving letters from friends and family back home. These letters gave them much-needed boosts to their morale, for they reminded the soldiers that they were loved and supported. The letter that no one wanted to get, however, was the so-called "Dear John" letter. These were notes in which girlfriends or wives explained that they wanted to end their relationship with the soldier, usually so they could build a relationship with another man. These letters often crushed the spirit of soldiers who received them.

Writing in his memoir *Brothers in Arms: A Journey from War to Peace,* Marine Lieutenant William Broyles, Jr., recalls how devastating "Dear John" letters could be to men who were fighting for their survival every day in Vietnam: "Every three or four days we would get resupplied by helicopter. With our rations and our ammunition and our medical supplies would come a large red sack of mail, which each squad leader passed out with a running commentary, much of it obscene. But every now and then someone got a Dear John, which was almost as bad as stepping on a mine. Then all the laughter stopped and everyone moved away, leaving the victim to read and reread the letter alone. After a while, some close buddy would come up with a deck of cards and maybe a . . . delicacy like peaches and pound cake with melted chocolate. The two of them would talk quietly and everyone else would clean their rifles or dry their socks in silence. A Dear John was a calamity for the whole platoon. It took days to recover."

committed by American, South Vietnamese, and Communist forces increased. Indeed, both sides engaged in terrible acts of violence against the enemy, including murder, rape, torture, and the mutilation of dead bodies. Viet Cong guerrillas, for example, sometimes tortured and murdered chiefs of rural villages in order to force the rest of the community to assist them. Some U.S. troops, meanwhile, threw captured enemy soldiers out of helicopters or cut off the ears of dead Vietnamese to keep as souvenirs.

The worst atrocity committed during the war was the My Lai Massacre of March 16, 1968. On that day a squad of American soldiers commanded by Lieutenant William Calley swooped down on a small village and murdered hundreds of unarmed Vietnamese women, children, and elderly people. But many other terrible acts took place throughout the war. "Cruel acts occurred on both sides with nauseating frequency," wrote former Vietnam journalist Charles C. Moskos, Jr., in *War Crimes and the American Conscience*. "As a day-to-day participant in the combat situation, I was repeatedly struck by the brutal reactions of soldiers to their participation in the war."

Caputo confirmed that the war in Vietnam was a savage and merciless one. "Whether committed in the name of principles or out of vengeance, atrocities were as common to the Vietnamese battlefields as shell craters and barbed wire," he wrote in *A Rumor of War*. "American soldiers learned that Vietnam was not a place where a man could expect much mercy if, say, he was taken prisoner. And men who do not expect to receive mercy eventually lose their inclination [desire] to grant it. . . . Out there, lacking restraints, sanctioned [given approval] to kill, confronted by a hostile country and a relentless enemy, we sank into a brutish state. The descent could be checked only by the net of a man's inner moral values, the attribute that is called character. There were a few—and I suspect Lieutenant Calley was one— who had no net and plunged all the way down, discovering in their bottommost depths a capacity for malice [desire to see others suffer] they probably never suspected was there."

In the following excerpt from his memoir, Caputo recalls how his grief and anger over the deaths of his fellow soldiers caused him to take revenge on a nearby Vietnamese village.

Wounded U.S. soldiers.
Reproduced by permission of AP/Wide World Photos.

Philip Caputo (1941–)

Philip Caputo first entered Vietnam in March 1965, when the first U.S. Marine combat forces landed in that war-torn country. When he began his tour of duty in Vietnam, Caputo was confident that the mighty U.S. forces would smash the Communist threat to South Vietnam within a matter of months. But the American march to victory floundered in the steamy jungles and rugged mountains of Vietnam. For U.S. soldiers, the war turned into a terrifying, frustrating, and deadly contest for survival in a strange land. During this period, Caputo admitted that his "convictions about the war . . . eroded to almost nothing."

Caputo spent some of his time in Vietnam tracking U.S. and enemy casualties. He hated this duty, however, and actually volunteered for a combat assignment in order to escape it. As a result, Caputo spent his last months in Vietnam as an infantry officer leading Marines on combat patrol in the South Vietnamese countryside. Near the end of this assignment, he ordered several of his men to kidnap two suspected Viet Cong guerrillas from a remote village. The soldiers then killed the two men, as Caputo had hoped they would.

Caputo initially viewed the kidnapping mission as a success, but he later learned that both of the men had been South Vietnamese youths seeking protection from Viet Cong military recruiters. This realization horrified

Things to remember while reading the excerpt from *A Rumor of War*:

- When American combat troops first arrived in Vietnam, they expressed great confidence in their ability to quickly defeat the Viet Cong and their North Vietnamese allies. As the months passed, however, U.S. soldiers began to recognize that the war would be a long and bloody affair. This realization had a negative impact on the morale of many soldiers.

- Vietnam was not the first war in which acts of savagery took place. Military historians agree that acts of ruthlessness and cruelty are an unfortunate characteristic of all wars, whatever their time and place.

Caputo and deepened his anguish about the war. The U.S. military called for an investigation into the incident. Caputo was only punished with a letter of reprimand, but years later he expressed shame and regret about his part in what he called the "murder" of two innocents.

After ending his tour of duty in Vietnam, Caputo left the Marine Corps and became a journalist. In 1975 he returned to South Vietnam to cover the fall of Saigon to Communist forces. Two years later, he published A Rumor of War, a dark and honest account of his experiences in Vietnam. This memoir quickly became known as one of the finest books ever written about the war. Since A Rumor of War was published, Caputo has become a successful novelist.

Caputo has made two other trips to Vietnam since the war ended in 1975. In 1990 he traveled there with a group of American writers who had served in the conflict to meet with several Vietnamese novelists and poets who had fought with the North Vietnamese Army. And in 1999 he returned to Vietnam to revisit the trails and villages where he and his comrades had fought and died. Months later Caputo described the visit as one that helped him heal old spiritual wounds associated with the war.

- The average age of U.S. soldiers who served in Vietnam was only 19. By contrast, the average age of an American soldier in World War II was 26. Most U.S. combat soldiers who fought and died in the jungles of Vietnam, then, had attended high school proms and graduation parties only a few months earlier. Many observers believe that the young ages of American troops contributed to the savagery that prevailed among some combat units in Vietnam. They believe that the inexperience and youth of the soldiers made them more likely to resort to excessive violence and cruelty as a way of warding off the fear and helplessness that they felt.

- Despite the vicious nature of the war in Vietnam, many American veterans express pride in their service. As Myra

MacPherson observed in *Long Time Passing: Vietnam and the Haunted Generation*, "even those who found the war a tragic, shattering waste and wore peace symbols on their helmets know a sense of honor in doing their own job well, in helping others to live, in having survived."

Excerpt from Philip Caputo's memoir A Rumor of War

*In late October an enemy battalion attacked one of our helicopter bases, inflicted fifty casualties on the company guarding it, and destroyed or damaged over forty aircraft. Two nights later, another **Viet Cong** battalion overran an outpost manned by eighty marines from **A Company**, killing twenty-two and wounding fifty more. The usual ambushes and booby traps claimed daily victims, and the **medevac** helicopters flew back and forth across the low, dripping skies.*

*The **regiment**'s mood began to match the weather. We were a long way from the despair that **afflicted** American soldiers in the closing years of the war, but we had also traveled some emotional distance from the cheery confidence of eight months before. The mood was **sardonic, fatalistic,** and **melancholy.** I could hear it in our **black jokes** "Hey, Bill, you're going on patrol today. If you get your legs blown off can I have your boots?" I could hear it in the songs we sang. . . . One, "A Bellyful of War," was a marching song composed by an officer in A Company.*

Oh they taught me how to kill,
Then they stuck me on this hill,
I don't like it anymore.
*For all the **monsoon** rains*
Have scrambled up my brains,
I've had a belly-full of war.

Oh the sun is much too hot,
*And I've caught **jungle rot**,*
I don't like it anymore.
I'm tired and terrified,

Viet Cong: North Vietnamese guerrilla fighters.

A Company: A military division.

Medevac: Medical evacuation.

Regiment: Military unit of ground troops.

Afflicted: Suffering from pain or distress.

Sardonic: Scornful.

Fatalistic: Feeling of having no control over one's future.

Melancholy: Sad or depressed.

Black jokes: Angry or cruel humor.

Monsoon: Weather season marked by heavy rain and winds.

Jungle rot: Skin infection common among soldiers in Vietnam.

I just want to stay alive,
I've had a belly-full of war.

So you can march upon **Hanoi**,
Just forget this little boy,
I don't like it anymore.
For as I lie here with a pout,
My intestines hanging out,
I've had a belly-full of war.

There was another side to the war, about which no songs were sung, no jokes made. The fighting had not only become more intense, but more vicious. Both we and the Viet Cong began to make a habit of atrocities. One of 1st Battalion's radio operators was captured by an enemy patrol, tied up, beaten with clubs, then executed. His body was found floating in the **Song Tuy Loan** three days after his capture, with the ropes still around his hands and feet and a bullet hole in the back of his head. Four other marines from another regiment were captured and later discovered in a common grave, also tied up and with

GIs carrying a fellow soldier who has been wounded out of the jungle during the war.
Reproduced by permission of AP/Wide World Photos.

Hanoi: Capital of North Vietnam.

Song Tuy Loan: River in South Vietnam.

Philip Caputo   157

their skulls blasted open by an executioner's bullets. . . . A twenty-eight man patrol was ambushed by two hundred **VC** and almost **annihilated**. Only two marines, both seriously wounded, lived through it. There might have been more survivors had the Viet Cong not made a **systematic** massacre of the wounded. After springing the ambush, they went down the line of fallen marines, pumping bullets into any body that showed signs of life. . . . The two men who survived did so by crawling under the bodies of their dead comrades and **feigning** death.

We paid the enemy back, sometimes with interest. It was common knowledge that quite a few captured VC never made it to prison camps; they were reported as "shot and killed while attempting to escape." Some **line companies** did not even bother taking prisoners; they simply killed every VC they saw, and a number of Vietnamese who were only suspects. The latter were usually counted as enemy dead, under the unwritten rule "If he's dead and Vietnamese, he's VC."

Everything rotted and **corroded** quickly over there: bodies, boot leather, canvas, metal, morals. Scorched by the sun, **wracked** by the wind and rain of the monsoon, fighting in alien swamps and jungles, our humanity rubbed off of us as the protective **bluing** rubbed off the barrels of our rifles. We were fighting in the cruelest kind of conflict, a people's war. It was no orderly campaign, as in Europe [during World War II], but a war for survival waged in a wilderness without rules or laws; a war in which each soldier fought for his own life and the lives of the men beside him, not caring who he killed in that personal cause or how many or in what manner and feeling only contempt for those who sought to impose on his savage struggle the **mincing distinctions** of civilized warfare—that code of battlefield ethics that attempted to **humanize** an essentially inhuman war. . . . Butchery was butchery, so who was to speak of rules and ethics in a war that had none?

[After enduring a period as an officer in charge of counting American and Communist casualties, Caputo volunteers to join a combat unit. He accounts for this change by listing boredom, emotional exhaustion associated with identifying bodies, and a furious desire to avenge the deaths of friends who had died. In December 1965 his platoon is assigned to clear Viet Cong guerrillas out of a village. During the mission, Caputo's unit endures vicious firefights, deadly sniper fire, long marches through a region called Purple Heart Trail because of its minefields, and nights of monsoon rains. They then are hit by a mortar attack that may have been accidentally launched by friendly forces.]

VC: Viet Cong.

Annihilated: Destroyed completely.

Systematic: Carrying out a step-by-step plan; methodical.

Feigning: Pretending.

Line companies: Troops operating in areas closest to the enemy.

Corroded: Dissolved or worn away.

Wracked: Twisted or beaten.

Bluing: A protective substance used on rifles.

Mincing distinctions: Elegant or refined rules.

Humanize: Make human.

The shells seemed to take forever to fall. For what seemed a long time, we heard the **lunatic chorus wailing** *in the sky, our bodies bracing for the coming shock, hearts* **constricted,** *all thoughts suspended. Then the storm struck. The shells, impacting about twenty-five yards from the* **perimeter,** *exploded one after another, creating one enormous blast that went on for five minutes.* **Shrapnel** *flew overhead with a sound like that of taut steel wires snapping. Jones and I, huddled beside each other like two frightened children, pressed ourselves against the earth. I wanted God to shut that roaring out of my ears. Make it stop. Please God, make it stop. . . . [The shelling finally ends, and Caputo climbs out of his foxhole to check on his men.]*

I crawled out to the edge of the perimeter and called to Smith's **fire-team.**

"Yes, sir," Smith said in a whisper.

"You guys all right?"

"Outside of being cold, wet, miserable, hungry, and scared . . . we're just fine, sir."

"No casualties?"

"No, sir. Because I'm black, the shells couldn't see me."

I laughed to myself, thinking, They're all right, the best you could ask for. They've been through a fire-fight and a shelling and they're making jokes about it.

[Caputo learns that a Christmas cease-fire has been called, and that his platoon has been ordered to return to their base. Delighted, the unit begins marching out of the jungle. As they pass a small Vietnamese village, a landmine blows up in their midst.] Still slightly stunned, I had only a vague idea of what had happened. A mine, yes. It must have been an **ambush-detonated** *mine. All of Pryor's squad had passed by that spot before the mine exploded. I had been standing on that very spot, near the tree, not ten seconds before the blast. . . . Oh God—if I had remained on that spot another ten seconds, they would have been picking pieces of me out of the trees. Chance. Pure chance. Allen, right beside me, had been wounded in the head. I had not been hurt. Chance. The one true god of modern war is blind chance. . . .*

A rifleman and I picked up Sergeant Wehr, each of us taking one of the big man's arms. . . . A **corpsman** *cut Wehr's trouser leg open with a knife and started to* **dress** *his wounds. There was a lot of blood. Two marines dragged Sanchez up from the* **paddy.** *His*

Lunatic chorus wailing: Screaming of the incoming shells.

Constricted: Tightened.

Perimeter: Outer edge of their position.

Shrapnel: Shell fragments from an explosive weapon.

Fire-team: Squad of combat soldiers.

Ambush-detonated: Explosion that is triggered by a nearby ambusher.

Corpsman: Soldier trained in giving medical treatment.

Dress: Bandage.

Paddy: Rice field.

A Helicopter Pilot Talks about Evacuating Wounded Soldiers

In 1966 Glenn Munson published a collection of letters written by American soldiers who served in Vietnam. This book, *Letters from Vietnam*, included the following letter written by airman Glen Kemak to his family:

> It's no fun carrying 50 or 60 guys who are laid out on a stretcher moaning and crying and bleeding all over the place. It's a good thing that I am not home now, after all the bad stuff that I've seen over here. If anyone ever started talking about our position in Vietnam, and burning their draft cards, and all these protest marches—I swear I would kill him.

> People don't realize what's going on over here. It is horrible, believe me, just plain rotten. These poor Army and Marine troops are living like animals and fighting for their lives every day they are in the field. Some come back, but some don't. I've carried some of the ones that didn't, and it makes you sick. Every time I carry these bodies in canvas bags and wounded GIs I get sick inside. You may think that I'm like a baby when I tell you that I have cried when I've carried these guys, but it's no lie, and I'm no baby for doing it.

Compresses: A soft bandage that is used to control bleeding.

Landing zone: An area that can be used by aircraft to land and take off.

Envelop: Cover or bury.

face had been so peppered with shrapnel that I hardly recognized him. Except for his eyes. The fragments had somehow missed his eyes. He was unconscious and his eyes were half closed; two white slits in a mass of raspberry red. Sanchez looked as if he had been clawed by some invisible beast. . . .

I slid down the embankment and splashed over to where the corpsman, Doc Kaiser, was working to save Corporal Rodella. There were gauze and **compresses** all over his chest and abdomen. One dressing, covering the hole the shrapnel had torn in one of his lungs, was soaked in blood. With each breath he took, pink bubbles of blood formed and burst around the hole. . . . I tried talking to him, but he could not say anything because his windpipe would fill with blood. Rodella, who had been twice wounded before, was now in danger of drowning in his own blood. It was his eyes that troubled me most. They were the hurt, dumb eyes of a child who has been severely beaten and does not know why. It was his eyes and his silence and the foamy blood and the gurgling, wheezing sound in his chest that aroused in me a sorrow so deep and a rage so strong that I could not distinguish the one emotion from the other.

I helped the corpsman carry Rodella to the **landing zone**. His comrades were around him, but he was alone. We could see the look of separation in his eyes. He was alone in the world of the badly wounded, isolated by a pain none could share with him and by the terror of the darkness that was threatening to **envelop** him.

Then we got the last one, Corporal Greeley, a machine-gunner whose left arm was hanging by a few strands of muscle; all the rest was a scarlet mush. . . . Carrying him, I felt my own anger, a very cold, *very deep anger that had no specific object. It was just an icy, **abiding** fury; a hatred for everything in existence except those men.*

*[Caputo calls for helicopter evacuation of the wounded soldiers.] The helicopters swooped in out of the **somber** sky, landing in the green smoke billowing from the smoke grenade I had thrown to mark the **LZ**. . . . We laid the casualties on the stretchers and lifted them into the **Hueys**, the rain falling on us all the time. The aircraft took off, and watching the wounded soaring out of that miserable patch of jungle, we almost envied them.*

*Just before the platoon resumed its march, someone found a length of electrical detonating cord lying in the grass near the village. The village would have been as likely an ambush site as any: the VC only had to press the detonator and then blend in with the civilians, if indeed there were any true civilians in the village. Or they could have hidden in one of the tunnels under the houses. All right, I thought, tit for tat. No cease-fire for us, none for you, either. I ordered both rocket launcher teams to fire **white-phosphorus** shells into the hamlet. They fired four altogether. The shells, flashing orange, burst into pure white clouds, the chunks of flaming phosphorus arcing over the tress. About half the village went up in flames. I could hear people yelling, and I saw several figures running through the white smoke. I did not feel a sense of vengeance, any more than I felt **remorse** or regret. I did not even feel angry. Listening to the shouts and watching the people running out of their burning homes, I did not feel anything at all.*

Abiding: Long-lasting or enduring.

Somber: Dark or gloomy.

LZ: Landing Zone.

Hueys: Military helicopters used to transport soldiers.

White-phosphorus: Explosive and fiery substance.

Remorse: Guilt or sadness.

Did you know . . .

- In conflicts like World War II and the Korean War, American soldiers entered the military knowing that they would remain in the service until the war was over. During the Vietnam War, however, soldiers served only one-year tours of duty before being released from their military obligations. Many observers believe that the one-year tour contributed to a decline in military performance. They claim that as support for the war dwindled, U.S. soldiers became preoccupied with completing their individual year of ser-

U.S. soldiers wait in a North Vietnamese bunker before their next assault on Hill 875 in Dak To, Vietnam.
Reproduced by permission of Corbis Corporation.

vice and going home. In some cases their desire to avoid death in a seemingly hopeless war led them to disobey direct orders. "My men refused to go—we cannot move out," one lieutenant told his commanding officer in 1969, when told to attack a North Vietnamese military position. "Some of them have simply had enough—they are broken. There are boys here who have only 90 days left in Vietnam. They want to go home in one piece."

- Viet Cong and North Vietnamese forces saw terrorist activity as a legitimate weapon to use in the Vietnam War. "Viet Cong guerrillas used terror, including systematic murder and kidnapping of civilians, as an indispensable—and in their eyes legitimate—weapon for breaking down government control over the population and establishing their own," wrote Graham Cosmas in *Encyclopedia of the Vietnam War.*

- When America learned about the My Lai Massacre, many U.S. citizens expressed public support for William Calley and the other soldiers who were accused of war crimes. In fact, Calley was defended by both conservative and liberal political groups in the United States. Both sides charged that Calley was a pawn in the larger debate over the war. Supporters of American military involvement claimed that Calley's actions were being distorted and that he had actually done his duty in Vietnam. Antiwar activists, meanwhile, claimed that blame for Calley's actions should be placed on America's immoral political and military leadership. Support for Calley remained strong even after his conviction as a mass murderer. These expressions of support angered many Vietnam veterans. As Colonel Harry G. Summers, Jr., a Vietnam veteran and military historian, stated, "[American support for Calley] compounded the tragedy [of My Lai] for it rendered a major disservice to the overwhelming majority of American combat soldiers who risked their lives to protect—not harm—the men, women, and children of South Vietnam."

Sources

Bilton, Michael, and Kevin Sim. *Four Hours in My Lai.* New York: Viking, 1992.

Bourne, Peter G. *Men, Stress, and Vietnam.* Boston: Little, Brown, 1970.

Boyle, Richard. *The Flower of the Dragon: The Breakdown of the U.S. Army in Vietnam.* San Francisco: Ramparts Press, 1972.

Caputo, Philip. *A Rumor of War.* New York: Henry Holt, 1977.

Caputo, Philip. "Prisoner of Hill 52." *National Geographic Adventure.* Winter 1999.

Ebert, James R. *A Life in a Year: The American Infantryman in Vietnam, 1965–1972.* Novato, CA: Presidio, 1993.

Helmer, John. *Bringing the War Home: The American Soldier in Vietnam and After.* New York: Free Press, 1974.

Mahedy, William P. *Out of the Night: The Spiritual Journey of Vietnam Veterans.* New York: Ballantine Books, 1986.

Moskos, Charles C., Jr. *War Crimes and the American Conscience.* New York: Holt, Rinehart & Winston, 1970.

Myers, Thomas. *Walking Point: American Narratives of Vietnam.* New York: Oxford University Press, 1988.

O'Brien, Tim. *If I Die in a Combat Zone.* New York: Delacorte Press, 1973.

Julie Forsythe

*Excerpt from an interview about her
experiences in Vietnam, 1972–75*

**Published in Kathryn Marshall's *In the Combat Zone:
An Oral History of American Women in Vietnam*, 1987**

Thousands of American women served in Vietnam during the war years. In fact, some estimates place the total number between 33,000 and 55,000. The U.S. Department of Defense estimates that nearly 7,500 of these women served in the American military, while the Veterans Administration places the number of American military women in Vietnam at over 11,000. The numbers are uncertain because the government did not keep separate military records by gender at that time. In addition, there were no official records of civilian (non-military) women serving in Vietnam.

During the Vietnam War women who pursued a military career were segregated into special branches of the service and not allowed to participate in combat. The main opportunities for women in the American military were in the nursing and administrative fields. Most of the women in the American armed forces in Vietnam served as nurses. But about 20 percent served in various administrative roles, such as clerks, typists, information officers, air traffic controllers, map-makers, decoders, and photographers.

"I'm sure things are desperately poor [in Vietnam] and probably still incredibly beautiful. But whatever's happened, it's their [the Vietnamese's] country now, and I'm glad of that."

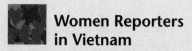

Women Reporters in Vietnam

In addition to the women who served as military nurses and civilian relief workers, more than 70 women journalists reported on the war from Vietnam. Although women accounted for only a small fraction of the hundreds of war correspondents in Vietnam during the conflict, they reported for such major news media as the Associated Press, United Press International, the National Broadcasting Company (NBC), *Newsweek,* and the *New York Times.* Two women journalists were killed in Vietnam, three were wounded, and four were taken prisoner.

In addition to those who served in the military, many American women also served as civilian relief workers during the Vietnam War. These women worked with a number of international organizations, including the Red Cross, the Agency for International Development, the Peace Corps, and International Voluntary Services. Some civilian aid workers, like Julie Forsythe, helped the Vietnamese people who suffered the effects of the war. They applied their skills in schools, orphanages, and hospitals in the South Vietnamese cities and countryside. Other civilian women supported the American troops by putting on shows, organizing games, or setting up entertainment centers at base camps where off-duty soldiers could play cards and shoot pool.

Nurses in the Vietnam War

The majority of the American women who served in Vietnam worked in a medical capacity, treating wounded U.S. soldiers or Vietnamese people. The U.S. military began recruiting women out of nursing schools in 1965. In some cases nurses entered the military through programs in which the government paid the cost of nursing school in exchange for a year of service in Vietnam. Nurses serving in the U.S. Army were stationed at hospitals throughout South Vietnam. U.S. Navy nurses served on special hospital ships off the coast of Vietnam, while U.S. Air Force nurses cared for patients on evacuation flights.

Female nurses were commissioned officers in the U.S. military, and they were required to be at least twenty-one years old. But many lacked practical experience. In fact, 60 percent of the military nurses who served in Vietnam had less than two years of experience, and 36 percent had less than six months. But even the most seasoned battlefield nurse might not have been prepared for the severe injuries nurses routinely treated in

300 — 1500

Vietnam. "No one told them, nor could they know, they would experience a level of trauma in Vietnam that nurses had never confronted before in wartime," Laura Palmer wrote in the *New York Times Magazine*. As army nurse Ruth Sidisin recalled in *In the Combat Zone,* the injuries were "like a grotesque form of 'can you top this,' because each time you thought you'd seen the ultimate, something else would come along."

There were several reasons that Vietnam War wounds tended to be more severe than the ones that nurses had treated in previous wars. For one thing, the widespread use of helicopters in Vietnam allowed wounded soldiers to be transported to hospitals very quickly. "Helicopters made the difference," Palmer noted. "Soldiers who would have died on the battlefields in World War II and Korea were evacuated to hospitals, sometimes within minutes of being wounded."

Another reason for the severity of wounds in Vietnam was the type of weapons that were used. Many soldiers and

U.S. Army nurses in front of the showers that had been revamped for their use. Previously, the showers had been for men.
Reproduced by permission of AP/Wide World Photos.

civilians were injured by mines or bombs rather than bullets. "In the Vietnam War, the small arms used by both sides were specifically designed to inflict massive, multiple injuries," Kathryn Marshall wrote in *In the Combat Zone.* "Even nurses with backgrounds in trauma surgery were unprepared for the kinds of injuries they saw." For example, huge blast wounds were common. Amputations of multiple limbs were routine. Nurses also frequently saw burns so severe that they went down to the bone.

"The typical soldier who arrived for treatment had many different types of injuries. It was unusual to see a single gunshot wound. More likely, nurses would work on someone who suffered from multiple traumatic injuries," Elizabeth M. Norman explained in *Women at War.* "For example, a navy nurse remembered one patient who had stepped on a land mine and lost both legs. The impact of the blast perforated his eardrums. He also fractured both arms when he hit the ground."

In addition to serious war wounds, military nurses and civilian aid workers in Vietnam treated a number of rare diseases that they had not been taught to treat, such as typhoid, tuberculosis, and dengue fever. "Nurses also found themselves in wards filled with patients diagnosed with tropical diseases like malaria, cholera, even snake and monkey bites," Norman noted. "There were the exotic diseases of bubonic plague and tetanus, usually found only in nursing textbooks." In addition, some military nurses worked in drug wards, where they treated soldiers who had become addicted to marijuana, cocaine, opium, or heroin. These drug problems became more frequent as the war progressed, for hard drugs were cheap, extremely potent, and widely available in Vietnam.

Remarkably, only 2 percent of the patients who made it to American military hospitals died of their injuries or illnesses. Fast evaluation by helicopter saved some lives, while medical advances meant that more serious wounds could be treated successfully. But this high survival rate left many people—both American soldiers and Vietnamese villagers—with lasting disabilities. "Although it salvaged lives, this system also created a dilemma about the quality of life left for some of the men," Norman wrote. "Nurses spoke of the guilt and confusion they felt when they sent severely disabled patients home."

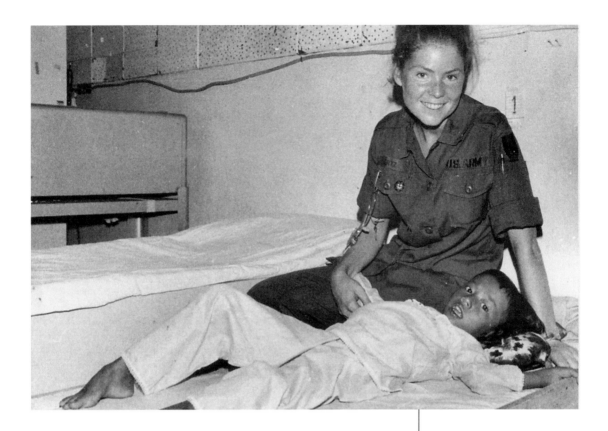

A U.S. army nurse treating a child in a children's ward in a South Vietnam surgical hospital.
Reproduced by permission of AP/Wide World Photos.

In general, military nurses and civilian relief workers in Vietnam worked long, grueling shifts in medical facilities that often overflowed with patients. They saw young American men and Vietnamese women and children suffering from terrible wounds on a daily basis. Because they were women, they were often expected to provide emotional support as well as medical treatment to these patients. In addition, the nurses often faced physical danger themselves due to guerilla warfare and the lack of clear battle lines. "Because a terrorist bomb could be planted anywhere and a midnight mortar attack could hit a hospital or office, women were sometimes in as much danger as any of the males in the same vicinity," David K. Wright noted in *Perspectives: A Multicultural Portrait of the Vietnam War*. In fact, eight female nurses died during the Vietnam War.

Overall, the nurses and relief workers who served in Vietnam reported that they experienced moments of deep satisfaction during their service, when they were able to make the difference between life and death for a fellow human being.

But these moments were overshadowed by their feelings of fear, anger, and sorrow over the suffering they witnessed.

Things to remember while reading the excerpt from the interview with American relief worker Julie Forsythe:

- Julie Forsythe served as a civilian relief worker at a rehabilitation center for severely injured Vietnamese people. Since she was not a member of the armed forces, and she treated Vietnamese victims of the war rather than U.S. soldiers, her experiences differ somewhat from those of American military nurses. Still, she saw the same kinds of traumatic injuries and felt the same range of emotions as many nurses.

- In the excerpt, Forsythe discusses the damage that American bombing, burning, and use of herbicides (harsh chemicals that kill plants) did to the once-beautiful country. Before the Vietnam War the South Vietnamese countryside was lush and green. Farmers tended rice paddies (wet fields where rice is grown) in fertile river valleys. The surrounding hillsides were covered with jungles of trees and plants. But U.S. troops found that the jungles provided ideal hiding places for the Communist guerilla fighters known as the Viet Cong. They also realized that the rice paddies and rural villages were good sources of food and supplies for the Viet Cong. To eliminate these sources of support for the enemy, the U.S. military used more than 14 million tons of explosives and sprayed millions of gallons of herbicides on the South Vietnamese countryside during the Vietnam War.

- Forsythe also talks about some of the effects the war had on the Vietnamese people, including hunger, disease, emotional trauma, and physical wounds. The destruction of the South Vietnamese countryside with bombs and herbicides took a terrible toll on the people who lived there. Many people were killed or suffered crippling injuries. Many others left the rural villages where their families had lived for generations and became refugees.

- In her interview, Forsythe describes a visit to My Lai, a small village in Quang Ngai province near the rehabilita-

Julie Forsythe

Julie Forsythe grew up on a Quaker dairy farm in New Jersey. The Quakers, formally known as the Society of Friends, are a religious group that has traditionally opposed war. During the Vietnam War, many Quakers became conscientious objectors and were released from military service on the basis of their religious beliefs. But many other Quakers went to Vietnam as civilian relief workers, hoping to help the victims of the war.

After graduating from Oberlin College in 1971 with a degree in religion, Forsythe accepted a position with the American Friends Service Committee as a civilian relief worker in Vietnam. In 1972 she was assigned to a rehabilitation center in Quang Ngai province where Vietnamese people were treated for serious war wounds, like amputated limbs, severe burns, and paralysis. During her three years of service in Vietnam, Forsythe learned to speak Vietnamese fluently. She spent a great deal of time among the Vietnamese people and developed deep sympathy for them.

Unlike most Americans, Forsythe remained in Vietnam after the U.S. troops were withdrawn in 1973. In fact, she was in Saigon in March 1975, during the final North Vietnamese push for control of the South. When it became clear that Communist-led North Vietnam was going to win the war, many people tried to flee the country. They were afraid that the North Vietnamese would take violent revenge on anyone associated with the American side. Forsythe witnessed scenes of mass hysteria as refugees desperately tried to escape from South Vietnam.

But Forsythe stayed in Saigon when the Communist forces arrived and took over the South Vietnamese government. North Vietnamese soldiers questioned her, but she recalled that they treated her politely and then let her go. In October 1975 she returned to the United States and married the American doctor she had worked with in Vietnam. The couple have two children and live on a farm in Vermont.

tion center where she worked. My Lai was the site of a massacre in 1968. U.S. troops entered the village in search of enemy forces, then proceeded to murder hundreds of unarmed civilians, including elderly people, women, and children. When news of the massacre reached the United States in 1970, it triggered strong emotions of shame, disgust, and anger among millions of ordinary Americans.

But the children Forsythe met in My Lai could not understand why Americans viewed what happened there as unusual. After all, the Vietnamese people were exposed to violence and suffering every day during the war.

- At the end of the excerpt, Forsythe expresses her hope for the future of Vietnam, now that it has been reunited under a Communist government. Unlike many Americans, Forsythe remained in Vietnam after the American troops withdrew in 1973. She was in the South Vietnamese capital of Saigon in 1975, when North Vietnamese forces took over the city and won the war. Many Americans believed that the fall of South Vietnam to communism would be disastrous both for the Vietnamese people and for U.S. interests around the world. But Forsythe got to know many Vietnamese during her time at the rehabilitation center. She came to believe that they should be allowed to form their own government and rule themselves, free from interference by the United States or other countries.

North Vietnamese soldiers patrolling Saigon after its fall in 1975. Saigon was renamed Ho Chi Minh City after the deceased North Vietnamese leader.
Reproduced by permission of Corbis Corp.

Excerpt from the interview with Julie Forsythe:

You never get over the sense of green and flowers in Southeast Asia. Coconut palms, mango trees—the villages are really beautiful, especially where the mountains come down to the coast. And Saigon [capital of Vietnam]. You know, the earliest Western travelers there— the Portuguese were there in the 1600s—talk about walking on the roads out of Saigon and being entirely overwhelmed by the smell of **orchids.** Because, you know, the trees were just everywhere full of orchids. Of course, by the time I got there the Americans had done a fairly nasty job.

That's why there were so many diseases—the whole economy was wrecked. For instance, the U.S. came in with bulldozers and plowed down the **hedgerows,** right through the irrigation system. We messed up the fields and left **Agent Orange** in the hills, so every spring there were floods. Yeah, all the wells were messed up, too—you can't just wreck an environment the way we did and not leave a lot of nasty footprints. **Typhus. Bubonic plague.** Polio. All kinds of diseases from lack of public health and a completely destroyed economy.

Yeah, it used to be a beautiful country.

I wasn't prepared for a lot of things I saw. Like the prison wards. Or once I was in surgery and they were doing **amputations**—this was right after I got to Quang Ngai—and I nearly passed out. Horrible. But the kids were the worst. Up to 40 percent of our patients were kids—we saw about a thousand people a year—because the kids are the ones who take the ducks out and take the water buffalo down to the river. And some yo-yo leaves a landmine in the path and—pop! That's it. No, I wasn't prepared for how many kids were so badly damaged.

A lot of them came in with no arms and legs. And we saw kids with neck injuries from **shrapnel,** so that they were entirely paralyzed. At times we took over the hospital's burn unit, where we saw the kids who'd been napalmed. **Napalm** is really grim stuff. What's so disgusting about it is that only oil stops the burning. Water doesn't stop the burning, so when kids get hit with napalm they run into the river and the stuff keeps burning—they keep burning. And listen, the most disgusting thing you've ever seen in your life is a child who's just totally burned. Right down to the muscle. It's very, very painful, and the treatment is brutally long. It's almost impossible to undo that kind of damage. Maybe under extremely sanitary conditions—which we didn't have—and with horrible, really horrible, scar tissue.

Other burns we saw were due to **black marketeering.** A lot of airplane fuel was ripped off from the Air Force and sold as cooking fuel. And when it ignited—whoom! Really disgusting, those body burns.

We did the best we could for our patients, under tough conditions. There never seemed to be enough of us, though. The center had a Vietnamese staff of sixty. They included the **prosthetists,** the physi-

Orchids: A type of plant with showy flowers.

Hedgerows: A row of shrubs or trees separating fields.

Agent Orange: A toxic chemical sprayed on the Vietnamese countryside to kill crops and other vegetation during the war.

Typhus: A severe disease caused by a microorganism that usually occurs in unclean conditions.

Bubonic plague: A highly contagious disease caused by a bacterium that is sometimes carried by rats.

Amputations: Surgical removal of limbs or other body parts.

Shrapnel: Metal fragments from exploded bombs, artillery shells, or land mines.

Napalm: A highly flammable form of jellied gasoline used to burn areas of the Vietnamese countryside during the war.

Black marketeering: The process of buying and selling stolen goods through unofficial channels.

Prosthetists: A person who designs artificial body parts and trains patients to use them.

cal therapists, the people who made limbs, a maintenance depart-ment, a schoolteacher, a social worker, a nurse, and a physician's assistant. The Americans were my husband, Tom—he was the doc-tor—a physical therapist who was training the Vietnamese, a hus-band-and-wife team who were codirectors, and me. I did all the jobs that fell in the cracks.

*My position was great, because I got to relate to everybody. I got to take patients back to their homes, for instance—which meant I was out in the countryside much of the time. And I did the books. I emptied the trash. I made trips to **Danang** to get pipe—we made all our own wheelchairs out of electric **conduits**, American military sur-plus. So I'd always have to go to the black market and scrounge. And let's see. I learned to make legs from a Vietnamese who'd invented the paddy leg. You know what a paddy leg is? Well, suction is a terrific force, and if you're going to work in a rice **paddy** with a **prosthesis** on, the foot will be sucked off. So this guy invented a very, very small foot that you could screw on, with a suction-release valve at the bot-tom. That way people could still go on being rice farmers even if they were **amputees**.*

*And we did nutritional evaluations. I remember once Tom and I went up to the mountains to do an evaluation on a hill tribe. It was pretty desperate—they were pretty much living on leaves. Not long after we got to the village a woman came out of a hut and grabbed me. "I want to show you a picture of my son," she said. "He was killed in the fighting." So I went inside. She showed me the picture, and then she started **keening** and weeping. And there was nothing I could do. Nothing but sit very quietly, listening to her. So that's what I did. I just sat and listened.*

I don't know why that memory jumps out any more than the oth-ers. Because things like that were so much a part of what went on.

*Or another time. One of my other jobs was taking tourists around. **My Lai** was very close to us, and it was a place American tourists often wanted to go. Not that there were a lot of tourists, but occasionally people would come. Reporters, for instance. So I'd take them across the ditch to My Lai. And one time we were standing there when some Vietnamese kids came up and stood with us. "Well," I said to the kids, "is there anything you want to say?" And one of them asked, "Why do you Americans think this place is so different from any other place?" You see, My Lai had been blown up seven times. And there we were, Americans, focused on a single moment in what we think of as history.*

Danang: A large city on the coast of central Vietnam where a U.S. Marine base was located.

Conduits: A pipe or tube for protecting electrical wires.

Paddy: A wet field used for growing rice.

Prosthesis: An artificial device used to replace a missing body part.

Amputees: People who have had a limb or other part of their bodies surgically removed.

Keening: A loud wail of mourning for the dead.

My Lai: A hamlet in Quang Ngai province where U.S. troops killed hundreds of unarmed Vietnamese civilians in March 1968.

*Oh, the stories. Like you're planting rice and a bullet goes astray and—bang!—you're a **quadriplegic**. Or I could tell you a story about a woman who went home and poisoned her son as soon as they left the center. The child was a **paraplegic** and she couldn't take care of him with all her other responsibilities. . . .*

*I'd **give my eyeteeth** to go back and see what the Vietnamese have done. I sincerely hope they're not as **militarized** now. I'm sure things are desperately poor and probably still incredibly beautiful. But whatever's happened, it's their country now, and I'm glad of that.*

What happened next . . .

Upon returning to the United States, American women suffered many of the same problems as male Vietnam veterans. For example, thousands of female veterans suffered from post-traumatic stress disorder (PTSD), a set of psychological problems caused by exposure to a dangerous or disturbing situation, such as combat. These women struggled to cope with symptoms like depression, flashbacks, nightmares, and angry outbursts.

To some American women who served in Vietnam, life at home seemed dull and unrewarding compared to the danger and excitement of the war. Many nurses who had been responsible for saving lives in Vietnam suddenly found themselves changing bedpans in American hospitals. As a result, many female veterans felt alienated from society. They had trouble sharing their experiences with other people and felt that no one could understand their feelings. "You didn't feel there was anything you ever could enjoy again because you really were immersed in death," nurse Joan Furey explained to Palmer. "Other people seemed shallow. You felt a strong allegiance to the dead."

To make matters worse, the women who served in Vietnam did not receive much support from the American people, the U.S. government, or male veterans' groups. In fact, many people did not even realize that women had served in Vietnam. "Because their numbers were smaller and because they

had worked for such a variety of organizations, the women were more isolated . . . than the men were," Marshall noted.

Immediately after the war ended, the Veterans Administration—a U.S. government agency responsible for providing medical care, insurance, pensions, and other benefits to American veterans—claimed that military women were not eligible for counseling services, medical treatment, or other benefits. But in 1979 a group of female military nurses organized the Vietnam Veterans Association Women's Project to bring attention to the issues they faced. The resulting publicity led the U.S. Congress to investigate charges that the Veterans Administration discriminated against women.

Finally, in 1993 the women who served in Vietnam received some public recognition for their service to their country. A bronze statue of three female nurses and a wounded soldier was dedicated in Washington, D.C. General Colin Powell, chairman of the joint chiefs of staff and America's highest-ranking Vietnam veteran, spoke at the dedication ceremony. "I didn't realize, although I should have, what a burden you carried," he noted. "For male soldiers, the war came in intermittent flashes of terror, occasional death, moments of pain; but for the women who were there . . . and for the nurses in particular, the terror, the death, and the pain were unrelenting, a constant terrible weight that had to be stoically carried."

A memorial statue of Lt. Sharon A. Lane, a member of the U.S. Army Nurse Corps who was the first woman killed by hostile fire during the Vietnam War. The statue stands at the entrance to Aultman Hospital in Canton, Ohio. *Photograph by Ron Schwane. Reproduced by permission of AP/Wide World Photos.*

Did you know . . .

- In 1973, when U.S. troops were withdrawn from Vietnam, the government ended the military draft—an involuntary process used to select men between the ages of 18 and 26 for military service. Throughout the war the draft was criticized for unfairly targeting the poor and minorities. When the draft was eliminated it resulted in a shortage of military personnel. Over the next few years large numbers of women joined the U.S. armed forces to help make up the shortage. In fact, the percentage of women in the American military increased from 2 percent in 1972 to over 8 percent in 1980. The influx of women encouraged the U.S. government to end the practice of segregating male and female recruits into separate branches of service. It also led to expanded career opportunities for women in the military.

Sources

Marshall, Kathryn. *In the Combat Zone: An Oral History of American Women in Vietnam.* Boston: Little, Brown, 1987.

Norman, Elizabeth M. *Women at War: The Story of Fifty Military Nurses Who Served in Vietnam.* Philadelphia: University of Pennsylvania Press, 1990.

Palmer, Laura. "The Nurses of Vietnam, Still Wounded: Only Now Are They Healing Themselves." *New York Times Magazine,* November 7, 1993.

Saywell, Shelley. *Women in War.* New York: Viking, 1985.

Van Devanter, Lynda, with Christopher Morgan. *Home before Morning: The Story of an Army Nurse in Vietnam.* New York: Beaufort Books, 1983.

Walker, Keith. *A Piece of My Heart: The Stories of Twenty-Six American Women Who Served in Vietnam.* Novato, CA: Presidio, 1985.

James Stockdale

Excerpt from an account of his experiences as a prisoner of war
Published in *In Love and War* by James and Sybil Stockdale, 1984

During the Vietnam War, thousands of soldiers on both sides of the conflict were captured and imprisoned by enemy forces. These prisoners of war (POWs) included infantry soldiers, fighter pilots, and other military personnel, as well as people who participated in the conflict by spying, recruiting, or providing other direct assistance to the enemy army.

As the Vietnam War progressed, neither the Communist leadership of North Vietnam nor the U.S.-supported government of South Vietnam paid much attention to international guidelines on proper treatment of POWs. These guidelines were detailed in the Geneva Conventions, a series of international agreements that had been developed through the nineteenth and twentieth centuries.

According to the terms of the Geneva Conventions, POWs were supposed to receive "humane treatment," including adequate food, shelter, and medical care. But both North and South Vietnam subjected many of their war prisoners to horrible treatment. For example, both sides tortured some of their prisoners in order to punish them or gain information. In addition, many captives received very poor food, shelter, and med-

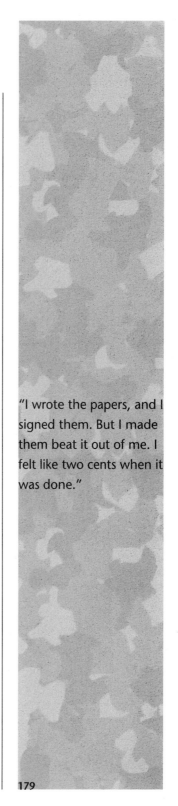

"I wrote the papers, and I signed them. But I made them beat it out of me. I felt like two cents when it was done."

The Geneva Conventions

The Geneva Conventions are a series of international agreements designed to protect wounded soldiers, prisoners, and civilians during times of war. As of the mid-1990s, 178 nations around the world had agreed to abide by the terms of these agreements.

The first Geneva Convention was adopted in 1864. This international law was created in response to grim accounts of the suffering that wounded soldiers endured during Italy's war of independence in 1859. It called for all nations to provide protection to sick and injured soldiers on the field of battle. This first convention is also credited with sparking the creation of the International Red Cross, a relief agency that continues to operate in war-torn regions of the world. The second Geneva Convention was passed in 1868. It expanded the rules of the first convention to include sailors wounded in battles at sea.

The third Geneva Convention was passed in 1929. This agreement instructed nations to recognize that prisoners of war (POWs) had certain basic rights such as medical care and adequate food and shelter. It called for prisoners to be treated humanely and released to their own people once a war ended. The fourth and last Geneva Convention was passed in 1949. This agreement replaced the first three conventions, providing additional guidance on the way in which wounded and captured soldiers should be treated. The 1949 convention also extended protection to civilians caught in war. In 1977 the international agreement amended the Geneva Convention of 1949 by extending protection to people caught up in civil wars and people engaged in violent conflicts that had not formally been declared as wars. People protected under these rules include journalists and religious, medical, and humanitarian aid personnel.

ical care. Some prisoners spent years wearing the same tattered uniforms in which they had been captured.

American soldiers were not spared from this terrible treatment. In fact, their North Vietnamese captors singled them out for special attention, since they believed that their true enemy was the powerful United States, not the weak South Vietnamese government.

Since most of the Vietnam conflict was fought in South Vietnam, relatively few U.S. soldiers were captured and imprisoned. The Communists recognized that the time and effort involved in transporting American servicemen captured in the South all the way to prison camps in the North was too great. But they did imprison several hundred American pilots who were shot down during bombing or surveillance missions over North Vietnam.

Over the course of the war, North Vietnam held approximately six hundred U.S. servicemen in POW camps scattered across their territory. Most of these men were pilots shot down in air raids, but about fifty were infantry soldiers captured in ground fighting. The first of the U.S. pilots to be shot down and captured was Navy pilot Everett Alvarez, Jr. Other notable pilots captured over the ensuing months included Commander James Stockdale, Lieutenant Colonel Robinson Risner, Commander Jeremiah Denton, Lieutenant Commander Richard Stratton, and Lieutenant Commander John McCain III, son of Navy Admiral John S. McCain, Jr.

The Communists maintained POW camps in both North Vietnam and Cambodia, but most of the camps were scattered around the capital city of Hanoi. Prisons maintained by the North included Cu Loc (nicknamed the "Zoo" by American POWs), Xam Ap Lo, and "Alcatraz." The most notorious of the North Vietnam POW camps, however, was Hoa Lo Prison. This facility, nicknamed the "Hanoi Hilton" by its American inmates, housed many of the American POWs during the final years of the war.

Living conditions in the Hanoi Hilton and other POW camps were terrible. American prisoners were locked for days at a time in dank, humid cement cells that reeked of urine, sweat, and vomit. The only companions that many prisoners had were the rats, mosquitos, and cockroaches that infested the camps. Medical care was practically nonexistent in almost all the camps. In addition, most of the POWs received only meager portions of spoiled food and contaminated water. Forced to live on maggot-infested meat, moldy bread, and polluted water, many American POWs contracted painful viruses or serious diseases.

The worst aspect of prison life for the American pilots and other soldiers, however, was their captors' use of torture. The North Vietnamese prison officials, known as the Camp Authority, inflicted horrible torture on many of the American

American POW is paraded through a village by North Vietnamese soldiers during the war.
Reproduced by permission of Archive Photos.

inmates. Interviews with American POWs after the war, in fact, indicate that approximately 95 percent of them were tortured between 1965 and 1969. In some cases these torture episodes pushed prisoners to the brink of death or actually killed them.

During the early years of the Vietnam War, North Vietnam denied that it tortured its prisoners. Some American antiwar activists defended the North's claims of innocence. These

Con Son Prison and the Vietnamese "Tiger Cages"

During the course of the Vietnam War, South Vietnam used an old French colonial prison on Con Son Island as one of its primary jails. This prison, located about fifty miles off the coast of Vinh Binh province, held a wide range of prisoners, including captured Viet Cong guerrillas, North Vietnamese prisoners of war, and suspected political enemies of the government.

In 1970, however, Con Son Prison became a subject of intense controversy in the United States. At that time, a group of U.S. lawmakers who visited the facility reported that its prisoners were being badly mistreated and, in some cases, subjected to torture-like conditions. The Congressional delegation was particularly troubled by the widespread use of "tiger cages" at Con Son. These "tiger cages" were small cement cells in which prisoners were sometimes chained. Some prisoners were kept chained in these cramped cages for so long that they became paralyzed from the waist down. When the American lawmakers reported on the miserable conditions at Con Son, the prison was quickly cited by the U.S. antiwar movement as further evidence that the war in Vietnam was immoral.

activists—some of whom were given limited tours of the POW camps by Communist officials—charged that the stories of POW torture were outright lies. Eventually, however, clear evidence of Communist torture began to mount. When this happened, the Communists switched public relations tactics. They declared that captured American pilots were war criminals rather than prisoners of war and therefore not covered by the rules of the Geneva Conventions.

The Communists used torture for a variety of reasons. Sometimes they wanted to gain military information from their prisoners. On other occasions, they used torture as a weapon to maintain order and obedience in the camps. Finally, the North Vietnamese resorted to torture in order to force American POWs to confess to "war crimes" on camera or sign statements criticizing U.S. involvement in the war. They even tortured American servicemen into signing documents praising the North for their "humane treatment" of their prisoners. The Communists valued these "confessions" because they thought that the docu-

Nearly nine hundred of the prisoners in the Qui Nhon, South Vietnam, POW camp were women.

Reproduced by permission of AP/Wide World Photos.

ments would help them turn American and world public opinion against U.S. involvement in Vietnam.

Most of the American POWs resisted their captors to the best of their abilities, even though they knew that the guards would punish them for their defiance with torture sessions. Some prisoners even took extraordinary risks to transmit messages about their condition to U.S. officials. Navy pilot Jeremiah Denton blinked the word "torture" in Morse Code with his eyelids when his captors forced him to confess to "war crimes" to reporters from other Communist countries. The U.S. government used film footage of this interview as evidence that North Vietnam was torturing American POWs.

The American POWs also developed a tapping code so that they could communicate with fellow POWs held in other cells (POWs were often forbidden to speak to inmates in other cells). Using this code to exchange news and encourage one another to remain strong, the prisoners adopted a unified front against their captors. They also took steps to ensure that no American was forgotten. "The POWs had one mental exercise in common," wrote Robert Timberg in *The Nightingale's Song.* "They committed to memory the name of every prisoner they knew of, which eventually included almost all of the nearly six hundred aviators in captivity. The mind game was serious business. Suspicious of Vietnamese claims that they had made public an accurate prisoner list, the Americans wanted to be ready for any opportunity to smuggle out a complete roster."

These efforts helped boost the morale of the hundreds of American POWs held captive in North Vietnam and Cambodia. But the appalling conditions in which the inmates lived, year after year, still evoked feelings of hopelessness and despair in nearly every prisoner at one time or another. Indeed, each American POW waged a daily struggle to keep his bleak surroundings from extinguishing his dream of someday returning home to family and loved ones.

Over the years, several American pilots who were imprisoned during the Vietnam War have written about their wartime experiences. One of these men was U.S. Navy pilot James B. Stockdale (1923–), who was the highest-ranking American prisoner of war during the Vietnam conflict. Stationed with the USS *Oriskany* aircraft carrier, he was shot down on his two-hundredth mission over North Vietnam in September 1965. After his capture, Stockdale endured eight years of torture and long periods of solitary confinement at the hands of the North Vietnamese. Like all other Americans who were subjected to torture, he eventually confessed to illegal activities and signed antiwar statements. But Stockdale defied his captors throughout his imprisonment. In fact, he became an essential figure in organizing American POWs to resist their captors and remain hopeful of eventual freedom. His wife Sybil Stockdale also became a leading activist on behalf of American POWs during the war. She founded the League of Wives of American Vietnam POWs.

Returning POW James Stockdale being welcomed home by his wife and three sons.
Reproduced by permission of AP/Wide World Photos.

Things to remember while reading the excerpt from *In Love and War*:

- North Vietnamese prison authorities often used intimidation or torture to force prisoners to give up important military information, inform on fellow prisoners, make false statements about the treatment they received, or testify that their actions against North Vietnam were "crimes."

• No prisoner could withstand torture forever. But American pilots and other POWs who were forced to sign incriminating or anti-American statements nonetheless often felt great guilt afterwards. The POW support network that Stockdale and others established helped these prisoners to realize that they were still good soldiers who could take pride in their service.

• Stockdale was the highest-ranking officer in the POW camps in which he was held. He used this authority to pass along rules designed to help other POWs survive their imprisonment with dignity and hope for the future. Stockdale's actions, though, eventually got him in serious trouble with his captors.

Excerpt from James Stockdale's memoir
In Love and War:

Unity was our best hope. And in our prison, unity came automatically. Men of goodwill of the sort that inhabited those dungeons, faced with a torture system that made them write, recite, and do things they would never think of doing in a life of freedom, wanted above all else to enter a society of peers that had rules putting some criteria of right and wrong into their lives. Authority was not something that had to be imposed from the top; to be led, to obey fair and universal orders within the capability of all, was a right that this community of Americans demanded. A life of perfection was for them out of the question, but they all elected to take pain in a unified resistance program, to fight back against degradation.

To tell them "Do the best you can and decide for yourself how to resist" was an insult. They demanded to be told exactly what to take torture for. They saw that it was only on that basis that life for them could be made to make sense, that their self-esteem could be maintained, and that they could sleep with a clear conscience at night. . . .

Degradation: Humiliation.

Folly: A foolish act.

Submission: Surrender.

Ex-post-facto: Punishments delivered after a period of time has gone by.

To just issue the order "Do not bow" would have been **folly** and ultimately destructive of prisoner unity. The Vietnamese had gotten the drop on us with this bowing to every one of them at every meeting, and right now an order to refuse would have meant the beating of most of us into submission. That is, if the offense was committed inside the camp. But they couldn't afford to show their viciousness in public, and I had learned that ex-post-facto [after an event] punishments were more often than not halfhearted. They were overloaded with public

An American POW talks to a fellow prisoner through a doorport at a detention camp in Hanoi.
Reproduced by permission of AP/Wide World Photos.

James Stockdale (1923–)

Navy wing commander James Stockdale was stationed with the aircraft carrier USS *Oriskany* when he was shot down over North Vietnam on September 9, 1965, on his two-hundredth mission. His communist captors subjected him to years of torture and solitary confinement. But Stockdale resisted them throughout his captivity. On one occasion, he even tore his scalp to ribbons and bashed his own face in with a stool to prevent the Communists from filming a "confession" of his crimes. As the top-ranked naval officer in the North's POW camp system, Stockdale also organized other POW resistance efforts.

Stockdale was among the first POWs to return home in early 1973. After eight long years of captivity, he was finally reunited with his wife Sybil and his four young sons. Stockdale was promoted to rear admiral shortly after his return, and in 1976 he was awarded the prestigious Congressional Medal of Honor. "By his heroic action, at great peril to himself, he earned the everlasting gratitude of his fellow prisoners and of his country," stated the honor citation. In 1992 he served as the vice-presidential nominee for independent candidate H. Ross Perot in the presidential elections.

Sententiously: Briefly or tersely.

Make out: Do all right.

Shakedown: Initial interview or interrogation.

Tacit: Unspoken.

appearance commitments and had to concentrate on short-term pay-offs and often let long-term "lessons" slide. It was in public that the real prisoner humiliation came in, so 'Don't bow in public' was a good, practical, useful law. . . .

It would be the height of ignorance to order **sententiously**, "Make no confessions"; the toughest of the tough were forced to make them from time to time. But I thought that if everybody applied his post-torture skill and cunning to the problem of avoiding the use of the word crime in confessions, we could do it, and thereby take a lot of the emotional steam out of what they published. "Admit no crimes" thus became a law. . . .

My whole concept of proper prisoner-of-war behavior was based on sticking together. We were in a situation in which loners could **make out**. If, after the initial **shakedown**, you refused to communicate with Americans, there was **tacit** agreement that the Vietnamese would leave you alone; there would likely be no more torture, no confessions, no radio broadcasts, maybe not even another tough military-information interrogation. One interested only in keeping his own nose clean could score lots of points by remaining a loner. I asked everybody to give up this edge of individual flexibility and **get in the swim,** communicate, level with your American neighbors on just what-all you compromised, what information you had to give up in the torture room, to freely enter into **collusions** with Americans, to take your lumps together and, if necessary, all go down the tubes together. In this circumstance our highest value had to be placed on the support of the man next door. To ignore him was to betray him. The bottom line was placing unity over selfish interests. It was "Unity over Self." . . . In the spring of 1967 the orders were carried to every camp in the Hanoi prison system under my name as the senior American communicating in that system. . . .

[August 1967] As usual that night we made sure all the new arrivals in the hallway understood my standing orders and my name. A week later the **Camp Authority** became tense and ruthless and the **Thunderbird hallway** started to be vacated, cell after cell each day. One of those who got the orders, a young and dedicated navy pilot, had come into prison on the **crest** of such a wave of new **shootdowns** that he had just that afternoon been stashed in Thunderbird, even before he'd had his initial shakedown torture for current bombing-operations information. We didn't ask him how long he had been down, but had no idea he was that fresh-caught and inexperienced. That night they took him out and put him in the ropes [torture devices] and demanded that he give certain information. He innocently replied, "No, sir; that is against my commanding officer's orders." Cat [one of the guards] was called immediately, the ropes tightened, and the young man, like the best of men, was forced to give what they now knew he knew: what the orders were, and what my name was. The **purge** for more particulars about the complete chain of command was on. I knew it had been inevitable.

This purge affected many people, bringing torture to many and death to some. Norm Schmidt was taken to interrogation and never came back. Dan Glenn was tortured and in irons two months, interrogated mercilessly, and never let anything crucial escape his lips. Nels Tanner, on his one hundred and twenty-third day in leg irons in the **Mint,** was caught at communications, tortured, and made to reveal before movie cameras the content and meaning of my orders. Ron Storz was **buttonholed** and told to come across with information on me, and his response was to take the pen they asked him to

Get in the swim: Join the effort.

Collusions: Secret agreements.

Camp Authority: North Vietnamese prison officials.

Thunderbird Hallway: Cell block in the prison camp.

Crest: Front.

Shootdowns: American planes shot down by North Vietnam.

Purge: Campaign to find and neutralize troublemakers.

Mint: Cell block in the prison camp.

Buttonholed: Detained for interview.

Unprecedented: Never seen or experienced before.

Paraphernalia: Equipment.

Mao: (1893–1976) Reference to Mao Zedong, leader of People's Republic of China (1949–59) and chairman of China's Communist Party until his death.

Pigeye: North Vietnamese guard.

Incited: Encouraged.

Criminals: American POWs.

Purchase: Hold or position.

Out of business: Unable to resist any longer.

Greasy: North Vietnamese guard.

Vy: North Vietnamese guard.

Big Ugh: North Vietnamese guard.

Dossiers: Reports.

Compatriots: Persons born, residing, or holding citizenship in the same country.

Two cents: Terrible.

write it with and jam it nearly through his left arm. He carried a big scar from that the rest of his short life. . . .

[Prison authorities tortured Stockdale for some time, then transported him to a new room he had never seen before.] An **unprecedented** array of people and **paraphernalia** were there to meet me. A long table was against the wall opposite the door; and behind it . . . were at least half a dozen Vietnamese officers I had never seen before. The man in the center was portly and spoke English. I mentally nicknamed him "**Mao.** " Behind me was a semicircle of about ten riflemen, bayonets fixed and pointing toward the floor. **Pigeye** was up front where I expected to see him, and he had there as his assistant torturer the big kid who had been at the Zoo as a recruit. . . .

Mao opened the proceedings by stating, "I have not been here long, but I have heard a lot about you and it's all bad. You have **incited** the other **criminals** to oppose the Camp Authority."

[Pigeye then punched Stockdale and placed him in a rope torture device,] amid extraordinary shouting from both the table and the ring of soldiers behind. Somewhere in this excitement, as my head was being forced down . . . Pigeye, I think by mistake, looped the rope under my left (broken) leg and around my neck and took a **purchase** on forcing my head down to my left knee, rather than to my right knee as he had done before. My leg was bending backward, giving at the knee, when suddenly—pop!—there went that hard-won cartilage.

Pigeye heard it, everybody heard it, but nobody could acknowledge it. I was **out of business.** I submitted, and told them all they wanted to hear. Yes, I had opposed the Camp Authority and I had incited the other criminals to oppose the Camp Authority. The whole thing ended there sort of self-consciously, with everybody filing out and me sitting there on the floor. I was not to be able to get up for over a month.

Three weeks were spent on the floor of that . . . room while I was worked over alternately by **Greasy** and **Vy,** with able assistance from Pigeye or **Big Ugh** as needed, as "war crimes" **dossiers** on myself and all my leading senior **compatriots** were compiled. I wrote the papers, and I signed them. But I made them beat it out of me. I felt like **two cents** when it was done.

What happened next . . .

In late 1969 the treatment of American POWs began to change for the better, though torture and other punishments remained ever-present threats. The quality of food, shelter, and medical care at most of the camps improved, and inmates were given more opportunities to interact with one another.

Many historians believe that this change came about as a direct result of the 1969 death of North Vietnamese leader Ho Chi Minh. They contend that his death triggered a reassessment of government policies toward the POWs. Communist leaders realized that the POWs would be valuable bargaining chips in any negotiations to end the war. They also belatedly recognized that their abusive treatment of the prisoners was hurting their efforts to divide the American people. Indeed, the American public had become deeply divided over many aspects of the Vietnam War by 1969. But nearly all Americans were united in their concern for the well-being of the POWs.

In early 1973 the United States and North Vietnam reached agreement on a treaty to end the war. Threatened with a withdrawal of U.S. support, the South Vietnamese government reluctantly went along with the treaty. Under the terms of this agreement, called the Paris Peace Accords, all prisoners of war held by South and North Vietnam—including the Americans—were supposed to be released within 60 days. In addition, each side was supposed to account for all prisoners who had died in captivity during the war.

In the two months following the agreement, a major exchange of prisoners took place. The South Vietnamese government based in Saigon released 26,880 POWs to North Vietnam's Communist government. In return, the Communists delivered 5,336 South Vietnamese prisoners. Both sides complained that the other failed to release all prisoners, however. These complaints eventually resulted in the release of another 5,000 Communist POWs and 600 South Vietnamese POWs, but some historians believe that the South continued to hold thousands of alleged enemies of the state in prison.

When the Paris Peace Accords were signed, North Vietnam immediately turned over a list of 591 American POWs who would be returned by the deadline. These men all were released. In accordance with U.S. Military Code of Conduct, American soldiers who had been held captive for the longest period of time returned home first. The first group, which included pilots who had been held captive for as long as nine years, flew from Hanoi to a U.S. base in the Philippines on February 12, 1973. Upon disembarking from the plane, Jeremiah Denton, who had been held captive for seven years, declared that "We are honored to have had the opportunity to serve our country."

Over the next several weeks, the American POWs returned to a jubilant United States. Dozens of parades and homecoming celebrations were held to welcome them home, and President Richard Nixon hosted a special White House dinner in their honor. Most Americans agreed that the POWs deserved this outpouring of affection. But the celebrations reminded some Vietnam veterans and their families that most Americans who served in the war had been ignored or mistreated upon returning home.

The MIA controversy

The homecoming also failed to convince some Americans that all POWs had been released by the Communists. In fact, one of the greatest controversies that currently surrounds the Vietnam War is the question of whether American soldiers who served in the conflict are still alive and being held captive in Indochina. Many Americans believe that there is a significant likelihood that some soldiers listed as "Missing in Action" or "MIAs" are actually POWs. A national poll held in the early 1990s indicated that about two-thirds of Americans believe that the Vietnamese are still holding American soldiers prisoner. But many scholars and historians flatly reject this theory. They charge that the theory is based on emotion rather than any credible evidence of POW/MIA survivors. Nonetheless, the issue significantly impacted relations between the United States and Vietnam after the war.

The MIA issue first emerged in the mid-1970s, spurred by Vietnam veterans and families of soldiers listed as missing in action. Citing reports of "live sightings" of American POWs still held in Vietnam, these activists formed a number of support groups to publicize their cause. The most powerful of these organizations were the National League of Families of

American Prisoners and Missing in Southeast Asia and Voices in Vital America (VIVA).

In 1975 a special House of Representatives committee chaired by G. V. "Sonny" Montgomery, a Mississippi Democrat, was created to determine if any Americans listed as POWs or MIAs were still being held by Vietnam. After 15 months, the committee concluded that "no Americans are still being held alive as prisoners in Indochina, or elsewhere, as a result of the war in Indochina." But this investigation failed to put the issue to rest.

In the late 1970s and 1980s activists working on behalf of the MIA issue claimed that "sightings" and other evidence showed that American MIAs remained alive in Vietnam, Laos, and Cambodia, where they endured terrible abuse. The evidence cited by the MIA groups ranged from photographs to eyewitness testimony. Many of these activists claimed that the U.S. government knew of the situation but chose to cover it up for its own reasons.

Around this same time, the continued imprisonment of American soldiers in Vietnam became a major plot element in numerous American films and books. Films like *Rambo: First Blood, Part II*—which featured a storyline in which a lone Vietnam veteran defeats villainous Vietnamese and backstabbing American officials to rescue a group of POWs—contributed to the growing belief in many American neighborhoods that U.S. soldiers might still be trapped in Vietnam. POW/MIA organizations, meanwhile, raised millions of dollars to publicize their beliefs.

As public demands to learn the fate of all American MIAs intensified, the U.S. government launched a series of investigations. In nearly every instance, the investigators learned that the "evidence" was wrong or falsified. Investigators also pointed out that although nearly 2,300 Americans remained officially "unaccounted for" from the war in Indochina, approximately 1,100 of these soldiers were known to have been killed in action. They were listed as "unaccounted for" only because their bodies had never been recovered (for example, many of these MIAs were pilots whose planes had been seen crashing into the sea or exploding in mid-air). Finally, historians noted that every major war in world history has featured combatants who die without ever being identified or having their bodies recovered. For example, H. Bruce Franklin pointed out in *M.I.A. or Mythmaking in America* that approximately 78,750 Americans remain unaccounted for from World War II.

Nonetheless, the U.S. government continued to pursue possible evidence that MIAs were alive in Indochina. Throughout the mid-1980s, for instance, the Department of Defense claimed that "it would be irresponsible to rule out the possibility that live Americans are being held [in Indochina]." This viewpoint was actively encouraged by President Ronald Reagan and other lawmakers who believed in the possibility of living MIAs. Lawmakers who were not convinced by the MIA conspiracy, meanwhile, were reluctant to say so. They feared that if they declared their true feelings, they would be called unpatriotic or viewed as participants in a vast government scheme to hide the truth from the American people.

Still, the MIA activists did not escape criticism during this period. Many people felt that the activists' theories about Vietnam's decision to keep American prisoners and U.S. government cover-ups were not very believable. In addition, some activists were accused of using the MIA issue to increase their own personal fortunes, even though their insistence on the existence of U.S. POWs gave false hope to the families of American soldiers who had disappeared during the war. "The myth of live POWs has been an unhappy burden on the American people," claimed Susan Katz Keating in *Prisoners of Hope*. "It has fostered mistrust and falsified the national history. More important, it has destroyed the lives of MIA families."

A Rolling Thunder Rally held in Washington, D.C., on May 24, 1998, called on the government to locate POWs and MIAs of Vietnam and other wars.
Photograph by George Bridges. Reproduced by permission of AP/Wide World Photos.

Others charged that the MIA groups were manipulated and misled by lawmakers, veterans, and others who opposed U.S. reconciliation with Vietnam. Finally, some observers contended that efforts to prove that American MIAs remained alive in Indochina was basically an effort to rewrite the history of the Vietnam War in America's favor. Franklin, for example, claimed that the theory that American POWs continue to be held in Vietnam "proves undeniably the cruelty and inhumanity of the Asian Communists, the fortitude and heroism of the American fighting man, and the noble cause for which the United States fought in Indochina." Despite such criticism, however, groups devoted to the MIA issue remained very strong throughout the United States.

In the early 1990s the governments of the United States and Vietnam slowly moved toward normal relations after years of animosity and distrust. This was made possible in large part by Vietnam's willingness to meet a wide range of U.S. demands designed to determine the status of American troops still listed as missing in action in Indochina. Vietnam opened its wartime military records and cooperated with U.S. efforts to find and retrieve the bodies of American servicemen scattered across Indochina.

These actions failed to satisfy many POW/MIA groups in America, but they helped convince the Clinton administration to lift a long-time trade embargo (prohibition of trade) against Vietnam in 1994. President Bill Clinton—who had himself avoided serving in Vietnam because of his student status—was greatly helped in this effort by the support of the U.S. business community and three respected Senators who had served in Vietnam—John McCain (a former POW), John Kerry (a leader of Vietnam Veterans Against the War), and Bob Kerrey (who lost a leg in combat and received the Medal of Honor for his service). America established normal diplomatic ties with Vietnam one year later, in 1995.

Did you know . . .

- The American antiwar movement was a source of special pain to many POWs. Most of the prisoners fiercely defended U.S. involvement in Vietnam. Their belief that they were part of a noble mission helped them to endure the terrible prison conditions in which they lived. Understandably, then, they expressed intense dislike for the antiwar activists who claimed that America was engaged in an immoral war.

- Only one American soldier listed as missing in action in the Vietnam War has been found alive over the years. Robert Garwood was captured in South Vietnam in 1965 and reportedly spent the next two years as a prisoner. Garwood later claimed that he remained a prisoner throughout the war. Dozens of American POWs and combat troops, however, report that Garwood willingly joined the Communist forces in 1967. In 1979 Garwood returned to the United States. One year later he was convicted by a military court of assault on a POW and collaborating with the enemy. Since that time, he has repeatedly claimed that dozens of other American POWs were held captive in the North after the war. But most of these claims have been proven false, and many former POWs view him as an untrustworthy figure who betrayed his countrymen.

Sources

Denton, Jeremiah A. *When Hell Was in Session*. New York: Reader's Digest Press, 1976.

Franklin, H. Bruce. *M.I.A. or Mythmaking in America*. Brooklyn, NY: Lawrence Hill, 1992.

Hubbell, John, with Andrew Jones and Kenneth Y. Tomlinson. *P.O.W.: A Definitive History of the American Prisoner-of-War Experience in Vietnam, 1964–1973*. New York: Reader's Digest Press, 1976.

Jensen-Stevenson, Monica, and William Stevenson. *Kiss the Boys Goodbye: How the United States Betrayed Its Own POWs in Vietnam*. New York: Dutton, 1990.

Keating, Susan Katz. *Prisoners of Hope*. New York: Random House, 1994.

Maurer, Harry. *Strange Ground: Americans in Vietnam, 1945–1975, An Oral History*. New York: Henry Holt & Company, 1989.

Stockdale, James, and Sybil Stockdale. *In Love and War*. New York: Harper & Row, 1984.

Legacies of the War

4

In January of 1973 the Paris Accords were signed and the United States withdrew its military forces from Vietnam. Two years later, North Vietnamese troops captured the South Vietnamese capital of Saigon to end the war. Once the war ended, the Communist leaders of North Vietnam reunited the two halves of the country to form the Socialist Republic of Vietnam. The government then seized control of all farmland and business activities and placed new limitations on the rights of the Vietnamese people. These changes made life very hard in Vietnam, and millions of Vietnamese fled the country to look for a better way of life.

Some of the people who fled the country after North Vietnam's victory in 1975 had supported the South Vietnamese government or its American allies. They worried that the country's new leaders would consider them enemies and take revenge on them. Others left Vietnam because they held religious or political views that would make it difficult for them to live under Communist rule. These people worried that they would be persecuted (harassed or attacked because of their beliefs) by the new government. Finally, some people fled

As the American evacuation of Vietnam drew to a close in 1975, Vietnamese scaled the walls of the U.S. Embassy in Saigon trying to reach the last of the departing helicopters. *Reproduced by permission of AP/Wide World Photos.*

because they believed that Vietnam would suffer widespread poverty as it struggled to recover from the destruction of the war. In an excerpt from the book *Hearts of Sorrow: Vietnamese-American Lives,* a South Vietnamese businessman named Phuong Hoang recalled his decision to flee Vietnam after the Communist takeover in 1975.

In the United States, meanwhile, memories of the Vietnam conflict haunted the country for many years. Lawmakers, historians, and ordinary citizens all argued about the reasons for America's defeat and the reasons for the deep divisions that appeared in the country during the war. After a while, most Americans seemed to want to pretend that the war never took place. This attitude made America's Vietnam War veterans feel neglected and forgotten. But people's feelings finally began to change in the 1980s. Americans continued to disagree about U.S. actions and attitudes in Vietnam, but they showed a greater willingness to move on and look to the future together. Veterans, meanwhile, finally began to receive recognition for the sacrifices they made in service to their country.

An important part of the healing process was the dedication of the Vietnam Veterans Memorial in Washington, D.C., in 1982. Today, the memorial is the country's best known tribute to the American soldiers who fought and died in the Vietnam War. This monument—also known as "The Wall"—features the name of every American man and woman who died in the war. Thousands of people have left cards, letters, souvenirs, and other mementoes at the Wall over the years in memory of those whose names are etched there. In one such letter, published in *Shrapnel in the Heart: Letters and Remembrances from the Vietnam Veterans Memorial,* a woman named Linda Phillips Palo mourns the deaths of three of her best friends in Vietnam.

Phuong Hoang

Excerpt from a statement about his
experiences as a refugee, 1975–76

Published in *Hearts of Sorrow: Vietnamese-American*
***Lives*, edited by James Freeman, 1989**

After the Vietnam War ended in a North Vietnamese victory in 1975, huge numbers of South Vietnamese people began leaving the country. Some of these people had supported the South Vietnamese government or its American allies. They worried that the country's new leaders would consider them enemies and take revenge on them. Other people wanted to leave Vietnam because they held religious or political views that would make it difficult for them to live under Communist rule. These people worried that they would be persecuted (harassed or attacked because of their beliefs) by the new government. Finally, some people fled because they believed that Vietnam would suffer widespread poverty as it struggled to recover from the destruction of the war.

Many people immigrate to foreign countries in search of opportunities to provide a better life for their families. But the people who decided to leave Vietnam after the war were not typical immigrants. In fact, the people who fled Vietnam were considered refugees. Refugees are forced to leave their homeland out of fear of persecution. Refugees often must leave quickly under dangerous circumstances. Sometimes they are

"When we set out on our journey, we had no idea what would happen to us or what country would allow us to land. All we knew was that we had to get out, even at the risk of losing our lives."

forced to leave belongings and loved ones behind. In addition to the struggles of adapting to a new culture, which are common to all immigrants, refugees "must also come to terms with the *losses* of the past that include home, country, family, work, social status, material possessions, and meaningful sources of identity," James Freeman commented in *Hearts of Sorrow*.

The first wave of refugees began departing South Vietnam shortly after North Vietnamese troops captured the capital city of Saigon in April 1975. Most of these people were high-ranking government officials or military officers and their families. These refugees had an easier time than many of the people who left Vietnam later. In fact, many refugees in the first wave received assistance from U.S. officials and military advisors who were still in Saigon. They were taken to temporary receiving stations on nearby islands in American military transport planes. There they learned to speak English and were processed for entry into the United States. As a result, most of the first wave of 130,000 refugees had successfully resettled in America by the end of 1975.

But a much larger second wave of refugees began fleeing Vietnam the following year. After winning the war, the Communist leaders of North Vietnam reunited the two halves of the country to form the Socialist Republic of Vietnam. They then introduced a series of changes designed to transform Vietnam into a socialist society. For example, the government took control of all farmland and business activities and placed restrictions on the lives of the Vietnamese people. These changes created terrible hardships for the Vietnamese. Before long, hundreds of thousands of Vietnamese people decided that they could not live under the new government. A similar situation arose in Cambodia and Laos), the countries along Vietnam's western border. Communist forces took control of those countries and instituted harsh reform policies that convinced many people to leave.

Rather than military officers and government officials, the second wave of refugees from Indochina consisted mostly of ordinary citizens. Many of these people were very poor and unable to read or write. Some of the refugees walked over land into nearby Thailand, but most attempted to escape Vietnam's poverty and repression (denial of basic rights and freedoms) by leaving the country by water. They set out from

the coasts in a variety of small boats and rafts. Many of the boats were overcrowded and had very little food, water, or other supplies on board. Most of the refugees headed for Thailand or the island nations of Malaysia, Singapore, Hong Kong, or the Philippines. This second wave of refugees from Vietnam, Cambodia, and Laos became known around the world as the "boat people."

Even if they succeeded in gaining passage on a boat, the refugees still faced a difficult and dangerous journey to freedom. After all, they had to cross hundreds of miles of open ocean in small, poorly equipped vessels. Many of the boats sank during storms. Thousands of refugees died at sea from drowning, exposure to the elements, hunger, thirst, or disease. To make matters worse, Thai pirates roamed the seas and attacked the overloaded boats. The pirates robbed passengers of their food, water, and valuables, and they often raped or kidnapped the women on board. An estimated 30 percent of the refugee boats departing Vietnam were attacked by pirates.

U.S. personnel and civilians evacuating Saigon in 1975. *Reproduced by permission of AP/Wide World Photos.*

Many of the boat people also had trouble finding a place to land. Between 1976 and 1978, hundreds of thousands of refugees from Vietnam, Cambodia, and Laos landed in nearby Malaysia, Singapore, Thailand, Guam, and the Philippines. But these countries were relatively poor and lacked the facilities to handle such large numbers of new people. As a result, the refugees were forced to live in unpleasant conditions in overcrowded refugee camps for months or years until they were allowed to enter a wealthier nation like the United States.

Eventually, the number of refugees became too great for the Southeast Asian nations to handle. Caring for the refugees placed a huge strain on their economies, food supplies, and living space. The local people grew to resent the refugees and began pressuring their governments to stop accepting them. In fact, sometimes local people would line up on beaches and throw rocks at refugee boats to prevent them from landing. In 1979 the leaders of several Southeast Asian nations announced that they would no longer allow the boat people to land.

In the late 1970s wealthy countries such as the United States, Canada, France, and Australia increased their immigration quotas in order to accept some refugees. But these countries did not want to appear too generous, because they did not want to encourage more people to attempt the dangerous journey.

People in the United States also changed their views of the Vietnamese refugees over time. At first, America welcomed the refugees. After all, many people in the first wave of refugees had helped the United States during the Vietnam War. In addition, the refugees generally opposed communism—a viewpoint that was supported by the U.S. government and many American people. Finally, the United States had a long history of helping refugees from World War II and other conflicts.

But as the second wave of refugees from Indochina began pouring into the United States, some Americans began to resent them. At the time, the U.S. economy was in bad shape, and many people were unemployed. Some people worried that the refugees would take jobs that might otherwise be filled by Americans. Others believed that they would

end up paying higher taxes in order to support the newcomers. Many Americans still felt great sympathy for the boat people and wanted to help them. But many others pressured the U.S. government to reduce the number of Indochinese refugees it allowed into the country.

Over time, the United Nations and a variety of international relief organizations came up with funds to help the boat people. They also convinced the Vietnamese govern-

A barge packed with Vietnamese refugees escaping from the port city of Danang after it fell to North Vietnamese forces on March 30, 1975.
Reproduced by permission of AP/Wide World Photos.

ment to institute the Orderly Departure Program, which allowed a certain number of people to leave the country each year. This program gave people hope that they could immigrate through legal channels and helped reduce the flow of boat people making the dangerous journey out of Vietnam by sea.

Nevertheless, the flow of refugees from Vietnam continued into the early 1980s. By 1987 more than 1.5 million refugees from Vietnam, Cambodia, and Laos had resettled in other parts of the world. Over 800,000, or more than half of the refugees, ended up in the United States. Canada, Australia, and France each took in more than 100,000 Indochinese refugees.

The narrator of the following excerpt, Phuong Hoang, was an educated man who worked as a teacher in one of the central provinces of South Vietnam. After North Vietnamese forces took control of his town, Phuong Hoang began to worry about the safety of himself and his family under Communist rule. He decided to leave the country. He then purchased a boat and spent the next year learning to operate it and secretly storing supplies for a voyage to the Philippines. With the help of an Italian freighter captain, Phuong Hoang and his family survived their journey and eventually resettled in the United States.

Things to remember while reading the excerpt from Phuong Hoang's statement:

- In the excerpt, Phuong Hoang mentions that the Communist soldiers who searched his home were amazed at his modern conveniences, such as his television, ceiling fan, and flush toilet. He claims that the soldiers had not seen these items before because North Vietnamese citizens were forced to join the army at a young age, so they knew no other life. In general, North Vietnam was less technologically advanced than South Vietnam during the war. The American forces brought a great deal of technology to the South, and U.S. soldiers also influenced some Vietnamese to adopt modern conveniences. But Phuong Hoang was different from many people, even in South Vietnam. The majority of the people were poor farmers who lived in rural villages, and only the educated and wealthy people had televisions or electricity.

- Phuong Hoang recalls that the new Communist government required him to attend reeducation sessions every day for a month, but his situation could have been worse. Immediately after the Vietnam War ended, about 400,000 South Vietnamese people who were viewed as threats to Communist rule were sent away to be "reeducated," or forced to go along with the government. These people included not only former South Vietnamese government officials and army officers, but also doctors, lawyers, teachers, journalists, engineers, and other intellectuals. They were held in prisons that had been used during the war or sent away to work farms, sometimes for a period of years. Many were forced to perform hard labor and received very little food. Some of the people Phuong Hoang says disappeared may have been sent away during this time, while some others may have been killed.

- Phuong Hoang describes some of the restrictions the Communist government placed upon the people's basic freedoms. For example, he could not travel freely or speak with certain friends, and his activities were always watched and viewed with suspicion. Many people in South Vietnam found this situation intolerable, especially educated people. Such repression was one of the reasons that many Vietnamese fled the country as refugees.

- Phuong Hoang discusses some of the careful preparations he made before beginning his dangerous journey to freedom, including stockpiling gasoline, food, water, and other supplies. Many of the "boat people" left Vietnam with less advance preparation than he did, and many used smaller or less seaworthy boats. For this reason, more than 10 percent of the refugees died at sea. Still, most of them— like Phuong Hoang—felt it was worth the risk.

- Once they are picked up by the Italian freighter, Phuong Hoang and his family have trouble finding a country that will accept them. For a few years in the late 1970s, there were so many refugees leaving Indochina that some countries decided that they could not afford to become involved.

Excerpt from Vietnamese refugee Phuong Hoang's statement:

*In my town, there were only low **Communist** soldiers, not officers. If people made them angry, the soldiers would kill them and go on. I saw this happen in the market. A soldier grabbed hold of a man and said, "Two days ago you sold me a watch, and it doesn't work. That's wrong. I'll kill you for that." He raised his gun.*

The women in the market cried and pleaded with the soldier, "That man did not know the watch was bad; he bought it from someone else and just sold it to you."

The soldier pushed them aside, shot the man, and left. We lived in an area like that; it's not right at all to kill people just because someone feels like it.

*When the American soldiers were in our town, they did not act this way. Sometimes on holidays they drank a lot and sang loudly, but that was all right; they were good. They'd walk around the town, and say hello to people; we liked them. Our own soldiers also had good discipline, and good weapons, unlike the Communists, so I could not understand how we lost so quickly. The Communists did not know anything about modern life. What they had was good **propaganda**, a lie.*

*Within a few days, the Communists came to every house and searched them. They were quite **bewildered** and uneasy at what they saw. "What's this?" they asked, pointing to our ceiling fan and our electric lights. When I turned on the fan, they ducked. One young man decided that it was a machine to cut off the heads of prisoners.*

"Don't you know?" I asked. "Haven't you ever seen one?"

"Never." When they were small children, they had been picked up and taken to the jungle, where they had been taught how to fight. That's all they knew. They had no understanding of the city. "What's that?" they asked, pointing to the television set. I told them about it, explaining that it was like a movie, but not a real movie. When they saw the toilet bowl, they wanted to know what we wash in it. They were so young and strange. They wore a peculiar uniform; they talked in a funny way, and they expressed very different opinions and ideas.

Communist: Followers of communism, a political system in which the government controls all resources and means of producing wealth. By eliminating private property, this system is designed to create an equal society with no social classes. In effect, however, it often limits personal freedom and individual rights.

Propaganda: Information or ideas that are spread in order to promote one cause and do damage to the opposing cause.

Bewildered: Puzzled or confused.

When they talked to us, they used words we did not understand; their customs were unfamiliar to us. They had never seen a watch. They assumed that our floor was made of mud, so after drinking some tea, they poured the rest on our tile floor. To their amazement, the liquid was not absorbed. . . .

I was forced to attend **reeducation sessions** each day for one month. There the Communists said that with a rifle they shot down **B-52** planes. One South Vietnamese man laughed and said, "I cannot believe this. A B-52 flies so high that a rifle cannot shoot that far."

You know what happened? The next day that man had disappeared. When we saw this, we worried about our own situation.

Each day we had to listen to them boast and lie, "Our army is so courageous, so powerful, we beat the American people! We beat the South Vietnamese Army! Life in South Vietnam is **fictitious**; the prosperity of South Vietnam is fictitious!" Day after day they repeated the same thing. We could not live with that, so after a while I said to a teacher who was a friend of mine that we had to find some way to get out of Vietnam. This was very difficult, because the Communists were watching us at all times. It would take us about a year of careful preparation before we dared to attempt an escape.

If we wanted to visit a friend a few kilometers away, we needed a special pass. To get it, we had to answer questions: "Why do you want to visit your friend? What subject will you discuss with him, and for how long?" It was terrible. When two people talked together, the Communists would come by and ask, "What did you talk about with that person? Tell me."

This was the most terrible aspect of the Communist government; we could not talk together because every time, they would ask, "What did you talk about? Was it against the government?" They were always listening to overhear us. . . .

By now life had changed a lot. I could not trust anybody, even my wife or children, for **inadvertently** they might say something that could **incriminate** us. When my children came back from school, they told me that their teacher asked them, "What did you eat at dinner? Did you have chicken or pork? Did you have a lot of it? What are your father's opinions about our government? Does he like it or dislike it?"

My children were old enough so that I told them, "Never listen to those teachers; when they ask, just say that you don't know."

Reeducation sessions: Training programs in which citizens received favorable information about the Communist government and were strongly encouraged to cooperate with it.

B-52: A model of American warplane used to drop bombs on Vietnam during the war.

Fictitious: False or imaginary.

Inadvertently: By accident; without meaning to.

Incriminate: Arouse suspicion of guilt or give evidence against in a crime.

*Education had now become nothing: no English, no French, just the history of **Ho Chi Minh** and **General Giap**, and work in the gardens, that's all. . . .*

*For one year we lived like this. We learned that all the promises of the Communists were lies. They talked one way and did another. They claimed that all people would be equal, not too rich or too poor. Everyone would plant rice, and it would be divided with the poor. All houses would be divided equally. There would be no more unemployment. And there would be freedom: people would be able to go anywhere and do what they liked. It took only a few days to find out that everything they said turned out to be the opposite of what life would be like under their rule. . . . They claimed to have **liberated** us from a bad government; instead, they had **enslaved** us.*

*Not long after I had completed my month of reeducation, a former student of mine came to my house and asked if I wanted to escape from Vietnam. He said that lots of students wanted to flee, and he mentioned several whom I knew. I replied, "No, this is my home, and I am happy here." I didn't trust him; I thought he might be an agent for the Communists. A couple of months later, he returned and asked again. This time, I thought that maybe we could trust him. I asked my friend, the teacher, what to do. We invited that young man to a restaurant, and while we gave him food and drink, we **investigated** his mind.*

The student said, "I have a fisherman's permit that allows me to take a boat out to sea." This was quite valuable, for the Communists controlled the seashore to prevent escape. City people were not allowed to walk along the coast, and boats were not allowed to pass from the river into the sea without a valid permit. And people who wished to buy or sell their boats also needed a permit from the Office of Marine Products.

*My friend and I bought a boat, 12½ by 3½ meters [about 41 feet long and 11 feet wide], for 35 million **piasters** in pre-Communist currency, a lot of money. We paid both the seller and the Office of Marine Products. Our payment was half in money and half in gold. In addition, we paid another 3 million piasters for fishing nets. Instead of staying at home, I could now go out fishing.*

*Although we had a boat, we did not know how to **navigate**. Neither we nor the student with the fishing permit had ever done anything like this. We did not even know how to anchor the boat. . . .*

*Around three in the afternoon, the fishermen would go out to fish. They would stop at a Communist **checkpost** located just before the river*

Ho Chi Minh: (1890–1969) Vietnamese Communist leader who became the first president of North Vietnam in 1954 and led the North during the Vietnam War until his death.

General Giap: Vo Nguyen Giap (1911–), a North Vietnamese general and Communist Party leader during the Vietnam War.

Liberated: Freed.

Enslaved: Turned into a slave.

Investigated: Studied or examined closely.

Piasters: Vietnamese money.

Navigate: Steer or operate over a specific course.

Checkpost: An area where official inspections are performed.

emptied into the sea. After showing their permits, the fishermen would proceed to the open sea. If their permits had expired, they could be sent to jail; that happened to one of my friends. My son, my friend, and I also pretended to go out to fish. The problem was that our fishing net was too big and heavy for the three of us. We caught hardly any fish.

Our real purpose was to learn how to navigate. Once out at sea, with no mountains or landmarks, how could we tell north from south, east from west? We needed a compass, but at first we could not find one. A person caught buying a compass would be thrown in jail because the authorities assumed that such a person was trying to escape. We studied the stars in the night sky. I found that there was a kind of star cluster in the west. I didn't know its name, but I recognized the shape of the stars. Every night I would look for it. Finally I also took the chance and bought a small Japanese pocket compass. I still have that compass. I worked with it until I learned to use it. I also found an old tattered map of Southeast Asia that had been published in a newspaper. I measured the angle to the east that I needed to follow; then I measured the distance from my home town to **Manila**, the intended destination for my escape: it was about 1,500 kilometers [900 miles]. I drew a bigger map which I put in my boat. . . .

For one year, I learned and practiced navigation, changing oil, and fixing the diesel engine. I also bought small quantities of fuel, a gallon at a time, and sometimes only a liter or a quart so that I did not attract attention. Had I bought large quantities, the authorities would have noticed, asked me what I used it for, and might have taken me to jail. . . . In the afternoon, my friend and I would go out in the boat and remain on the sea overnight. Our aim was to transfer some of the diesel fuel in small cans to a larger tank, originally taken from a truck, that we had transported and hidden between rocks and covered with grass and leaves on an island nearby. Usually the Communists were on the lookout for people carrying a lot of fuel, water, and food, signs of an intended escape. Those people they put in jail. Since we carried only small quantities at any one time, the Communists did not suspect us when they searched us. . . .

Then one day in August, the guards [at the checkpost] stopped me. They said, "Month after month you go out, but you bring back no fish. You don't look like a fisherman. What do you do? Do you have relatives in another country beyond Vietnam?"

"No," I lied. "I had a little fish which I salted already." I am not surprised that they questioned me. I looked and behaved differently from fishermen. . . .

Manila: Capital city of the Philippines, an island nation in eastern Asia.

The Hmong People of Laos

The ethnic Hmong population of Laos stood as one of America's steadiest allies during the Vietnam War. This tribe of hardy highland farmers had long been a part of French Indochina. When armed resistance against French colonial rule erupted in the 1940s and 1950s, Hmong warriors fought on both sides. By the early 1960s, however, the majority of the tribe was in the anti-Communist camp.

U.S. agents took advantage of tribal animosity toward the Communists, building Hmong guerrilla groups that included thousands of tribesmen. By the mid-1960s the Hmong were recognized as one of the U.S. military's best weapons in Laos. The Hmong conducted countless guerrilla raids against North Vietnam's Ho Chi Minh Trail and other Communist supply lines and bases throughout Laos. They also rescued American pilots who were shot down, blocked Communist raids, and guarded Laotian radar installations used by U.S. aircraft in their bombing runs over Laos and North Vietnam. These Hmong troops were supervised by Laotian commander Vang Pao, who was a Hmong himself. At the peak of Hmong involvement in the war, Vang Pao commanded nearly 30,000 soldiers from the tribe.

As time passed, though, the war's violence took a heavy toll on the Hmong. U.S. bombing raids destroyed many of their farms and fields. In addition, the Hmong population (approximately 250,000 before the war) lost many of its youngest and strongest men to the war. A U.S. Air Force study, for example, stated that "by 1971, many [Hmong] families were down to the last surviving male (often a youth of 13 or 14), and survival of the tribe was becoming a major concern."

As the Hmong people lost their young men and their farms to the war, they became dependent on rice shipments and medical supplies from the United States for their survival. This dependence made the Hmong even more vulnerable to the war's cruelties. For example, when a few Hmong villages tried to stop Vang Pao from drafting their teenage sons into the Laotian military, he threatened to cut off their shipments of rice and other supplies. Faced with starvation, the Hmong villages had no choice but to go along with Vang Pao's demands.

When the governments in South Vietnam, Cambodia, and Laos all fell to Communist forces in 1975, the Hmong tribespeople expressed great fear for their future. Convinced that the victorious Communists would punish them for their wartime opposition, thousands of Hmong families fled into Thailand. Most of those who stayed behind—an estimated 100,000 Hmong—were murdered or imprisoned by Laos's new Pathet Lao Communist government.

In 1996 there were still more than two thousand Hmong living in refugee camps such as this one northeast of Bangkok, Thailand. These people were to be resettled in the United States after more than twenty years of living in camps. *Photograph by Charles Dharapak. Reproduced by permission of AP/Wide World Photos.*

Those Hmong who escaped to Thailand endured terrible conditions in their new home. Crowded into disease-ridden refugee camps, many Hmong families struggled to survive on meager supplies of food and water. Thousands of Hmong tribespeople died from malnutrition and disease during these first few years, despite the efforts of the United Nations and various international relief agencies.

In the late 1970s Hmong families began migrating to the United States from the refugee camps in Thailand.

Between 1975 and 1995, an estimated 110,000 Hmong refugees resettled in America. They were initially sprinkled throughout the country. As time passed, however, Hmong families concentrated in several areas of the country. Today, large Hmong American populations can be found in Wisconsin, Minnesota, and California. Some Hmong have found jobs working on farms or in factories, but they still have the highest percentage of families on welfare of any Southeast Asian immigrant group.

Sometimes boat people would be detained in refugee camps such as this one in Hong Kong.
Reproduced by permission of Corbis Corporation.

I think the officials realized that I was not what I claimed. "You cannot go out there unless you have a permit," they said. "Let us see your papers."

I replied, "I have applied for a permit at the Office of Marine Products. Please let me go out this afternoon only. I just need to catch fish to feed my family. If by tomorrow I don't have a permit, then okay, I'll stay home." I knew that I would have to leave the next day. Because I was not a fisherman, I could not get a renewal of the permit.

I took the boat out, anchored it near the island, and returned to shore in a small bamboo raft about three feet wide.

The following day, Sunday, August 8, 1976, at eight in the morning, my friend and I led our families to the small raft. We were dressed in swimming suits, nothing else. It appeared that our little group was going out to swim, fish, and have some fun. At that moment, neither my wife nor my four teenage children had any idea that this was to be their last day in Vietnam. I had told no one in my family of my plans, not even my son who sometimes went with me out on the boat, for I feared that by accident they might say something that could betray us.

The raft held only a couple of people. I made several trips back and forth between the shore and the island until all 19 people were on the larger boat. As they climbed aboard, I said, "We are leaving our country. Get into the boat quickly and lie down so that you are not seen. If the patrols spot you they will shoot us."

They were surprised; they had had no warning; they had carried nothing with them. Everything had been left behind, including their clothes. On the boat, I had stored water in diesel cans and some special dry food that contained vitamins. I expected to supplement our food by fishing along the way.

I turned over the engine, **accelerated**, and fled as fast as we could away from a shore that we would never see again. For two hours we went at full speed. At that point I figured we probably were safe, since the Communists used patrol boats that were no faster than ours. None of the passengers in the boat said anything. They were too seasick.

For three days and four nights we traveled eastward. On the journey, we did not talk. I spent my time fishing and bailing out water. Along the way, we passed several ships. We called to be rescued, but they did not stop. On that fourth night, when we were within 100 kilometers [62 miles] of Manila, the sea became quite rough; it was terrible, with huge waves battering us. We would have died had we not been saved by an Italian oil tanker traveling between South Korea and Saudi Arabia. Not only did the captain save us, he also attached and pulled along our boat. Later we were able to sell it in Saudi Arabia; we received $3,000 in U.S. currency.

The captain of that tanker was formerly from **East Germany**. He picked us up because he realized that, as he had done years before, we were fleeing from Communist **oppression**. He offered to put us ashore in a free country. For two days we anchored in Singapore while he tried to get permission for us to land; Singapore refused. We traveled to Saudi Arabia, where we remained for two weeks while the ship was loading oil. The other family that had escaped with us had relatives in Canada. At that point, the Canadian government accepted them. My family remained on the ship. We went to Madagascar, South Africa, Angola, then up to Spain, into the Mediterranean Sea to North Africa, and finally to North Italy. Our journey took two and a half months. In Italy the **International Rescue Committee** processed our application, and ten days later we flew to the United States to begin a new life in an unfamiliar land.

Accelerated: Increased speed.

East Germany: Eastern part of Germany that was taken over by a Communist government following World War II.

Oppression: Abusive use of power or authority.

International Rescue Committee: A relief organization that helped refugees.

Some people from my town had fled before the Communists arrived in 1975. As far as I know, my family was only the fourth to escape once the Communists took over. Later, many others would escape. But when we set out on our journey, we had no idea what would happen to us or what country would allow us to land. All we knew was that we had to get out, even at the risk of losing our lives. We were very lucky to have been saved by that captain. Looking back on it now, our sea voyage, with only a toy compass to guide us, was very dangerous. Still, it would have been better to die at sea than to live another day under Communist rule.

What happened next . . .

According to Edward F. Dolan, author of *America after Vietnam: Legacies of a Hated War,* the refugee crisis "ranks as one of the war's greatest legacies, a legacy that is marked by tragedy, hardship, and hope—tragedy because it has uprooted so many people from their homes, livelihoods, friends, and cultures; hardship because their journeys to freedom were marked always with danger and the threat of death; and hope because the flight has always held out the promise of fresh and successful lives in new lands for all."

About half of the Indochinese refugees who ended up in the United States settled in California, mostly in the Los Angeles and San Francisco areas. Other states with large refugee populations include New York, New Jersey, and Illinois. Many of the refugees managed to build successful lives in their new country through hard work and determination. In fact, many Vietnamese refugee families pooled their money in order to open their own businesses. Some areas of American cities have been revitalized by the addition of Vietnamese grocery stores, restaurants, and gift shops. On average, though, the refugees from Indochina have not obtained the standard of living enjoyed by white Americans, or even that of non-refugee Asian immigrants, like Japanese Americans.

Many refugees experienced problems as they tried to establish themselves in the United States. For example, some refugees struggled to learn English. Their poor command of the language often cost them jobs and other opportunities. In addition, many refugees faced discrimination in housing, education, or employment due to their race. Sometimes the people in poorer American communities resented the refugees and lashed out against them with violence. Many Vietnamese refugees settled in Florida, Mississippi, and Texas and became fishermen on the Gulf of Mexico. But some local fishermen grew angry when the Vietnamese crowded into their traditional fishing grounds. In some cases, the Vietnamese had their fishing nets cut or their boats damaged by local fishermen.

Other refugees had trouble understanding and adjusting to their new culture. The problem of adapting to the new culture sometimes caused conflict in refugee families with children. While the parents tried to preserve some of their Asian traditions, the children often found it easier to succeed in American society if they behaved more like Americans. "Both parents and children often feel deep discomfort about this conflict between parental authority and children's freedom," Freeman wrote. "The parents see themselves as sacrificing for their children, who abandon them; the children see themselves as performing well, yet their parents reject them because of their social behavior."

Did you know . . .

- The United States did not always welcome immigrants from Asian

A refugee remembers his family being executed by North Vietnamese soldiers during a protest of Vietnam's Communist government. *Reproduced by permission of AP/Wide World Photos.*

nations. For example, one of the earliest American immigration laws, the Chinese Exclusion Act of 1882, was passed specifically to prevent Chinese laborers from entering the country. Later, the National Origins Act of 1924 banned immigrants from any part of Asia. These policies began to change in 1952, with the passage of the McCarran-Walter Act. This law eliminated race as a barrier to immigration and set special rules for refugees fleeing from violence or repression. In 1980 President Jimmy Carter signed the Refugee Assistance Act, which increased the number of refugees admitted from Southeast Asia and established programs to aid in their adjustment to American society.

- Before 1970 only 11 percent of all immigrants to the United States came from Asian nations. Instead, most immigrants came from Europe (39 percent) or Latin America (38 percent). But between 1970 and 1979, the flow of refugees from Vietnam, Cambodia, and Laos increased the percentage of immigrants from Asia to 34 percent. This percentage was second only to immigrants from Latin America, who made up 41 percent of the total coming to the United States during those years. Between 1980 and 1984, Asians made up the largest proportion of immigrants to the United States at 48 percent, while the number of immigrants from Latin America dropped to 35 percent.

- All of the Vietnamese refugees who came to America are not the same. For example, they practice three major religions—Catholic, Buddhist, and Confucian. They also belong to a wide variety of ethnic groups, including Khmer (Cambodian), Hmong, Montagnard, Tonkinese, and Annamese.

- Vietnamese Americans continue to observe many traditions in their new country, including the annual Tet holiday, the lunar new year. It is celebrated each year in late January or February, during the full moon before the spring planting season. In U.S. communities with large populations of Vietnamese immigrants, the Tet festivities are held in large fairgrounds. People decorate booths with colored lanterns, set off fireworks, perform religious ceremonies, eat festive meals, and exchange gifts with family members.

Sources

Caplan, N., et al. *The Boat People and Achievement in America*. Ann Arbor: University of Michigan Press, 1989.

Dalglish, Carol. *Refugees from Vietnam*. London: Macmillan, 1989.

Dolan, Edward F. *America after Vietnam: Legacies of a Hated War*. New York: Franklin Watts, 1989.

Freeman, James, ed. *Hearts of Sorrow: Vietnamese-American Lives*. Palo Alto, CA: Stanford University Press, 1989.

Grant, Bruce. *The Boat People*. New York: Penguin, 1979.

McGwire, William. *Recent American Immigrants: Southeast Asians*. New York: Franklin Watts, 1991.

Strand, P. J. *Indochinese Refugees in America*. Durham, NC: Duke University Press, 1985.

Linda Phillips Palo

Letter left at the Vietnam Veterans Memorial, July 20, 1985
Published in *Shrapnel in the Heart*, edited by Laura Palmer, 1987

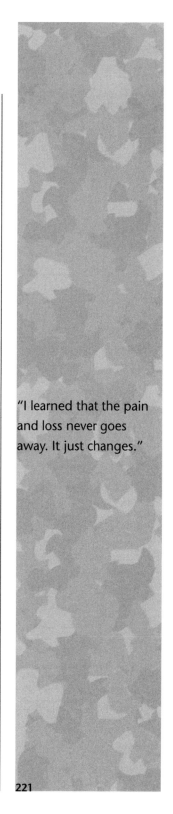

When American Vietnam veterans returned home to the United States, many of them felt ignored and rejected by their country. The Vietnam War had caused so much pain and unhappiness that most Americans seemed to want to forget that the conflict had ever taken place. As a result, neither the nation's surviving veterans nor those soldiers who were killed in Vietnam received any meaningful recognition outside of their small circle of family and friends. In 1982, however, their sacrifices and service were finally recognized by their nation with the formal dedication of the Vietnam Veterans Memorial in Washington, D.C.

The idea for the memorial originated with Jan Scruggs, a Vietnam combat veteran. In 1979 he founded the Vietnam Veterans Memorial Fund to raise money for the construction of a monument honoring the men and women who gave their lives in the war. As Scruggs began his fund-raising efforts, he emphasized that he had no wish to make any political statements about American involvement in the war. He simply wanted a memorial that would pay tribute to the 58,000 Americans who were killed in Vietnam.

"I learned that the pain and loss never goes away. It just changes."

Jan Scruggs (left), the Vietnam combat veteran who originated the idea for a Vietnam memorial, and Maya Lin (right), the art student whose design was chosen for the memorial.
Reproduced by permission of AP/Wide World Photos.

"There was a great deal of difficulty in getting this project off the ground," admitted Scruggs in *Writings on the Wall*. "Most Vietnam veterans were primarily concerned with jobs, Agent Orange [a chemical used in wartime that was widely blamed for veterans' postwar health problems], and other issues relating to themselves." Gradually, however, the fundraising efforts of Scruggs and his supporters began to pay off. They eventually gathered more than $8 million from more than 650,000 private contributors. These donors included both people who had supported American involvement in Vietnam and activists who had protested against the war. The federal government did not contribute any money to the memorial fund. But Congress did agree to set aside a two-acre section of land for the memorial in Washington, D.C.'s Constitutional Gardens, between the Washington Monument and the Lincoln Memorial.

In August 1980 Scruggs's organization announced a nationwide competition to come up with a suitable design for the memorial. The design competition attracted more than 1,400 entries. These submissions were reviewed by a distinguished panel of sculptors and architects. On May 1, 1981, the panel of judges announced that the winning memorial design had been submitted by Maya Lin, a twenty-one-year-old Chinese American art student at Yale University. Her design called for a long, V-shaped wall of polished black granite which would be engraved with the names of American soldiers killed or missing-in-action in Vietnam.

The selection of Lin's entry triggered a tremendous uproar of controversy. Her design was much different from the traditional statue memorials of earlier wars, and some people hated it. Critics—including some Vietnam veterans—said the design was grim and depressing and did not honor America's fallen Vietnam War soldiers. One Vietnam veteran described Lin's design as a "black gash of shame," and the Marine Corps League charged that it was "an insult to the memory of those it is intended to memorialize." As the debate continued, many critics voiced genuine concerns about the proposed memorial. But some opponents resorted to racist remarks about Lin's Asian heritage in an effort to erode support for her design.

The controversy bothered Lin. She defended her submission by stating that "I felt a memorial should be honest about the reality of war and be for the people who gave their lives." The commotion also deeply upset Scruggs and other people who believed that Lin's design offered a powerful tribute to the Americans who lost their lives in Vietnam. In fact, many Americans—including the Veterans of Foreign Wars (VFW) and other veterans' groups—rallied to support Lin's design. But opponents continued to fight it, and conservative lawmakers successfully blocked its construction.

Work on the memorial began only after the two sides agreed on a compromise. Under the terms of this agreement, a statue of three young American soldiers and an American flag would be added to the two-acre plot near Lin's memorial. Lin objected to the installation of the statue, which was designed by sculptor Frederick Hart. She thought that her memorial design and the proposed statue were of such different styles that they would not look good together. But the Vietnam Veterans Memorial Fund members convinced her that her memorial might never be built without the inclusion of the statue.

Dedication of the Wall

The Vietnam Veterans Memorial, popularly known as the Wall, was formally dedicated on Veterans' Day weekend in November 1982. Thousands of Vietnam veterans traveled to the nation's capital for the ceremony. They were joined by family members, as well as the friends and families of soldiers who had been lost in the war. As the dedication ceremony unfolded, thousands of Americans received their first opportunity to see the Wall for themselves.

The memorial designed by Lin featured two tall walls set in the ground, each nearly 250 feet long, that meet at a V-shaped angle. Constructed of polished black granite, the Wall had a mirror-like surface that reflected both the sky and the faces of those who stood before it. Visitors to the Wall also saw that the names of all 58,000 American soldiers who had been lost in Vietnam were engraved on the wall's surface in the order in which they died (names are periodically added to the wall as casualty records are updated and corrected). As the weekend progressed and the people roamed up and down the Wall's length, it became clear that most visitors approved of the design.

In the weeks and months following the dedication of the Vietnam Veterans Memorial, the controversy over Lin's design faded away. It was replaced by a widespread recognition that the Wall was in fact a powerful tribute to those who died while serving their country. "The anguish of the Vietnam War is present here but not in a way that does any dishonor to veterans," wrote Paul Goldberger in the *New York Times*. "This memorial . . . honors the veterans who served in Vietnam with more poignancy [emotional power], surely, than any ordinary monument ever could."

Indeed, the Wall became known as a place where those who had lost friends and loved ones could go to grieve and remember in a special way. Many visitors commented that the wall's design gave them a feeling of intimacy with loved ones who were killed or had disappeared in Vietnam. They liked being able to touch or trace the names of their lost sons, brothers, fathers, husbands, and comrades. They also treasured the opportunity to leave offerings—photographs, letters, flowers, childhood keepsakes, and other items—at the Wall in memory of friends and family.

A Mother Mourns the Loss of Her Son

Countless parents of men who were killed in Vietnam have visited the Vietnam Veterans Memorial since its dedication in 1982. Many of them return to the Wall again and again to mourn their lost sons, leaving letters or momentos from the past such as childhood toys or photographs. The following letter left at the Wall, from one grief-stricken mother to her long-dead son, was published in *The Wall: Images and Offerings from the Vietnam Veterans Memorial*:

Dear Bill,

Today, I come to this memorial, this black wall. I come to put flowers and a letter, not because it's a special day, like your birthday or Memorial Day. But just because it's Tuesday, and just because I love and miss you so and want the whole world to know.

The other day I saw a picture of Elvis Presley on a poster in a music store window. Under his picture it read, "Remember I lived, forget I died." I stood looking at this for a long time, wondering how you could possibly forget that

someone you loved so much had died.

Yes, I remember that you lived. I remember our laughter together and our tears when your rabbits died and especially when your grandparents died. I remember when you would get mad at me because you had to do the dishes or carry out the trash or be in bed a certain time on school nights.

But I can't forget that you died. I will never forget the day I heard of your death. I will never forget the long days of waiting for your body to be returned from Vietnam. I will never forget the millions of tears I have shed. And I can't forget the terrible hurt because you are not with me and never will be again.

I have cried many, many tears since you left us because I saw no reason for you to die then and I see no reason now.

But this I do know, you are happier with God in heaven than you could ever be on earth. So forgive me, my son, my Billy, when I cry because most of my tears are for me, I guess, because you are not with me and I miss you so.

Mom

Soon after its unveiling, the Vietnam Veterans Memorial became one of the nation's most beloved and revered monuments. "From the moment of its dedication, the wall . . . seemed to give physical form to a whole nation's feelings of pain and loss," explained Arnold Isaacs in *Vietnam Shadows*. "The controversy over the design . . . quickly faded from view, to be replaced by images of veterans, children, parents, and other visitors shedding healing tears and finding solace in the sight and touch of the names. The wall quickly became one of the most-visited of all Washington's attractions, and certainly the most emotionally compelling. Some veterans still wouldn't go, but others found themselves returning again and again. 'It is exactly the right memorial,' said a retired three-star general, 'for that war.'"

The story of one letter left at the Wall

One of the many letters that has been left at the Vietnam Veterans Memorial over the years was written by Linda Phillips Palo, a woman who lost three of her best friends in the war. She grew up in Orchard Park, New York, with Bill Mason, Douglas Henning, and Gary Townsend. "We were children without turmoil," recalled Linda Phillips Palo in Laura Palmer's book *Shrapnel in the Heart.* "It was this idyllic little town, picture perfect."

As they grew older, Linda and her friends often talked about their futures. Doug and Bill, for example, dreamed of relocating to the Colorado Rockies and opening an outdoors camp for city kids. But as American involvement in Vietnam deepened, growing numbers of Orchard Park's young men joined the military. "It became a ritual," wrote Palmer. "Before someone went off to war, the gang from Orchard Park High School would gather at the local pizza place to talk, drink beer, and try to be supportive. In Linda's church, departing soldiers were called to the altar and given a Bible to take with them to Vietnam."

As the war progressed, Doug, Bill, and Gary all voluntarily joined the U.S. armed forces and were sent to Vietnam. Bill became a medic. But four months after his arrival in Vietnam, his mother had a terrible nightmare that he was in a fire and was calling to her. As it turned out, her son had died that same night. Bill had run into a burning tank to rescue a fellow soldier during a fight with enemy troops. But before he could drag the injured man to safety, the tank was hit by a rocket and both men died in the flames. Four months later, Doug was killed in a firefight while on patrol. A short while later, Gary died in a fierce battle against Communist forces. All three men received the Silver Star for heroism.

The *Mayaguez* Incident

Even after the Vietnam War ended, U.S. forces continued to clash with Communist forces on the high seas. The best-known postwar incident took place on May 12, 1975, when Communist troops from Cambodia seized the American commercial ship the *Mayaguez,* while it was cruising in the Gulf of Thailand, near the Cambodian coast. The Cambodian soldiers took the ship's 30-man crew hostage and transported them off the vessel.

This incident took place only a few weeks after the governments of both Cambodia and South Vietnam had been taken over by Communist forces. Mindful of this fact, U.S. President Gerald R. Ford and members of his administration believed that America needed to prove that it remained a strong nation willing to use force when necessary. Acting on intelligence reports that stated that the hostages were probably being held on the Cambodian island of Koh Tang, Ford approved a military rescue of the hostages.

On May 15, 1975, air force helicopters landed a party of U.S. Marines on Koh Tang. They were supported by an arsenal of U.S. ships and aircraft but encountered fierce resistance from Cambodian troops stationed on the island. Eighteen U.S. soldiers were killed in the ensuing battle, and another fifty were wounded. No crew members were found in the assault. Around this same time, however, the U.S. Navy regained possession of the *Mayaguez,* which had been abandoned by the Cambodians.

Later in the day, the mystery of the whereabouts of the *Mayaguez* crew ended when the U.S. destroyer *Wilson* spotted the men adrift at sea in an old fishing boat. The crew members had been put in the boat by their Cambodian captors, who wanted to end the clash. The *Wilson* rescued the men and delivered them to safety. With the crew accounted for, Ford then ordered air strikes against military targets on the Cambodian mainland. Some members of Congress and the American press criticized Ford for the bloody rescue effort and the bombing runs. They argued that the administration used the *Mayaguez* incident to deflect attention from the recent loss of Vietnam to the Communists. But many others defended Ford. They charged that the president's use of force was an appropriate response to the taking of American hostages.

Back home, the deaths of her three friends contributed greatly to Linda's strong opposition to the war. She eventually became an active member of the antiwar movement. She also continued her education, earning a master's degree in American studies. Linda then became a movie casting director in Hollywood. But although the years passed by quickly, she never forgot her friends who had died in Vietnam.

In 1985 the Orchard Park High School graduating class of 1965—of which Linda, Doug, Bill, and Gary had all been a part—held a twentieth anniversary reunion. But before going to the reunion, Palo made a special trip to the Vietnam Veterans Memorial, which had been dedicated three years earlier. Once she arrived at the Wall, the emotional impact of its black granite surface and engraved names became overwhelming. "I put my hand up there and the wall felt cold, so I put my face up against it and these incredible sobs started," she recalled. "Once that happened, and I could lay my face against the wall and sob, it gave me my freedom. . . . It was like saying good-bye to someone you love. . . .You hate to let go. But I felt like I had closed one door—not to forget them, but the door of rage and anger was finally closed."

Things to remember while reading Linda Phillips Palo's letter . . .

- As the war progressed, growing U.S. casualties dramatically reduced public support for the conflict. The deaths of neighborhood boys, nephews, sons, and old boyfriends had a great personal impact on countless American families and communities. Grief and mourning over these losses eventually led many Americans to adopt a negative and skeptical view of the war. In fact, the antiwar movement in the United States included many people who had lost close friends or family members in Vietnam.

- Voluntary enlistment in the U.S. armed services was much more common in the early stages of the Vietnam War, when American patriotism and confidence was at its peak. When the conflict turned into a bloody stalemate (standstill), however, the U.S. military was forced to rely more heavily on the draft to recruit new soldiers.

Letter by Linda Phillips Palo, left at the Vietnam Veterans Memorial:

July 20, 1985

Dear Gary, Doug and Billy,

Well, that time has rolled around and the Class of '65 is having its 20th year reunion. Cheers, cheers for Old Orchard Park High School.

Don't be afraid that you will not be remembered. We all talked about you in 1975 and our thoughts are with you. I think of you all— often.

Doug—they moved your house off the boulevard onto a new street. Your death was a real shock, especially since you were so **adamant** *about hating guns.*

Billy—I'm sorry that we never lived out the fantasy of running into each other in a supermarket with batches of children.

And yes, Gary, I still talk too much.

I had to come. I live in Los Angeles now and I could not have gone to that reunion without first coming here.

After you all died, I guess two boyfriends and several friends gone was a bit too much for me and I pretty much screwed up for ten years. Two boyfriends is just too much, too much, too much.

Now I'm much better. More responsible. I learned that the pain and loss never goes away. It just changes. Sometimes I think it is more painful now. And I'm still mad.

All three of you hold a special place in my heart. I'm just sorry you had such little time to spend here.

Years later
I can never hear
the sound of a helicopter
Without remembering
What I have lost.

In leaving today
tears stain
the window of the airplane

Adamant: Feel strongly about something.

on the runway.
It has not rained
in L.A. for months
It rains today.

I have had
twenty years
now
to reflect on this
madness
And it is always the same.

—Linda Phillips Palo

Thinking of you,
Linda

What happened next . . .

Today, the Vietnam Veterans Memorial remains one of America's most beautiful and emotionally powerful monuments. It is also the most visited site in Washington, D.C., with an estimated 2.5 million visitors each year. And the memorial continues to be updated as U.S. casualty lists from the war are corrected. (As of Memorial Day 1997, the Wall contained the names of 58,209 Americans who served in Vietnam.)

Visitors who go to the Wall also continue to leave photographs, letters, and other offerings in memory of the men and women who gave their lives in service to their country in Vietnam. Officials of the National Park Service, which maintains the memorial, collect and catalog these items at a climate-controlled warehouse in Maryland. "The collection [of items] is now a memorial in itself," wrote Michael Norman in *The Wall: Images and Offerings from the Vietnam Veterans Memorial,* "a remembrance of sacrifice apart from the lodestone [something that strongly attracts] of black polished granite on a quiet capital green."

Did you know . . .

- Since the Vietnam Veterans Memorial was dedicated, designer Maya Lin has become a widely respected sculptor and architect. She has exhibited many sculptures in museums and galleries. She has also produced several other well-known public monuments, including the *Civil Rights Memorial* (1989) in Montgomery, Alabama. In 1995 Freida Lee Mock's film on Lin's life and career, called *Maya Lin: A Strong Clear Vision,* won an Academy Award as best documentary of the year.

A U.S. Marine veteran remembers a slain friend from the war when he visits the Vietnam Wall Experience, a traveling replica of the Vietnam Veterans Memorial Wall in Brooklyn.
Reproduced by permission of AP/Wide World Photos.

- The two angled walls of the Vietnam Veterans Memorial meet together so that they point exactly to the northeast corners of the Washington Monument and the Lincoln Memorial.

- In 1993 another statue was added to the area around the Vietnam Veterans Memorial. This statue, by sculptor Glenna Goodacre, honors the thousands of American nurses who served in Vietnam.

- The Wall has become a very important symbol to Vietnam veterans over the years. They see the memorial not only as a tribute to fellow soldiers who were killed in the war, but as a sign that their nation finally recognized that American soldiers deserved respect and appreciation for serving their country in Vietnam. The Wall is so highly valued by Vietnam veterans that they maintain a constant vigil at the site.

- In 1984 a mobile half-sized replica of the Vietnam Veterans Memorial was constructed and unveiled to the public. This model, known as The Wall That Heals, has been presented in cities and towns all across America ever since. It is a very popular attraction, especially for people who do not have the financial resources or the physical health to travel all the way to Washington, D.C., to see the original memorial.

Sources

Hass, Kristin Ann. *Carried to the Wall: American Memory and the Vietnam Veterans Memorial.* Berkeley: University of California Press, 1998.

Isaacs, Arnold R. *Vietnam Shadows: The War, Its Ghosts, and Its Legacy.* Baltimore: Johns Hopkins University Press, 1997.

Katakis, Michael. *The Vietnam Veterans Memorial.* New York: Crown, 1988.

Palmer, Laura. *Shrapnel in the Heart: Letters and Remembrances from the Vietnam Veterans Memorial.* New York: Random House, 1987.

Scruggs, Jan C., and Joel L. Swerdlow. *To Heal a Nation: The Vietnam Veterans Memorial.* New York: Harper and Row, 1985.

Severo, Richard, and Lewis Milford. *The Wages of War: When America's Soldiers Came Home—From Valley Forge to Vietnam.* New York: Simon and Schuster, 1989.

The Wall: Images and Offerings from the Vietnam Veterans Memorial. New York: Collins Publishers, 1987.

Where to Learn More

The following list of resources focuses on works appropriate for middle school or high school students. These sources offer broad coverage of the Vietnam War. For additional resources on specific topics please see individual chapters.

Aitken, Jonathan. *Nixon: A Life.* Washington, DC: Regnery, 1993.

Ambrose, Stephen E. *Nixon.* 3 vols. New York: Simon and Schuster, 1987–1991.

Anderson, David L. *Trapped by Success: The Eisenhower Administration and Vietnam, 1953–1961.* Lawrence: University Press of Kansas, 1991.

Appy, Christian. *Working-Class War: American Combat Soldiers and Vietnam.* Chapel Hill: University of North Carolina Press, 1993.

Becker, Elizabeth. *America's Vietnam War: A Narrative History.* New York: Clarion, 1992.

Berman, Larry. *Planning a Tragedy: The Americanization of the War in Vietnam.* New York: W. W. Norton, 1982.

Billings-Yun, Melanie. *Decision against War: Eisenhower and Dien Bien Phu, 1954.* New York: Columbia University Press, 1988.

Braestrup, Peter. *Big Story: How the American Press and Television Reported and Interpreted the Crisis of Tet 1968 in Vietnam and Washington.* Boulder, CO: Westview Press, 1977.

Butler, David. *The Fall of Saigon: Scenes from the Sudden End of a Long War.* New York: Simon and Schuster, 1985.

Buttinger, Joseph. *The Smaller Dragon: A Political History of Vietnam.* New York: Praeger, 1958.

Caputo, Philip. *A Rumor of War.* New York: Henry Holt, 1977.

Carroll, James. *An American Requiem: God, My Father, and the War That Came Between Us.* Boston: Houghton-Mifflin, 1996.

Caute, David. *The Year of the Barricades: A Journey Through 1968.* New York: Harper & Row, 1988.

Chandler, David P. *The Tragedy of Cambodian History.* New Haven, CT: Yale University Press, 1992.

Dareff, Hal. *The Story of Vietnam: A Background Book for Young People.* New York: Parents Magazine Press, 1966.

DeBenedetti, Charles, and Charles Chatfield. *An American Ordeal: The Antiwar Movement of the Vietnam Era.* Syracuse, NY: Syracuse University Press, 1990.

Dougan, Clark, and Stephen Weiss. *The American Experience in Vietnam.* New York: W. W. Norton, 1988.

Dougan, Clark, and Stephen Weiss. *The Vietnam Experience: Nineteen Sixty-Eight.* Boston: Boston Publishing, 1985.

Downs, Frederick. *Aftermath: A Soldier's Return from Vietnam.* New York: Norton, 1984.

Doyle, Edward, and Stephen Weiss. *A Collision of Cultures: The Americans in Vietnam, 1954–1973.* Boston: Boston Publishing, 1984.

Duiker, William J. *The Communist Road to Power in Vietnam.* 2nd ed. Boulder, CO: Westview Press, 1996.

Dung, Van Tien. *Our Great Spring Victory.* New York: Monthly Review Press, 1977.

Dunn, Peter M. *The First Vietnam War.* New York: St. Martin's Press, 1985.

Ebert, James R. *A Life in a Year: The American Infantryman in Vietnam, 1965–1972.* Novato, CA: Presidio, 1986.

Ehrhart, W. D. *Passing Time.* Jefferson, NC: McFarland, 1989.

Emerson, Gloria. *Winners and Losers: Battles, Retreats, Gains, Losses and Ruins from a Long War.* New York: Random House, 1976.

Engelmann, Larry. *Tears Before the Rain: An Oral History of the Fall of South Vietnam.* New York: Oxford University Press, 1990.

Eschmann, Karl J. *Linebacker: The Untold Story of the Air Raids over North Vietnam.* New York: Ivy Books, 1989.

Fall, Bernard. *Hell in a Very Small Place: The Siege of Dien Bien Phu.* Philadelphia: J. B. Lippincott, 1966.

Figley, Charles R., and Seymour Leventman, eds. *Strangers at Home: Vietnam Veterans Since the War.* New York: Praeger, 1980.

Fitzgerald, Frances. *Fire in the Lake: The Vietnamese and the Americans in Vietnam.* Boston: Little, Brown, 1972.

Franklin, H. Bruce. *M.I.A. or Mythmaking in America.* Brooklyn, NY: Lawrence Hill, 1992.

Freeman, James A. *Hearts of Sorrow: Vietnamese-American Lives.* Stanford, CA: Stanford University Press, 1989.

Gardner, Lloyd C. *Pay Any Price: Lyndon Johnson and the Wars for Vietnam.* Chicago: Ivan Dee, 1995.

Garfinkle, Adam. *Telltale Hearts: The Origins and Impact of the Vietnam Antiwar Movement.* New York: St. Martin's Press, 1995.

Gibson, James William. *The Perfect War: The War We Couldn't Lose and How We Did.* Boston: Atlantic Monthly Press, 1986.

Gitlin, Todd. *The Sixties: Years of Hope, Days of Rage.* New York: Bantam, 1987.

Goulden, Joseph C. *Truth Is the First Casualty: The Gulf of Tonkin Affair—Illusion and Reality.* Chicago: Rand-McNally, 1969.

Halberstam, David. *The Best and the Brightest.* New York: Random House, 1972.

Halberstam, David. *The Making of a Quagmire: America and Vietnam During the Kennedy Era.* Rev. ed. New York: Knopf, 1988.

Hammer, Ellen J. *A Death in November: America in Vietnam, 1963.* New York: Dutton, 1987.

Hawthorne, Lesleyanne, ed. *Refugee: The Vietnamese Experience.* New York: Oxford University Press, 1982.

Hellman, John. *American Myth and the Legacy of Vietnam.* New York: Columbia University Press, 1986.

Helmer, John. *Bringing the War Home: The American Soldier in Vietnam and After.* New York: Free Press, 1974.

Hendrickson, Paul. *The Living and the Dead: Robert McNamara and Five Lives of a Lost War.* New York: Alfred A. Knopf, 1996.

Herr, Michael. *Dispatches.* New York: Alfred A. Knopf, 1977.

Herring, George C. *America's Longest War: The United States and Vietnam, 1950–1975.* 3rd ed. New York: McGraw-Hill, 1996.

Herring, George C. *LBJ and Vietnam: A Different Kind of War.* Austin: University of Texas Press, 1994.

Herrington, Stuart A. *Silence Was a Weapon: The Vietnam War in the Villages.* Novato, CA: Presidio Press, 1982.

Hiebert, Murray. *Chasing the Tigers: A Portrait of the New Vietnam.* New York: Kodansha International, 1996.

Hubbell, John, with Andrew Jones and Kenneth Y. Tomlinson. *P.O.W.: A Definitive History of the American Prisoner-of-War Experience in Vietnam, 1964–1973.* New York: Reader's Digest Press, 1976.

Isaacs, Arnold R. *Vietnam Shadows: The War, Its Ghosts, and Its Legacy.* Baltimore: Johns Hopkins University Press, 1997.

Isaacs, Arnold R. *Without Honor: Defeat in Vietnam and Cambodia.* New York: Vintage Books, 1984.

Isaacson, Walter. *Kissinger.* New York: Simon and Schuster, 1992.

Johnson, Lyndon B. *The Vantage Point: Perspectives of the Presidency, 1963–1969.* New York: Holt, Rinehart & Winston, 1971.

Kahin, George M. *Intervention: How America Became Involved in Vietnam.* Garden City, NY: Doubleday, 1987.

Karnow, Stanley. *Vietnam: A History.* Rev. ed. New York: Viking, 1991.

Kearns, Doris. *Lyndon Johnson & the American Dream.* New York: Harper & Row, 1976.

Kimball, Jeffrey. *Nixon's Vietnam War.* Lawrence: University Press of Kansas, 1998.

Kolko, Gabriel. *Anatomy of a War: Vietnam, the United States, and the Modern Historical Experience.* New York: Pantheon, 1985.

Kovic, Ron. *Born on the Fourth of July.* New York: McGraw-Hill, 1976.

Kutler, Stanley I., ed. *Encyclopedia of the Vietnam War.* New York: Scribner's, 1996.

Levy, David W. *The Debate over Vietnam.* 2nd ed. Baltimore: Johns Hopkins University Press, 1995.

Lewy, Gunter. *America in Vietnam.* New York: Oxford University Press, 1978.

Maclear, Michael. *The Ten Thousand Day War: Vietnam, 1945–1975.* New York: St. Martin's Press, 1980.

MacPherson, Myra. *Long Time Passing: Vietnam and the Haunted Generation.* Garden City, NY: Doubleday, 1984.

Marshall, John Douglas. *Reconciliation Road.* Syracuse, NY: Syracuse University Press, 1993.

Mason, Robert. *Chickenhawk.* New York: Viking, 1983.

McMahon, Robert J., ed. *Major Problems in the History of the Vietnam War.* Lexington, MA: D. C. Heath, 1995.

McNamara, Robert S., with Brian VanDeMark. *In Retrospect: The Tragedy and Lessons of Vietnam.* New York: Times Books, 1995.

Moore, Harold G., and Joseph L. Galloway. *We Were Soldiers Once . . . And Young.* New York: Random House, 1992.

Morley, James W., and Masashi Nishihara, eds. *Vietnam Joins the World.* Armonk, NY: M. E. Sharpe, 1997.

Ngo Vinh Long. *Before the Revolution: The Vietnamese Peasants Under the French.* Cambridge, MA: MIT Press, 1973.

Nguyen Qui Duc. *Where the Ashes Are: The Odyssey of a Vietnamese Family.* Reading, MA: Addison-Wesley, 1994.

Nixon, Richard. *No More Vietnams.* New York: Arbor House, 1985.

Oberdorfer, Don. *Tet!* New York: Doubleday, 1971.

Olson, James, and Randy Roberts. *Where the Domino Fell: America and Vietnam, 1945–1990.* New York: St. Martin's Press, 1996.

Palmer, Laura. *Shrapnel in the Heart: Letters and Remembrances from the Vietnam Veterans Memorial.* New York: Random House, 1987.

Prados, John, and Ray Stubbe. *Valley of Decision: The Siege of Khe Sanh.* New York: Houghton Mifflin, 1991.

Prochnau, William. *Once Upon a Distant War.* New York: Times Books, 1995.

Rust, William J. *Kennedy in Vietnam.* New York: Scribner's, 1985.

Schell, Jonathan. *The Real War: The Classic Reporting on the Vietnam War.* New York: Pantheon, 1987.

Scruggs, Jan. *To Heal a Nation: The Vietnam Veterans Memorial.* New York: Harper & Row, 1985.

Shandler, Herbert Y. *The Unmaking of a President: Lyndon Johnson and Vietnam.* Princeton, NJ: Princeton University Press, 1977.

Shawcross, William. *Sideshow: Kissinger, Nixon, and the Destruction of Cambodia.* New York: Simon and Schuster, 1979.

Sheehan, Neil. *A Bright Shining Lie: John Paul Vann and America in Vietnam.* New York: Random House, 1988.

Simpson, Howard R. *Dien Bien Phu: The Epic Battle America Forgot.* Washington, DC: Brassey's, 1994.

Snepp, Frank. *Decent Interval: An Insider's Account of Saigon's Indecent End.* New York: Random House, 1977.

Spector, Ronald H. *After Tet: The Bloodiest Year in Vietnam.* New York: Free Press, 1993.

Starr, Paul. *The Discarded Army.* New York: Charterhouse, 1974.

Terry, Wallace. *Bloods: An Oral History of the Vietnam War by Black Veterans.* New York: Ballantine, 1984.

Thompson, James Clay. *Rolling Thunder.* Chapel Hill: University of North Carolina Press, 1980.

Turner, Fred. *Echoes of Combat: The Vietnam War in American Memory.* New York: Anchor, 1996.

VanDeMark, Brian. *Into the Quagmire: Lyndon Johnson and the Escalation of the Vietnam War.* New York: Oxford University Press, 1991.

Wells, Tom. *The War Within: America's Battle Over Vietnam.* Berkeley: University of California Press, 1994.

Westmoreland, William. *A Soldier Reports.* New York: Doubleday, 1976.

Wicker, Tom. *One of Us: Richard Nixon and the American Dream.* New York: Random House, 1991.

Wiegersma, Nancy. *Vietnam: Peasant Land, Peasant Revolution.* New York: St. Martin's, 1988.

Wiesner, Louis A. *Victims and Survivors: Displaced Persons and Other War Victims in Vietnam, 1954–1975.* Westport, CT: Greenwood,1988.

Wolff, Tobias. *In Pharoah's Army.* New York: Alfred A. Knopf, 1994.

Young, Marilyn B. *The Vietnam Wars, 1945–1990.* New York: Harper-Collins, 1991.

Zaroulis, Nancy, and Gerald Sullivan. *Who Spoke Up? American Protest against the War in Vietnam, 1963–1975.* Garden City, NY: Doubleday, 1984.

Index

Illustrations are marked by (ill).